I intended to zoom over the hill at treetop level. It would only be an identification run, but it would boost the recon team's morale. I reached out to the armament panel and flipped switches. The plane jolted as the big twenty-millimeter cannon slammed home.

"You're headed right for us, Hostage. We're in the crater," the team radio operator whispered hoarsely. "Get us out of here!" Suddenly I felt two small thumps, as though someone had kicked the tail of the plane.

"Goddam! Skipper, we just took a hit!"

"Yeah, I felt it, too. Everything still feels okay." I pushed the microphone switch forward to transmit.

"Danang DASC! Hostage. Thunderball definitely has to come out. We just took a couple of rounds ourselves. How are we doing on those bombers? Tell Stonepit Six that Thunderball has two WIAs. I've got some shooting to do now."

GROUND ATTACK—VIETNAM

The Marines Who Controlled the Skies

J. M. Moriarty

IVY BOOKS • NEW YORK

Ivy Books
Published by Ballantine Books
Copyright © 1993 by Michael Moriarty

Library of Congress Catalog Card Number: 93-91363

ISBN 0-8041-1065-4

Manufactured in the United States of America

First Edition: July 1993

To lieutenants the world over, without whom a squadron commander's life would be really dull;

and

To a generation of students who have heard most of these stories two or three times, and went out and bought the book anyway.

LET'S BRIEF

If you don't have a sense of humor, war can be a real drag. Let me tell a story to introduce this book, one which isn't all that funny, but an anecdote which pretty well sums up what we of Marine Observation Squadron 2 were doing in Vietnam during 1970.

In June of 1970, I had the occasion to emcee a variety show at the Marine Aircraft Group 11 officers club in Da Nang. The occasion was the going-away party for a man who was arguably the best-loved group commander MAG-11 had seen in a long time, and my job that night was to introduce the various comedy efforts on the part of the lieutenants from the six squadrons attached to the air group as they staged humorous skits to depict their squadrons' associations with the great man himself, Col. Grover "Meat Eyes" Stewart.

Meat Eyes himself was great and memorable; the skits and the humor were not.

The lieutenants assigned to the tactical jet squadrons of the air group—all-weather attack squadrons, VMA-225 and VMA-242, plus the VMCJ-1 photo and electronics countermeasures squadron—had all majored in some field of engineering in college, and while they were outstanding young men, deliberate, serious and exacting, they were not always a funny bunch of guys. The art and drama majors in the group, urbane gentlemen who could be counted on for a clever line or two, were to be found only in VMO-2, Marine Observation Squadron 2, the OV-10 Bronco squadron I was fortunate enough to command.

The aeronautical engineers of the A-6 Intruder squadrons had not written funny material, unless one found humor in math jokes and references to moving-target indicators. But as luck

1

would have it, on that night, neither had the witty English majors of our beloved VMO-2.

This added an additional measure of responsibility to the master of ceremonies, and as I sat uncomfortably through the dress rehearsal, two days before the show, and wondered just how in the world I had allowed our lieutenants to sucker me into emceeing this turkey, I made many notes on three-by-five cards to assist me in making light of things if the skits went as badly as I suspected they would.

I decided that the squadrons' shortfall in the humor department could be offset with dazzling statistics about sortie rates, bomb tonnage, and personal heroism, and I made copious notes on each of the squadrons' high points as I groaned over what the lieutenants thought were very funny lines, finding myself stumped only on the promotional information for the nonflying Marine air base squadron, which was responsible for the necessities of life in the air group such as food, shelter, and the ever-popular sewage-disposal problem.

As soon as the dress rehearsal was over, I told the actors how wonderful they were and suggested that they not give up their day jobs, or in the case of the A-6 pilots, their night jobs, and I put the three-by-five cards in my flight suit pocket and promptly forgot all about them.

For the next two days, I went about the business of running a squadron and didn't give the variety-show-skit night another thought until a few minutes before I was to climb up on the stage—at which time I dashed back to my quarters and thrashed through the pockets of my discarded flight suit at the bottom of a closet until I resurrected the notes.

Dressed for the occasion in freshly starched and ironed jungle utilities, I shuffled through the three-by-five cards as I hurried across the gravel road, back to the loud and smoky officers club building. I arrived just as the various troupes of squadron lieutenants were dragging their props up onto the tiny stage, and one of our former drama majors was struggling with the lighting.

Free booze, which had been flowing ever since the parade and formal change of command ceremonies that afternoon, enhanced the party attitude of the assembled air group, and I broke one of my own cardinal rules that night by having a few drinks and performing at the same time.

This was not a smart thing to do. Alcohol never made me as brilliant and clever as I thought I was. I didn't have time to read all of the notes, but I had done this sort of thing before, and I was confident that I would be able to muddle through with style and grace, no matter how horrible things got.

And in fact I did—until we came to an extra long break between one truly awful skit and another which was going to be just as bad, and which would take an extra minute or two setting up and involved the same Marine air base squadron, MABS-11, for which I had so much trouble inventing promotional notes.

I shuffled through my cue cards as the scenery change took longer and longer, and wished that I had numbered the damn things, and I prayed a little, in hopes that I had written myself some magical formula for a line of patter to get us into that last skit.

My prayers seemed to have been answered when I found the correct note card, but upon reading it I immediately suffered a "klong," which is generally defined as a cold rush of shit to the heart. In large letters across the top of the card was written the following: Tell Funny Joke.

Not too damn helpful. I felt beads of panic sweat popping out on my forehead and heard my inner voice chiding, "Well, what're you going to do now, Ace?" My informationally impaired brain raced through every joke I had ever heard in all of my thirty-seven years.

Fear is a great incentive. I relied on my years of intensive training for emergency situations, and I fell back on one of the tried-and-true standards of official Marine Corps doctrine: do something, even if it's wrong, and I proceeded to stretch out for two solid minutes one of the lamest attempts at a Morey Amsterdam joke Marine Aircraft Group 11 ever suffered; the visual punch line for which would become an unofficial squadron rebuke for every dumb idea I came up with for the rest of my tour.

And that's pretty much the way our war in Vietnam went in 1970. Some slipshod staff work every now and then, generally in the area of combat intelligence, caused grief and embarrassment, and like the story I just told, tactical operations often saw huge buildups, after which nothing happened.

Just about the time we thought we had everything under control, one of our enemies, either the Viet Cong or the more lethal snipers in Washington, came up with a new problem that would send us back to the drawing boards. Combat for a squadron commander that year was an unyielding sequence of hasty improvisations and crisis management.

Marine Corps aviation in Vietnam, from the beginning to the

end, was as professional a military organization as the world had ever seen. But as often as not, no matter how well trained we were, something unexpected popped up, and we had to wing it—just as I did that night on the MAG-11 officers club stage when I found refuge in a stale joke about a one-armed fisherman. While I didn't get any laughs that time, I muddled through and killed the required amount of time and made the next act look pretty good by comparison.

We muddled through admirably in Vietnam, too, and it is the purpose of this book to tell the story of one squadron's efforts during 1970 when the war was beginning to wind down, and when we were fighting a kinder, gentler war. The story is about the good times and the bad—mostly the good.

My twenty-year flying career ended as it began, flying propeller-driven airplanes manufactured by North American. I learned to fly in the old SNJ, and I flew my last military flight, in 1972, in an OV-10 Bronco.

During those twenty years, I had a lot of fun, preparing for the day when I would command a tactical squadron in combat, and then doing just that. In addition to telling a juicy war story about the Marine Corps' air war in Vietnam, I hope to provide some guidance to young aviators the world over who also aspire to squadron command.

Three names have been altered to avoid possible embarrassment, and I have taken liberties with the actual dates of two minor events, but everything in the book is as factual as my memory will permit. As reference material, I have relied upon my pilot's log book, my scrap books and notes, and Marine Corps history books found in the St. Petersburg public library.

ABOUT THE SQUADRON

As is the case with most squadrons, the history of Marine Observation Squadron 2 is not all that impressive. Squadrons do not do battle—pilots do. Except for organizations that reaped great publicity during World War II—Pappy Boyington's VMA-214 "Black Sheep" squadron comes to mind—a squadron's actual history is generally a series of administrative decisions, moves, and transfers.

Like most Marine squadrons, Marine Observation Squadron 2, VMO-2, came into being during World War II. Observation planes had been around almost forever, of course, beginning the minute someone realized that a man could see better from the air than from the top of a tree, and VMO-2 evolved from an artillery spotting squadron, VMO-251, in February of 1944.

Flying light OY-1 Grasshoppers (O for observation, and the letter Y stood for the manufacturer, Consolidated), the squadron got its first taste of combat in the Marianas, in support of the 2d and 4th Marine Divisions during the battles for Saipan and Tinian. On-board ordnance in those days consisted of handheld smoke grenades and an M-1 rifle, although I strongly suspect that some frustrated dive-bomber pilots, relegated to observation flying, kept a few explosive grenades in their pockets to toss at people they didn't like. The pilots of those light planes earned their keep spotting for artillery batteries and performing administrative chores, delivering mail and an occasional passenger.

In April of 1945, flying from aircraft carriers without benefit of tailhooks, the squadron supported 2d Marine Division in the battle for Okinawa, and laid claim to the first landing of an American plane on that island on the second day of the assault.

When the war ended, the squadron accompanied 2d Marine Division to Japan, to Isahaya on the southern island of Kyushu, where the pilots busied themselves taking pictures and carrying mail until they returned to the United States, where the squadron was deactivated in 1946.

The squadron was reactivated in 1951 but never heard a shot fired in anger during the advanced gunnery exercises in Korea. They made it as far as Japan in 1953, and in 1956 moved to Okinawa, where they set up shop near the beach in the Sukiran area until a base was built at Futemma. By this time they had traded in the old OY-1s for OE-1s (the letter *E* stood for Cessna) and picked up twin-rotor HOK helicopters (*H* for helicopter, *K* for Kaman), which added a new dimension to the squadron mission in that the HOKs could land at an infantry command post on top of a hill and haul the commander into the air to look at stuff.

The HOK was not always popular with the pilots. The twin rotors sometimes got in the way of each other, and in 1959, I remember attending an emergency meeting and hearing of VMO pilots turning in their wings after a succession of disastrous crashes.

In May of 1965, the squadron left the aging HOKs in Okinawa and moved the OEs into Da Nang as part of the 9th Marine Expeditionary Brigade. Twenty years of development saw the on-board ordnance improved to include hand-held smoke grenades and an M-16 rifle.

It was during this time that I got my first experience with the squadron. As the director, III MAF command center—a great title for a dumpy little guy who answered the telephone a lot—I was not allowed to fly in the combat area, so I sneaked in what little flight time I got during that tour flying in the backseat of an OE with Maj. Don Reilly, VMO-2's operations officer and one of the true aviation heroes of the early days of the war.

Almost as soon as the squadron arrived in Da Nang, it received UH-1E Hueys to replace both the OEs and those dying HOKs, and as soon as the air facility at Marble Mountain was constructed on the beach across the river from Da Nang, VMO-2 took up residence there, and stayed there until February of 1970.

The OV-10 Bronco joined the squadron in 1968, and in 1969 the Hueys were replaced with AH-1G Cobra gunships. These were loaners from the army because the navy would not buy a helicopter without rotor brakes or rotor stabilization. A few months later the Cobras were transferred out of the squadron—

a subject I cover in another chapter—and the squadron has flown nothing but OV-10s ever since.

VMO-2 returned to the United States in the spring of 1971 and has operated out of the airfield at Camp Pendleton in southern California since then, except for a brief stint during Operation DESERT STORM where it received national publicity as a result of the squadron commander being one of the first pilots blown out of the sky by an Iraqi missile.

What made VMO-2 unique was not the airplanes so much as the pilots and aerial observers who flew in them. In truth, the OV-10 was not always the best plane for the mission in Vietnam, and there were many occasions when the slow and vulnerable OE-1 Bird Dog would have been a more practical machine, when hearing and smelling the enemy was important. Also, the Huey had its good points: a crew of four, able to see more, and gunners able to shoot backward and sideways. There were many occasions when I would have liked to stop and hover over a spot and get a better look at suspicious bushes and caves.

What was impressive about VMO-2, then, was not its history and traditions, but rather what the squadron had become by the time I joined it in 1970. The different missions we performed are the meat of this small book, and I want to tell you about some of the things which were accomplished and which never made the history books.

EMERGENCY EXTRACT

"Hostage Six, Hostage Six, this is Thunderball!" The panicked voice crackled on the FM radio in a hoarse whisper. "Get us out of here!"

I pushed against the power levers as hard as I could, as though bending them over the front of the throttle quadrant would give me an extra knot of airspeed, and searched the terrain in front of me as I keyed the intercom switch.

"He's scared, Lee. You work with him while I get the cavalry out here. Find out what they're up against."

I was charged with a shot of adrenaline, and my fingers trembled as I flipped the radio selector from FM to UHF and switched to channel 4.

"Da Nang DASC? This is Hostage Six. Scramble the hot pad and launch the Mission 80 package. Send them to the Da Nang TACAN for now. Get the Basketball ready in case we have to play a night game. You copy?"

All of that sounds pretty strange now, years after the fact, but to those of us who spent our days and nights over the 1st Marine Division as the major link in the Marine air/ground team, it could have happened yesterday.

Let me explain it and tell you about a hornet's nest I walked into late one afternoon in May of 1970. It involved the emergency extraction of a division reconnaissance team from a hilltop about twenty miles northwest of Da Nang, and demonstrated just how quickly Marine Air could respond when the chips were down and infantry Marines' lives hung in the balance.

Hostage was the call sign for VMO-2, Marine Observation Squadron 2, and Six, universal signal for the commanding officer, was mine. Thunderball was a code name that year for one of the many reconnaissance teams of 1st Marine Division that lurked in the hills out in Indian country and detected enemy movement toward the operating regiments.

I was flying Mission 76-P that afternoon, which was the sixteenth and last of the standard daily reconnaissance flights that were VMO-2's bread and butter. The missions lasted two and a half hours, and I was scheduled to land just after dark. The only specific job the aerial observer and I had planned for the flight was to inspect carefully some trail activity in the hills around Thuong Duc, about thirty-five miles southwest of Da Nang.

Early that same morning, we had flown the Alpha mission, 76-A, the dawn patrol. Lt. Lee Gingras and I had seen all the telltale signs of enemy activity in an area that had been fairly quiet for a while. Now we were going to look at the same piece of real estate with the sun low in the west in hopes that we could turn up something more.

In time, the pilots and aerial observers of VMO-2 would sniff out a substantial enemy buildup in the Thuong Duc area and, within a few weeks, direct one of the most unusual air/ground operations of the war: the Blivot Drop. But today we were discovering the early signals.

The aerial observer in the back seat of my OV-10 Bronco was 2d Lt. Lee Gingras, a clean-cut young man who had received his commission after serving as a sergeant during his first tour in Vietnam. Lee had personally walked over much of the terrain that formed our battlefields, and his experience as an infantry Marine helped me through some sticky situations—one of which would arise in just a few minutes.

The Vu Gia River flowed toward the coast from the northwest and provided the enemy with a water route from the mythical Ho Chi Minh trail. The river was part of what we had labeled the "yellow-brick road," and the village of Thuong Duc lay at the point where it emerged from the mountains and entered the coastal flatland.

The nearest mountain ridge north of the river was what interested us, and I had asked the photo reconnaissance squadron, VMCJ-1, to make runs along the ridgeline at various times of day to photograph the spots we were looking at, but with the sun at different angles. I wish I had remembered to nail them down as to the time they were coming.

What we had seen at dawn had been only the remnants of a cook fire, a river crossing, and some human trails. It wasn't much, but it was enough to get our Sherlock Holmes juices flowing.

Lee Gingras was the aerial observer with whom I flew most of my missions, and it was he who spotted the cook fire that started a chain of events which would lead up to the major operation involving the entire 1st Marine Air Wing.

What he had seen at dawn was nothing more than a tree with a section of wilted leaves. Lee had good eyes. He pointed it out, and I dropped down to treetop level and opened all of the air vents.

The OV-10 was not air-conditioned, and through the air vents, we were able to smell traces of a wood fire, the heat from which had temporarily wilted the leaves above. We knew we had a cook fire. It wasn't gun smoke or artillery shell smoke, and natural jungle smoke had a smell all of its own.

River crossings were interesting, but they really didn't tell a whole lot. During the spring and summer, the rivers were shallow, and by looking straight down, a pilot could see footprints where feet had disturbed the thin layer of silt. Footprints told us where people were crossing, but they didn't tell us when.

Sometimes we were able to extrapolate an angle of travel where the footprints crossed the shoreline, and on one occasion, we were able to triangulate a base camp that way. But these prints, which appeared to have been made by two people, didn't give us any clues at all.

Trails in the tall grass were helpful. When an animal moved through an area, the trail of bent foliage was crooked, but a human, who was tall enough to see over the grass, walked in a straight line. These trails were human, but no longer visible in the late afternoon.

What we sought was a location between the river crossing and that cook fire. Two small waterfalls plummeted from the ridgeline to the north. Thin, white foam sparkled where the sunlight still played, and contrasted with rich, green foliage with brilliant scarlet trees, the name of which I never did learn.

It was beautiful, and for twenty minutes, we darted in and out of the ravines like a honeybee bent on cross-pollinating every flower in the valley.

The enemy was never so careless as to cook near a base camp, and we settled on a ravine within a hundred meters of the tree, one which seemed to satisfy all of the requisite needs of a campsite. The stream that trickled through it was quiet. No white water was visible. Charlie avoided noisy, rushing streams that masked the sounds of approaching troops.

We assumed that any campsite would be on the eastern slope of the ravine, defilade to artillery fire.

Lee Gingras marked it on his map as a "possible," and I added power and trimmed the plane for a climb to cooler air.

As we gained altitude and the temperature dropped to a comfortable level, we discussed jungle camouflage and one of my on-going crusades, a seemingly fruitless effort to find a color-blind aerial observer.

I wanted someone who would not be confused by camouflage. We almost had one a few weeks earlier, a lieutenant in the reconnaissance battalion, but at the last minute he backed out.

I had sicked the squadron lieutenants on him, and they had gone about it with the youthful enthusiasm of a fraternity rush, even offering a flight jacket with squadron patch as bait, but the young man was a naval academy graduate who didn't want to take a chance on hurting his career.

Suddenly—"Jesus! Look out!" Gingras grabbed the rear cockpit controls as he screamed and threw the OV-10 into a violent steep turn. "Look at that son of a bitch go!"

The OV-10 shuddered in jet blast as an F-4 photo plane streaked away to the north at five hundred knots. The gray jet was almost a blur against the dark green.

I steadied the plane back into level flight, my heart thumping like a trip-hammer, and verbally maligned the lineage of photo pilots. The squadron was only two hangars down from VMO-2, and still we couldn't get them to tell us when they were going to turn our busy little war into the Cleveland air races.

Gingras decided that he wanted to drop sensors in the area, ADSIDs in the ravines, Aqua Buoys in the trees.

The Aqua Buoy was an out-dated navy antisubmarine device, designed to bob in the water and listen for submarine noises. In Vietnam, we parachuted them into the trees to hang there for days and listen to the local sounds.

Bilingual people from the intelligence community listened to the sensors, and about three months before had taped the conversations of the Viet Cong as they tried to get one down out of a tree. The parachute was all tangled up in a branch, and they gave the junior man a saw and sent him up to cut the limb off.

He did, from the wrong side, and it was the first time in history both sides of a war were laughing their asses off at the same bizarre accident.

ADSIDs, aerial delivered seismic intrusion devices, were adaptations of the sensors used by oil company geologists. Dropped from OV-10s also, they plunged into the soft earth, leaving only their antennas above ground. The antennas were disguised as shrubbery. With them spaced along trails and transmitting on different frequencies, enemy footsteps could be detected by permanent Marine outposts that listened and watched from the hilltops.

The same people who listened to the Aqua Buoy transmitters also listened in on just about every radio frequency used in Vietnam, even our own. I know, because I was once put on report for cussing on the air.

The radio battalion screened our tactical frequencies for security slipups, like giving the enemy positions in the same code used for friendly positions and providing the enemy, who knew their position on the map, with some of our encryption. By 1970, someone had decided that our radio transmissions should be free of improper language, too, and I found my name on the monthly report for using the present participle of the big *F* word one day. I used it as an adverb, so maybe I deserved to be put on report.

A reconnaissance outpost was just to the right of our nose to the east, and I turned in that direction. Currently code named West Orange, the small fortress was dug into Hill 258, on the eastern face of the high ground called the Tennis Courts, and offered an incredible view from which Marines were able to observe everything that moved in the flatland labeled the Arizona Territory.

They had every optical viewing device known to man and a laser system that permitted them to pinpoint a target to a ten-digit grid coordinate—a square yard or so of terrain.

Eventually, the laser system would enable planes with "smart" bombs to hit ventilation shafts of buildings in downtown Baghdad, but in 1970, it was all still experimental.

It was boring work for the recon teams, especially during daylight hours when the Viet Cong took their naps, and a ritual diversion had developed over the months that began when an OV-10 approached the hill with all visible intent of buzzing the radio antennas and leaving prop blast in the drab brown trenches.

Any Marines standing outside the sandbagged bunkers were supposed to drop their pants and moon us as we flew by.

I never said we were sophisticated.

The object of the game was to sneak up on the outpost and catch them with their pants up. The OV-10's whine was so loud and distinctive, however, that we were seldom able to sneak up on anything.

I pushed the nose over and made the requisite pass, and we counted seven moons. Not a record, but a good turnout. I congratulated them on their attention to duty.

"West Orange? Hostage. Good show. Glad to see you're so alert."

"Thanks, Hostage. We try to do our bit for the morale of the zoomies."

"We appreciate it. Do you know there's a body hanging in your wire? A little to the south?"

"Yeah, we shot him last night."

"You going to just leave him there?"

"Well, truth is, we can't untangle him from the concertina wire. Got his weapon, though. Had a satchel charge with him. We'll get him loose after a while. He's downwind."

True story. I wrote it down on my knee board.

I returned to altitude, and the sun reappeared as we climbed above the mountains. The world became beautiful again, and I unscrewed the cap of my canteen and took a sip of water just as the FM radio interrupted.

"Cowpoke One One! Cowpoke Base, over!"

Cowpoke was the aerial observer call sign and there was urgency in the voice.

"Go ahead, Base. One One up," Gingras answered.

"Troops in contact, One One!" The voice spoke rapidly. "Thunderball. Sounds like they're in a peck of trouble. You'd better hurry."

Within the 1st Marine Division headquarters complex there was a small group of Marine aviators and radio operators who made the air/ground team work. The operation was called the Direct Air Support Center, DASC, pronounced the way it's spelled, and the mission was simple. Whatever the Marine on the ground needed, he got.

Before Vietnam, the DASC operated under a code name. Those who flew in Korea will remember it as Devastate Baker, but in the static air war around Da Nang, it had become senseless to attempt to mask the focal point of all air/ground support.

The infantry leader in the field called in with his request, and the DASC relayed the message to the wing, which passed it to the correct air group immediately. I've seen jets scrambled off the hot pad within three and a half minutes of the infantry's call. That wasn't a pilot running to his airplane. That was putting the wheels in the well on takeoff.

We in VMO-2 didn't think that was fast enough, so our aerial observers took turns sitting in the cramped DASC with an FM radio of our own. This was Cowpoke Base.

When something urgent came in, the duty Cowpoke called the nearest OV-10 immediately, which gave us a head start on the emergency. Two or three minutes was enough time to save lives.

Additionally, the aerial observers in the cockpits carried the map coordinates of every recon team in the field at the time, and in an episode such as this, Cowpoke Base had only to tell us who was in trouble.

All of this was illegal, of course, not a part of official Marine Corps doctrine, and so this short course in air/ground communications is included simply because when the next war comes around, everyone who remembers how to make the system work may be dead.

The twin-tailed OV-10 whined across Happy Valley as fast as it could and headed toward Elephant Valley. Lieutenant Gingras spoke on the intercom. "The coordinates are 814-773, Skipper. Head for the western end of the Razorback." He switched back to his FM radio, and that was when I made my initial call to the Direct Air Support Center.

"Okay, Thunderball, we're on our way." There was authority in Gingras's voice. "What's the situation?"

"Hostage Six, Thunderball. Gooners all over the place. You copy? They're coming up the hill after us. We got two casualties already. Get us out of here!"

There was a plea in the hushed voice, but I did not hear the tail end of the transmission. The UHF radio cut in.

"Hostage Six? This is Da Nang DASC, over." The voice was calm and businesslike.

"Go ahead, DASC. Six up."

"Hostage Six, we have a possible priority mission. I have the coordinates shackled. On the Whiz Wheel, set Bravo over Uniform. Are you ready to copy?"

I didn't have time to cuss. "Didn't you hear me, DASC? Forget the shackle code. We're almost there. Scramble the hot pad and get me some soft ordnance out here quick. Launch the

Mission 80 package and get a flare plane overhead in case we have to run this thing in the dark!''

"R-Roger, Six." The DASC controller's voice registered confusion. The manual he was working from didn't explain Cowpoke Base, although our man was sitting just six feet from him, and obviously this wasn't the same controller I had just talked to. Maybe he had been talking on the other phone.

"Are you sure the team has to come out? Their Six says he wants them to stay in the field."

"Negative, DASC! Do what I tell you! You've already wasted enough time. It's going to be dark pretty soon. Get those planes out here fast. I want the bombers just as fast as they can move!''

Gingras had been listening. "That's tellin' them, Skipper. Thunderball should be somewhere around a little hill just south of Razorback. There! You can see it now."

I set the gunsight at thirty-two mils and pushed the nose of the plane over toward the hill. The Razorback was a prominent, jagged, east-west ridgeline that looked very much like a dinosaur.

I intended to zoom over the hill at treetop level. It would only be an identification run, but it would boost the recon team's morale. I reached out to the armament panel and flipped switches. The plane jolted as the bolt of the big twenty-millimeter cannon slammed home.

"You're headed right for us, Hostage. We're in a crater on top of this hill!'' The team radio operator whispered hoarsely. "Get us out of here!''

At full power, the OV-10 fairly snarled as I buzzed the crater and turned sharply over the face of the hill. The radio operator keyed his microphone as we flew over, and I could hear the noise of my engines on the radio. In the background I could hear rifle fire, which over the radio sounded like harmless Fourth of July firecrackers.

Suddenly I felt two small thumps, as though someone had kicked the tail of the plane.

"Goddam! Skipper, we just took a hit! Pricks!''

"Yeah, I felt it too. Everything still feels okay." I pushed the microphone switch forward to transmit.

"Da Nang DASC! Hostage. Thunderball definitely has to come out. We just took a couple of rounds ourselves. How are we doing on those bombers? They have a TACAN fix?''

"Roger, 280 at twenty. Stonepit Six says he still wants the

team to stay in the field. Says they've only been out there a few hours.''

"I don't care what he says, DASC. You just do what I tell you. Tell him Thunderball has two WIAs. I've got some shooting to do now.''

"Roger, Hostage. The Mission 80 package is airborne. They know where you are.''

Mission 80 was the flight of CH-46 transport helicopters and Cobra gunships that inserted and extracted reconnaissance teams. Because Thunderball had been inserted only that day, chances were good that the extract would be conducted by the same pilots who flew them in.

"Roger the Mission 80 package.''

At the top of my climbing turn, the TACAN equipment received the Da Nang station. TACAN, like television, was VHF with line-of-sight restrictions and useless down in the valleys. As soon as the plane had enough altitude to clear the hills, the needle locked on, and the distance measuring equipment clicked to nineteen miles.

"DASC, my TACAN is 278 at nineteen.''

"Copy, Hostage. We're talking to Joyride on the land line now. I have a flight of two Fox Fours, and the flare plane is already airborne.''

"Skipper!'' Lee Gingras interrupted on the intercom. "Thunderball says the gooners are coming up the hill on two sides. See those ravines? The one on the east and the other to the west? The one on the west has two big craters on the far side. Right near the top.''

"I see them both. Is that where they want it? Up and down the ravines?'' I lowered the nose and put the eastern ravine in my sights as the plane gathered speed. I wrapped my finger around the trigger on the front of the stick.

"Right. Both ravines, and across the bush between them. Quick now!''

Brrr-Attt! The left sponson guns spewed 7.62-bullets into the ravine and formed a dotted line of tracer fire. I pulled up and away from the hill and positioned myself for the next run. I would play cat and mouse with the enemy for as long as it took for the bombers to arrive, anything to keep them away from the recon team. If I established any sort of repetitive pattern, Charlie would soon catch on and punch a hole in something important.

I flew around the hill, popped up, and then flew down the western ravine. The machine guns spurted fire again as I raked the entire avenue of approach. This time I pulled up straight ahead and soared out over the flat valley.

"They've stopped moving around, Hostage! Keep it up!"

Around again, up and down the ravines and across the face of the hill. When the left guns quit, I switched to the right.

I saved the twenty millimeter. This strafing was only suppressive fire to keep the enemy occupied. I strafed at random, first here, then there. Pick a run-in heading and spray a bush. Indiscriminate hosing. If I actually saw the enemy, it would be by chance.

Lieutenant Gingras switched off Thunderball's frequency during one of my wide sweeps. He tuned in Cowpoke Base quickly and instructed the duty aerial observer to get artillery up on the recon team's frequency in order that he might call in a storm of shells on the enemy as soon as the team was safely out.

He switched back in time for us to hear Thunderball call. The voice was strong now and no longer whispered.

"Hostage? We got a couple of moaners out there in that eastern ravine. Nice shooting."

I completed another firing run and released the pressure on the trigger as I pulled up. Moaners were good.

I had a theory, never proved, that the highly touted "screamers" were not as badly wounded as the "moaners" and would vent their emotions on the first hostile object they saw, generally the guy who just shot them. Moaners, on the other hand, just lay there and died.

"Roger on the moaners, Thunderball." I cut in on the FM radio. "Do you think you have them pinpointed now? We're going to run the fixed-wing in a couple of minutes."

"Right, Hostage. They're all through that eastern ravine and about halfway down the western ravine. Down where those rocks stick up. That's where all the shooting came from when you flew over."

He was interrupted by a new voice, strangely nasal in an oxygen mask, that cut in on the UHF.

"Hostage Six? This is Lovebug Two Zero Five, over."

"Okay, Thunderball, the jets are here. Bury yourselves in that hole when we start dropping. Lovebug Two Zero Five, Hostage. Come out to the 278 at nineteen."

Switching back and forth from radio to radio was a busy operation.

"Okay, DASC, Lovebug Two Zero Five just checked in. Where are those helicopters?"

"Roger, Six. We heard. They should be entering the valley right now. Your flare plane will be Ringneck One Zero Four." The flare plane was also known as the Basketball, mainly because their game was always played at night.

The controller spoke without emotion. The Direct Air Support Center was getting crowded. Word had spread around division headquarters quickly, and the cramped spaces were jammed with senior officers. After all, it was the best show in town that afternoon.

Two F-4 Phantoms streaked across the sky at twelve thousand feet, high enough to sparkle in the sun, which had already dropped behind the hills, yet low enough to leave black smoke trailing.

"Hostage Six, this is Lovebug Two Zero Five. Flight of two Fox Fours overhead with snake and nape. I have you in sight."

"Snake" stood for Snake Eye bombs, fin-retarded weapons that allowed a pilot to make a low-level drop, and still get away from the blast. When released, flat fins popped out and slowed the bombs. In the hands of a good pilot, the accuracy of Snake Eye bombs was deadly.

"Nape" was simply a contraction for napalm. Together with rockets and twenty millimeter, this ordnance was collectively called "soft ordnance"—as opposed to "hard ordnance," designed to crack bunkers and buildings.

"Roger, Lovebug. Good to see you." I zoomed out of my last strafing run and reset the switches on the armament panel. I selected Willie Peter, white phosphorus rockets, and the twenty-millimeter cannon and reset the gunsight to forty mils.

"Okay, Lovebug, here's the situation. We have a recon team in a crater on top of this hill under my left wing. See it? It's all by itself out here."

"Yeah, I think so." The F-4s descended to a lower altitude.

"Okay. There are two ravines leading up to the top of the hill. That's where the gooners are, and we're going to take them out. They're trigger happy, so I'll cover you in your runs. Target elevation is four hundred feet. Run in along the ravines southbound and pull out left. I'll mark at six and twelve o'clock. First run, I want your nape in the eastern ravine. You're going to be dropping within twenty-five meters of friendlies. Your wingman up to it?"

There was a moment of silence.

"Dash Two?" The flight leader spoke apologetically to his wingman. "Orbit high and dry for the first two runs."

"Dash Two, roger."

The wingman did not sound disappointed. I suspected that he was a young lieutenant. It was probably the twenty-five meters that got his attention.

A new voice sounded.

"Hostage Six? This is Scarface One One with Swift One Eight. We're five miles out. Have you in sight."

"Roger, Scarface. Set up your orbit east of the zone while I run the fixed wing."

Scarface and Swift acknowledged that they were the same Mission 80 package of aircraft that had dropped Thunderball off that morning.

"Okay, Lovebug." I armed the left rocket pod. "I'll put out marks at six and twelve o'clock in the eastern ravine. Line up on my smoke, and put your nape right in the middle."

"Hurry up, Hostage! They're coming up the hill again." Thunderball sounded anxious.

"We're working as fast as we can, babe."

I lowered the nose until the five-mil ring of the gunsight was on the ravine. Faster and faster the plane raced toward the target. *Whoomph!* The first rocket fired. I raised the nose slightly. *Whoomph!* The second rocket. Dense white smoke from the first rocket billowed squarely in the center of the top of the ravine, a scant twenty-five meters from the Marines in the crater. Then the second puff appeared downhill.

I pulled up in a tight left turn. The heavy G force pressed my rear end into the seat.

"Have at it, Lovebug!"

"Lovebug in."

The jet pilot turned his aircraft and aligned himself with the ravine, now clearly defined by the bright white phosphorous.

I studied the jet's flight path closely and climbed to a firing position. No margin for error here. I wouldn't clear Lovebug to drop until I was certain that the napalm fell clear of the recon team.

"Put your heads down, Thunderball!" Gingras warned. The Marines did not have to be told.

"They're down, man! They're down!"

"Wings level." The F-4 was in its run and on target.

"Cleared hot!"

The napalm tanks tumbled from the bottom of the F-4 as the

plane skimmed the tops of the bushes along the ravine. They ripped apart as they hit, and splattered fiercely hot, burning petroleum jelly down through the gulch in a gush of flame and black smoke.

"Right in there!" I put the pipper of my gunsight on the top of the ravine and mashed the red firing button on the top of the stick. The twenty-millimeter cannon chugged away, filling the cockpit with cordite we could both taste.

Shells exploded in bright, winking flashes along the length of the ravine. Two enemy soldiers panicked and ran out of the burning foliage, their clothing afire. The force of the twenty-millimeter shells picked them up and threw them down the hill. Damndest thing I had seen in a long time.

"Okay, Lovebug, now let's get the other side." I pulled up into a left turn, the whining engines at full power as the OV-10 fought for altitude.

"I'll put my first mark right in front of a big bunch of rocks. String your bombs along the trail that runs downhill from there."

I dropped my nose for the second marking run, and the F-4 maneuvered to an attack position. The jet pilot would not see his run-in heading until I marked it front and back.

Whoomph! Whoomph! The first rocket smashed into the rocks, showering sparks as it billowed. The second detonated at the base of the hill beside a thin trail that led away into the open flat land.

"Lovebug in."

"Roger, Lovebug. Continue. Okay, Swift? Scarface? Do it!"

The helicopters started toward the smoking hill as the F-4 hurtled downward. I pulled around tightly and watched the bomber level its wings in true alignment with the ravine.

"Wings level."

"Cleared hot."

I put the pipper of my gunsight on the trailing edge of the Phantom's tail and squeezed off a burst. Twenty-millimeter shells detonated in the rocks behind the jet as it flew by in its vulnerable low-level run. Four bombs separated from the jet's wing racks, and the fins popped open immediately, slowing the weapons as the F-4 sped away.

This guy was good. I was going to have to call him and tell him so.

Kee-rumph, rumph, rumph, rumph! The bombs detonated microseconds apart as they struck along the descending ravine. My plane was rocked by the shock waves of the 250-pound bombs. I released back pressure on the stick and allowed the plane to continue climbing in a shallow turn.

Suddenly, enemy soldiers broke and ran down the trail and out into the open terrain. My heart pumped as I horsed the plane around instinctively, buffeting in a near stall as I turned to the attack.

"Gooners in the open!" I fairly yelled over the radio. "Sic 'em, Scarface!"

I put the pipper of the gunsight behind one of the enemy and walked twenty-millimeter shells through the loping figure. Running men scattered in every direction.

"It's a Cobra target, Scarface! Give it one run, and then we'll go in for the pickup!"

"Roger, Hostage!"

The thin, sleek helicopter gunship darted in under me and picked off three more of the enemy in a hail of fire from its chin-turret Gatling gun. The gunship pilot turned back for another run.

"Hold it up, Scarface. Let's get Thunderball out first."

"There's a guy down there who has his hands up, Hostage! He's trying to surrender or something! What do I do?"

I didn't have an answer to that one. Gingras did. He keyed his UHF transmitter.

"The son of a bitch is making an ass of himself! Kill him, for Christ's sake! We've got work to do!"

There was a burst from the SUU-11 Gatling gun, then the Cobra pilot turned back to the hill. I wasn't too thrilled about Gingras's solution to the problem, but it was better than mine, which was none at all. I called the helicopter flight leader.

"Okay, you've got it, Swift. I'm getting out of your way now. I can lay down some Willie Peter for a smoke screen if want it."

"Thanks, Hostage. Don't think we'll need it now."

Puffs of forty-millimeter explosions dotted the brush around the crater as the gunships, now joined up in section, sniffed the hillside like bird dogs hunting quail. The front-seat gunners pumped grenade-size forty-millimeter shells from their swiveling turrets as though to flush their quarry.

"Okay, Swift. The zone looks good." The lead Cobra whirred out to meet the transport helicopter as it started in toward the flat top of the hill.

"Swift One Eight into the zone." The long, green helicopter

slowed to a hover beside the crater and settled gently to the ground. The rotor downwash raised a swirl of red dust, and the Cobra gunships kept their deadly turrets trained on the ground surrounding the crater.

Gingras and I watched anxiously. This was the critical moment. The next few seconds would see either a routine extract or a horror show. Charlie had been known to lie back until the helicopter landed, then press the attack anew. I was pretty certain Charlie didn't have anything to press with, but I had been wrong before. Then, "Hostage Six? Good evening, pardner! This is Ringneck One Zero Four, your friendly flare dispenser. Where do you want . . ."

"Stay the hell off the air, Ringneck!"

Gingras keyed the intercom, "Snippy, snippy!"

The Marines scurried out of the crater the instant the CH-46 touched down, then disappeared across the tail ramp and into the helicopter, carrying their wounded with them. The double-rotored aircraft lifted into a hover quickly, then lowered its nose and sped off in a right turn.

"Coming out right," the pilot transmitted after the fact.

I watched the helicopters join up and head out to the southeast toward Da Nang. I unscrewed the cap of my canteen and thought about my next act. I had to apologize to Ringneck. The voice was unmistakably that of Col. Grover "Meat Eyes" Stewart, the group commander. Also, it seemed like a good idea at the time to give that pitiful F-4 wingman some target practice. He was going to have to dump that ordnance somewhere.

While Lee Gingras talked with the cannon cockers about an artillery fire mission, I made my manners with Ringneck and called Lovebug Two Zero Five Dash Two.

I set him up for two east-to-west runs on the bushy area at the base of the hill where the moaners had supposedly been hiding and drew him a dotted line with Willie Peter.

I forgot that my gunsight was set for twenty-millimeter, and the smoke bloomed short of where I had aimed. It didn't make a whole hell of lot of difference because the Phantom pilot released his napalm too high anyway, and it splashed without forward momentum and made small, round, burning holes somewhere in Quang Nam Province.

My second marks were better, and so was his bombing, and he got to go home that evening feeling good about himself. I told a lie about the importance of his target, just as he was going to tell lies that night in the Chu Lai officers club.

By the time we crossed the Da Nang harbor and headed for the entry point to the giant air base, it was already dark, and if a pilot was approaching the area for the first time, he might think he was looking at any peaceful seaport city in the world, so brightly was it lighted.

Ships at anchor, swinging at the hook in the harbor, were clearly visible, and the hospital ships were the most brilliantly lighted. The German hospital ship was in its usual spot, and that was a good sign. It meant that there would be no rocket attacks that night.

No one ever proved it, but we had long been convinced that the neutral ship, which allegedly treated Vietnamese on both sides, received warnings of imminent attacks and put to sea out of harm's way until the danger had passed. Whether this was true or not, no rockets ever flew when the ship was in port. Additionally, there were very few fishing boats bobbing offshore in the South China Sea, and this, too, was a corroborating sign that it would be a peaceful evening. Each fishing boat was required by law to show a light at night, and when hundreds of little lights glimmered out to sea, it was fair warning that Charlie was up to no good.

I turned westward, virtually on top of the German ship, which was almost as brightly lighted as the *Queen Mary* in Long Beach, and called Da Nang Tower. They were using runway 34, which meant that we would not be flying over the city of Da Nang on the downwind leg, and this, too, was a cheerful note. As often as not, people took shots at us from their backyards as we turned off the 180-degree abeam position when we landed to the south.

After touchdown, I rolled out to the taxi turnoff, halfway down the runway, where the ordnance dearming crew awaited us. I sat there for a minute with my hands out of the cockpit and tasted the warm, moist air while the Marines saftied the guns and rocket pods, then I taxied into the squadron area.

Lieutenant Gingras and I agreed that a cold beer was the next major item on our agenda.

The next morning, I drove up to division headquarters to chat with G-2 about the intelligence information Lee Gingras was reading out at Thuong Duc, and I learned that in the course of my close-in strafing around the crater, one of my bullets had ricochetted off a rock and hit a Marine in the hand.

I went over to the recon battalion to apologize, and the kid bought me a Coke. His buddy, who I supposed was the radio operator, told me I sounded much taller over the radio.

COMBAT ART

There is nothing pretty about war except the airplanes that fly above it, like golden eagles soaring with grace and dignity over a garbage dump.

From above, my war in Vietnam was green. Many different shades of green mottled the flat farmland that extended south and west from Da Nang. Lush, dark green painted the low mountains, which extended eastward from the hazy gray-green high country to the west, extending like fingers to cradle that flatland. Olive-green, shallow rivers carried silt eastward to the sea from the mountains and fertilized the flatland along the way. And all of these blends were splattered randomly with the vulgar, bilious green of sulfurous water filling a thousand bomb craters.

My war in 1970 took place above the three regiments of 1st Marine Division, a tactical area of responsibility within I Corps, which covered most of Quang Nam Province in the northern part of the country.

The terrain was bowl shaped, ringed with low mountains, but open to the South China Sea to the east. The vast expanse of flatland was wonderfully fertile, and in better times, it was an agricultural paradise. The mountain fingers that extended eastward from the inland ranges cupped the earth protectively and ensured a steady supply of fresh water from the rivers that flowed from them.

Near the Vu Gia River, well to the south of the city of Da Nang, a hill rose unexpectedly from the flat ground and provided a fine vista of the huge farming acreage and several lesser rivers, which had for so long been used for nothing more than a battleground. Surveyors and cartographers had determined the elevation of the hill to be precisely fifty-five meters in height, and because of that, the rise was known to a generation of Marines as Hill 55.

Because of Hill 55's commanding presence, it had long been a focal point for military activity, and at the beginning of 1970, it was the command post for the 1st Marine Regiment.

In medieval times, a lord would have built his castle fortress there. The terrain sloped gently away from the crest of the hill, providing splendid fields of fire against any would-be attackers. The only protective cover available to invaders was the bushy foliage that grew quickly and abundantly in the incredibly fertile soil.

Denuding the land of that protective ground cover did nothing positive for the soil. An agronomist would have wept, but such harsh landscaping did deny cover and concealment to the enemy. And so, a lone engineer with a bulldozer spent his entire combat tour scraping away the bushes and grass from the acres and acres of terrain surrounding the barbed-wire fences of the regimental CP—itself so ugly a scar on the land that the mere sight of it might have caused a buzzard to puke.

Day after day, the unknown engineer—perhaps a farm boy temporarily displaced from his homestead—would crank up his tractor and chug on out to his fields to plow and scrape away that which nature intended to be there. As soon as he had cleared an acre, tiny shoots of green would pop up from the reddish brown earth and rear up to shout to the 1st Marines that they had been there first and would be around long after the Marines had gone.

It was a never-ending job for the lonely engineer, and to amuse himself, he had taken to creative artwork as part of his landscaping.

With nothing to do all day but drive that tractor and scour the countryside, he had become adept with the huge blade at the front of the machine. His rows were straight and clean, and in time, he found himself doodling, creating patterns of green and brown—a swirl here, a circle there. It was only natural that he would carve his initials, and then graduate to bigger and better things as he sweated under the burning sun.

His first effort was crude, but so it is with all artists. He began with a simple U S M C, and he had a lot of trouble with the letter *S*. The *U* and the *M* and the *C* were box shaped, and his lines relatively straight, but it would take him a month to perfect rounded letters.

We who flew over his artwork were the only ones who could appreciate his labor of love, and because it was the only show in town, appreciate it we most certainly did.

We named him the "Phantom Scraper," and his presentations were a joy to us all. Carefully, he would remove all of the offensive shrubbery around his work until it was framed in green, and then, just before he moved on to his next section of land, he would erase the message with his blade and begin again on a new canvas.

The Phantom Scraper's second presentation was more ambitious and certainly esoteric. USMC was obvious to anyone flying by and announced to the world the title of the lord of the manor. SEMPER FI, however, required some familiarity with his beloved Marine Corps and carried a message. While we assumed that his Latin was negligible, probably restricted to the Corps' motto, we appreciated his loneliness and understood his cry of frustration. Had he added the word MAC, all of us in the air would have known that he was giving us the finger.

After a few more USMCs, which saw a definite improvement in his lettering, especially the *S*, he was ready for the big time.

He had learned the art of scraping in a turn, how to angle the blade just right, and over the period of a week in early February, he produced a Marine Corps emblem. The artwork in the middle of the globe was crude, some horizontal lines and some squiggles to represent one of the earth's hemispheres, and his anchor tilted too much to the vertical plane. But a globe and anchor it was, and I wrote a letter of appreciation to the 1st Marines, commending his inspired artwork and the lift he gave to the spirits of the airmen of 1st Marine Air Wing.

This was not a smart thing for me to do, for the graphics ceased immediately. The never-ending scraping around the command post's perimeter continued, but without the engineer's signature creations. The regimental commander, or more probably one of his staff officers, apparently did not see a value to humor and art on a battlefield, and his talent was stifled forever. Or so we thought.

Some time around the middle of the month, we were electrified to see the beginning scars of what appeared to be a new creation. There were only a few straight lines on the first day, but our squadron ready room buzzed with excitement. We were easily entertained, and someone, probably this writer, drew a facsimile of his work on the graffiti blackboard.

Had a new engineer replaced the Phantom Scraper? Or, as some speculated, was our artist in residence getting short and preparing to rotate back to the States? Perhaps the 1st Marines had entered a renaissance period before they moved their CP to an area closer to Da Nang, but we were doubtful of that.

Within forty-eight hours, the Phantom Scraper had blocked out the framework for his message, but the words were indiscernible. All we could see was a series of ten vertical lines on the southern slopes of the hill which angled down to the river banks. There was a definite gap in the series, however, five on the left, five on the right, and we were positive that he was working on two words. We had seen SEMPER FI before, and we were fairly certain that wasn't it, and we eagerly awaited the outcome.

On the third day, horizontal lines appeared as Scraper began to flesh out his work, but he was not to tip his hand for a day and a half as he connected only the bottoms of some letters, forming what appeared to be hieroglyphics. He was toying with us, and he knew it. The anticipation was delicious. More and more pilots made a point of overflying Hill 55, and speculation was rampant.

On the evening of the fifth day, I noted that there had been no progress. Other acreage had been cleared, and I feared that he had been discovered and ordered to stop his foolishness. Or just maybe he was waiting for a dramatic moment, such as his departure from the 1st Marines, for we were beginning to suspect that his statement was not going to be a friendly one.

As in the original, biblical creation, he finished his work on the sixth day, and we all knew that on the seventh day he would rest, most probably on an airliner headed back to Okinawa, where he would be processed for his journey home.

The *F* was perfect, as was the letter *U*, but he had trouble with the *K* in the first word. Similarly, the *Y* that began the second word was awkward, diagonal lines not easy to accomplish with a bulldozer, but the *O* and the *U* were evenly spaced, and we applauded his outrage.

America loves a hero. The Phantom Scraper was certainly one of mine.

AH, YOUTH!

Over the years, people have wondered just how a mild mannered, junior high school English teacher ever made it as a cold, steely-eyed Marine. My answers have always been evasive, requiring me to remove my glasses and squint until I have focused on my inquisitors—which almost passes for steely-eyed—and then dazzle them with salty cuss words. But the truth of the matter is that the navy wouldn't have me.

I truly believed this at one time in my life. I received my first rejection at the age of five, about the time I gained national prominence as a champion boxer.

I was reared in Annapolis, Maryland, about two hundred yards from the main gate of the United States Naval Academy. Spike Webb, Navy's legendary boxing coach in the 1930s, invited my mother to enroll me in his navy-junior boxing program. My physician father, Anne Arundel County health commissioner in the early thirties, had recently passed away, and Spike—who seemed a little punchy to me, and talked out of the side of his mouth like Pat O'Brien—probably detected wimpiness in a young kid who was being raised in a household run by a woman trying to build a dental practice during the depression. Who knew how I really came to participate in his pugilistic program? Five-year-olds didn't spend too much time pondering cause and effect. But a boxer I became, and every Saturday morning, David Ansell would pack me on the handle bars of his bicycle, and off we'd go to the Naval Academy's McDonough Hall for our weekly workout on the punching bags.

They called me Mickey in those days. I was a southpaw trained in a right-handed stance, which made me a devastating contender, and I retired from the ring in 1937 with the fifty-pound crown in my pocket. I beat up a four-year-old for the title, sending him through the ropes with a haymaker that came all the way from the floor.

All of my punches were haymakers that came from the floor. We wore sixteen-ounce gloves, and I was only three feet tall, and the ends of the gloves dragged on the mat a lot. When I pulled a roundhouse left off the canvas and smacked my opponent in the face in that championship match, he crawled, crying and screaming, through the ropes, ran to his mother, and buried his face in her skirts. I'll never forget it.

I made the newsreels that day, and so did the kid who ran to his mother and wiped his snotty nose on her skirt. I got my picture in the *Baltimore Sun* as the referee held up my hand, and all the world saw my feet clearly a foot off the ground.

I was accepted as a boxer, and it was wonderful. The rejection came during those damn bicycle trips to McDonough Hall through the Maryland Avenue gate, which in the thirties and forties was the Academy's main gate. Either David Ansell wasn't a very good cyclist, or I wasn't an accommodating passenger, because on three successive trips to my boxing lessons, I fell off the bike and splattered my face on the pavement, causing large lumps to be a regular part of my profile. After the third spill in as many trips, as I lay there bleeding all over my blue and gold boxing uniform with NAVY lettered across the chest, the civilian gate guard, the "Jimmy Leg" as they were called in those days because of the clips they wore on their trousers when they made their rounds on bicycles, administered the rebuff. "Heaven help the navy," he muttered as he ministered to my wounds, "if they're ever dumb enough to put you in charge of anything."

My second rejection followed soon after. A rising star in the navy, a commander at the time, named C. Turner Joy—after whom a destroyer would be later christened to make his name synonymous with the beginning of the Vietnam War—moved in a couple of houses up from ours on Prince George Street. His young son, Duncan, and I were playing among the packing crates in the front yard as the movers carried the furniture inside. A board with a nail in it slipped in our hands and gouged Duncan's eye, and I was blamed for it. When it was believed that the injury might prevent him from following his father in the navy, I was advised in no uncertain terms that any efforts toward a similar career would not be in my best interests.

Whether or not any of that was true, of course, I had no way of knowing. But I believed it at the time, and spent a few years with the idea firmly implanted in my mind that if I were ever to put on a uniform, it had better be some color other than navy blue.

I joined my older brother in boarding school in 1941, at the age of eight, but I don't think Duncan Joy's eye was the reason why. I spent the next nine years at St. Paul's School for Boys in Baltimore, where I set no records. I was a decent student and generally did as I was told, and sang in the church choir with such future musical luminaries as Johnny Mann and Glen Yarborough.

My brother Peter was more adventurous than I, and before he graduated he was expelled a couple of times, once for stealing the school station wagon, which I thought was pretty daring—stupid, but daring—and running it up the ass end of a slopeback '41 Buick.

At St. Paul's, I developed a burning passion for journalism. I played varsity ball and participated in all of the proper clubs and activities, and fell in love a lot. But newsprint fascinated me, and I labored long and hard on the school publication, *the Monitor*, with a dream of one day writing for a big-city paper. The smell of the printing plant where we put the paper to bed was perfume to me, and I was convinced that a Linotype machine was the most wonderful invention of all mankind. When I had newsprint or galley proofs in my hands, I was certain that my future would be on somebody's city desk.

My mother's dental practice, however, gave rise to a cozy relationship with the Naval Academy, especially with the athletic department. This closeness had a powerful influence on both my brother and me. When football players and other stellar athletes arrived in Annapolis to enter the Academy and were rejected for dental reasons, good old Mom was there to patch up their mouths. In gratitude, the director of athletics saw to it that we always had tickets to the games and access to the Academy's great facilities.

World War II was an incredibly wonderful time for a young boy growing up in Annapolis with the Naval Academy as a vacation playground. During the war years, the top athletes in the country were playing for Army and Navy. They had all-Americans sitting on the bench, and being able to hang out with famous people like Clyde Scott and Pistol Pete Williams and Don Whitmire was a powerful influence on an impressionable youngster.

The majority of my childhood friends were navy juniors, sons and daughters of naval officers, most of whom also went to boarding schools. On weekends and holidays, I spent as much time in those huge navy quarters on Porter Road as I did in my own house.

Boarding school wasn't any less warlike. St. Paul's may have been a nice, church-run prep school, but during those wartime years we were pretty doggone militaristic. We lacked only uniforms and leadership, and it didn't take long to improvise both. After classes, we donned our battle jackets, which were covered with as many military patches as we could find, and headed for the woods behind the school, the hills and streams of which served as one of the truly great battlefields of the war. John Prosser Tabb had a genuine khaki army overseas cap, which made him our commanding officer.

I became quite comfortable with military people, and the structure of it all, and the day I turned seventeen I enlisted in the Naval Reserve at Fort McHenry, and got out of study hall every Tuesday night to don a sailor suit and journey down to South Baltimore for drills and lectures in navy lore.

When my brother graduated from St. Paul's, three years ahead of me, he went directly into the naval-air college program at Duke University, later to become an AD Skyraider pilot whose exploits in Korea are documented in books about that airplane. I went off to Washington and Lee University in 1950 to study journalism.

In those days, St. Paul's graduates went to one of three schools. We went either to Washington and Lee or the University of Virginia, or if going away to school was too traumatic, to Johns Hopkins University in Baltimore. I was taken with Washington and Lee's journalism program, and mightily impressed with Dean Frank Gilliam's recruiting pitch, so I packed myself off to Lexington, Virginia, to prepare myself for a career as a hard-hitting newspaperman. Additionally, I transferred to the Naval Reserve unit at Fishersville, Virginia, partly out of patriotism, but mainly because the Korean War was stirring up the draft boards again, and I was not interested in freezing my tail off in a foxhole over there.

My record at W & L was no more impressive than it had been at St. Paul's. I'll never forget Dean Gilliam's admonition when he informed me that I had lost my scholarship grant because I'd failed to maintain a *B* average. "Mr. Moriarty," he drawled as he delivered the bad news, "you have experimented, sir, in a self-administered course in sociology."

And so I had. I had a wonderful time. They didn't seem to

care whether I showed up for class or not, and I often did not. On top of that, when my mother bought me a car that would handle the mountains, I was over the hills and sniffing around Sweetbriar College three of four times a week. I wasn't in love, I was in heat, but I do not recall being very successful in that endeavor.

I was an enormous social success in that fraternity-oriented men's university, mainly because I knew the filthiest and most disgusting limericks ever written by human beings. Who ever said a private school education didn't prepare a man for the important things in life!

But my journalism career came to a screeching halt during my freshman year when it became apparent to one of the student literary giants that I was not a very good writer. T. K. Wolfe, Tom Wolfe, who has over the years proved himself to be a wonderful writer, ridiculed my submissions to the *Ring Tum Phi* student newspaper and *Southern Collegian* literary publication and damaged my delicate ego to the point that I screwed the cap on my pen and put it away for the next thirty years.

I was pissed off at T. K. Wolfe at the time and hated him for his haughty manner. But a single reading of those feeble literary efforts several years later made it painfully evident that his judgment had been correct and that he had probably done me a favor. Anyway, I began to lose interest in college.

By 1952, the "police action" was raging in Korea, and my brother was in the middle of it. With visions of being another Joe Foss, whose *Esquire* magazine foldout picture in an F6F Hellcat, with a dozen or so Japanese flags painted on the side, was the centerpiece of my bedroom art collection, I transferred to the Naval Air Reserve unit at NAS (Naval Air Station) Anacostia in Washington, D.C., in order to enter flight training through the Naval Aviation Cadet program. The navy needed pilots, and the reserve unit had a quota to fill, and I needed an excuse to quit college. As soon as I had the requisite sixty academic hours from Washington and Lee, I was off to Pensacola in July of 1952.

Preflight was about as much fun as a wet crossword puzzle. The military portion wasn't too tough. I knew my left from my right, and except for the day I stuck a sword in my eye, I do not recall any serious traumatic experiences. Physically, I suffered about as much as the next guy, but the heat of Pensacola that summer wasn't nearly as killing as the exhaustion I would suffer going through the army's jump school during the month of August ten years later.

It was the academic portion of the program that was my undoing. Engines were mysterious, just as electricity was magic, and I had to drop back a class about halfway through those grueling sixteen weeks, seventeen in my case, because I was absolutely unable to understand how the tip of a propellor blade traveled faster than the rest of the damn thing. Also, the fact that I navigated my classroom aircraft carrier into downtown Boise, Idaho, might have had something to do with my setback from Class 32-52 to 33-52.

But it was during Preflight that I decided to become a cold, steely-eyed Marine pilot and avoid a possible run-in with Adm. C. Turner Joy. Two incidents cemented this decision. During a physical training boxing class, I put my roommate's headlights out with a roundhouse left that came off the floor, and reinforced my childhood delusion that I was a tough guy. And about a week before graduation I had a religious experience.

The senior Marine aviator in the Naval Air Training Command was a tall, striking, and highly decorated colonel named Guy Morrow, whose reputation as a warrior was legendary. I had never seen the man up close before, but I knew a lot about his reputation as a hard-ass because I was interested in his daughter for a while there.

I was walking down the street, headed for the naval exchange from the cadet barracks, and as I approached the naval air training headquarters building, out came the famous man himself, swagger stick and all. Stung with the same shot of adrenaline I would experience many times in later years when I had to do something scary, I stiffened as though I had a ramrod implanted in my spinal column and snapped off the very best salute I knew how.

Colonel Morrow, about seven or eight feet tall as I recall, fixed me with a pair of gray eyes that really were steely and touched that swagger stick to his fore-and-aft cap in a manner that made Field Marshal Rommel look like a clergyman, and I damn near came unglued.

I knew then and there that I had to be a Marine. I had to be just like him, even though I wasn't exactly sure how I was going to grow two feet. That night in the barracks, I dazzled my roommates with the news that I was going to apply for a commission in the Marine Corps when I got to primary training at Whiting Field, which was where we could first apply because the selection board there in Pensacola didn't want cadets applying until after they had soloed so that they wouldn't waste time on people who couldn't fly.

The roommates were reluctant to accept my decision because they knew that I had been determined to become a navy AD Skyraider pilot, just like my brother, who was at that time in Korea, flying off the *Essex* with VA-55, and who had just been shot down and rescued in a harrowing episode of evasion and escape that left us all starry-eyed.

The story of my brother's exciting episode has little to do with my actual flight training, but it's a good one, and I include it here because it sheds some light on why I became such a stickler on the subject of cockpit discipline and survival in later years.

On 17 October 1952, Ens. Peter Manx Moriarty was blown out of the sky just south of Wonsan with a single shot from a new, radar-controlled antiaircraft gun the North Koreans had just received from the Russians. He didn't even have to bail out because the airplane disintegrated around him. The only damage to his person consisted of burns around his wrists, where he had rolled down his gloves, and on the right side of his face because he had unsnapped his oxygen mask.

He was captured immediately upon landing in his parachute, and a long, hairy episode of escape attempts ensued as squadron mates made firing runs on the position, causing the bad guys to scatter long enough for Pete to scamper off. But he wasn't able to run fast enough, and the bad guys, well-conditioned farmers for the most part, were able to catch him, take his .38 pistol away, and empty it out on him, missing all six times   which I still find hard to believe.

After about a half hour of this game of capture the Yankee, one Lt. Cmdr. Jim Franke came chugging into the area in his search-and-rescue helicopter, and in a coordinated attack-and-snatch operation with Attack Squadron 55's Skyraiders, Peter was picked up and whisked away. The helicopter picked up thirty-seven bullet holes from the fresh North Korean troops who had just arrived to complete the capture.

That's an abbreviation of the story that appears in Rosario Rausa's book about the airplane, entitled *Skyraider*; but what happened next, and didn't make it into his book, was equally fascinating to those of us who grew up on Prince George Street in Annapolis.

The closest ship to Wonsan at the time was a destroyer on picket duty, and because Pete didn't look too healthy with all of those burns, Franke, who received a Silver Star for his gutsy flying, decided to take him there for immediate treatment.

He was lowered down to the deck and taken to the sick bay and treated for his burns, after some really gruesome photographs had been taken. And then he was put to bed.

Now, there wasn't a spare bunk to be found on that little tin can, and so it was decided that he would be laid to rest temporarily in the bed of the junior watch officer, who would be on the bridge for another couple of hours and wouldn't be needing it anyway.

The ensign who owned the bed got off watch eventually and returned to his stateroom to see who this pilot was who had preempted the bunk. I suspect he had entertained ideas of using it himself and was a bit put out about it all, but any animosity disappeared the instant he stepped into the cramped quarters.

"Pete?" he gulped, pointing at a face he thought he recognized.

"Gordy?" my brother answered, probably not pointing because his wrists were all burned up.

Ens. Gordy Van Hook was our next-door neighbor in Annapolis. Small world.

Meanwhile, back in the training command, Peter Moriarty's little brother spent the next year or so going through all of the various stages of flight training without doing anything extraordinarily stupid.

The amount of flight time we amassed during flight training in the early fifties was incredible compared to what it is today. I finished up with just under four hundred hours, and today, with cost-cutting aircraft simulators and improved instructional techniques, a pilot just as well, and maybe better, trained can receive his wings with two hundred hours.

I received that much time in the SNJ alone (navy trainer manufactured by North American, called the T-6 in the air force). Today, SNJs are nostalgically referred to as "war birds," and travel around to air shows with all manner of warlike cosmetics, but we spent months and months grinding through our training maneuvers in the west Florida skies, knowing full well that our brightly colored, pansy-yellow airplanes were kiddy-car trainers.

It took nineteen flights just to solo in those days. That was a lot of flight time, and when the big moment arrived, it was virtually impossible for us to screw things up because we had been drilled so carefully that we performed by rote memory.

The check pilot on my A-19, "safe for solo," flight put me through my paces, spin recovery and a dozen or so different stalls, then had me shoot two or three touch-and-go landings at Pace Field, one of the outlying grass fields in the area. When he was satisfied that I could fly without killing myself, he told me to make a final landing and taxi over to the side of the field, where he got out of the plane and smoked a cigarette while I took off and shot a few landings without him.

I did as I was told, and each time keyed the intercom and reported, "Gear down, flaps down, prop full forward," to an empty rear cockpit.

We spent a lot of time flying with the canopies open. All takeoffs and landings, formation flying, and gunnery were performed alfresco, which was just fine in the summer time. But when the weather was cold, as happened even in Florida in the winter time, the cockpit grew a bit nippy. I used to wonder how pilots of open-cockpit planes in the old days could stand it.

In gunnery, at Barin Field, Foley, Alabama, each plane was fitted with a thirty-caliber machine gun, and that was pretty interesting. The back end of the gun was in the cockpit so that we could clear it when it jammed, and it fired through the propellor just like the Sopwith Camels my father flew during World War I when he was in the RAF, and when he probably froze his tail off too.

The instructor flew the tow plane, dragging a huge white sleeve about a thousand feet behind him, and graded our runs as we snarled around the target and snapped off short bursts of machine-gun fire. I don't recall that any of us got many hits, but our individual egos swelled measurably, and maybe I grew a few of those inches I needed.

I remember one afternoon when our instructor, Marine Cpt. Dayton Robinson, debriefed us after a flight, and beside my name on his knee-board grading sheet were the words: AW SHIT. I was pretty upset about that until he explained that it meant "angle wide, slightly high initial turn."

Taking the SNJ aboard an aircraft carrier was a kick. We practiced a lot on the outlying fields around Barin Field, grinding around the landing pattern for hours at a hundred feet, gear and flaps down, in SNJs that were equipped with tail hooks and had DON'T CRASH painted under the canopies in bright red letters, and shooting as many as fifteen practice carrier landings at a time until the instructor felt we were ready to "hit the boat."

I'll be honest. I don't remember much about my first carrier landing, aboard the tiny *Monterey*, a CV-L built on a Liberty ship hull. I remember turning off the "180," which was when the left wingtip was abeam the ship's smokestack, and I remember turning through the "90" and seeing the ass end of the ship and its wake as I staggered along at seventy-five feet and about seventy-five knots, but I don't recall anything else until I saw the plane director giving me the signal to get my feet off the brakes.

As I said, carrier takeoffs and landings were performed with the canopy open, the quicker to exit the plane should the pilot end up in the drink, the way we practiced in the "Dilbert Dunker" in the NAS Pensacola swimming pool. Because the straight-deck carrier steamed directly into the wind, the acrid stench that belched from the smokestacks became an exclusive naval aviation sensory experience that all old-time carrier pilots will carry to their graves. One sniff of number-six bunker-crude sulfur dioxide factory pollutant still propels me back to my youth with visions of aircraft carrier wakes and fantails and all manner of exciting memories.

Our instructor was the LSO for our carrier qualifications, the landing signal officer. He had brightly colored stripes sewn on the front of his flight suit, and one of the prettiest sights in the world for us was his dramatic "cut" signal as he slammed his right paddle against his left shoulder, just as you can see today in all the old carrier movies.

Another pretty sight was a brown shoe. After a man had landed aboard an aircraft carrier, he was entitled to wear brown shoes with his khakis and aviation greens, and this separated him from the black-shoe, surface navy. A twenty-year-old cadet who was able to sport that status symbol had to grow another six or seven inches overnight.

In advanced training, at NAS Cabaniss Field in Corpus Christi, Texas, I picked up over a hundred hours in the F6F Hellcat (the sixth fighter manufactured by *F*, Grumman), and it is difficult to describe the feeling of accomplishment in flying a "blue airplane" for the first time.

All navy and Marine tactical planes were painted dark blue until the mid-1950s, and that first "fam" flight in a blue airplane was a rite of passage right up there in importance with a man's first carrier landing and his wedding day—not as memorable as his first solo flight, but certainly greater than initial carnal knowledge. We had spent the better part of a year droning and whining around in high-visibility yellow airplanes, and that first flight in a blue airplane was a thrill young pilots today cannot imagine.

Our instructor in "Advanced," navy Lt. Vic Kreck, took the six of us in his training flight to the Cabaniss Field officers club, where we ceremoniously drank beer from a chrome-plated bomb shell. From that moment on, we were members in good standing in the international brotherhood of eagles.

When you were twenty years old, the Hellcat was a wondrous thing. The scent alone—avgas, oil, hydraulic fluid, and electrical smells—was perfume, and the rugged chugging of the R-2800 engine was damn near symphonic. As a kid, I spent many hours lying on my bed, staring at that picture of Joe Foss in his Hellcat and dreaming of the day when I too could fly one, and in advanced training I got to do it.

Flying out of Cabaniss Field, I broke a Hellcat one day over the Gulf of Mexico when I lost sight of a gunnery tow banner while attempting an overhead run—which we weren't supposed to do in the first place—and pranged into the steel bar that held the target together, pulling enough Gs to rip the wings off an ordinary airplane. It caused strike damage, even though I was able to nurse the plane back to base. I came out of that incident smelling like a rose when I bared my soul in front of the Student Pilot Disposition Board, the notorious "Speedy" board, and they presented me with the monthly safety award for being honest. They gave me a factory model of an F9F-8 Cougar as my prize, and I still have it.

I met my future wife at about that same time, one of the most beautiful women the state of Texas has ever produced, and I still have her too.

In December of 1953, I received my wings and Marine Corps commission after completing advanced carrier qualifications in the F6F back at Pensacola. After a wonderful Christmas leave—during which I may have finished growing those two feet I needed—I reported to the 2d Marine Air Wing at Cherry Point, North Carolina. I was absolutely certain that I would be assigned to one of the jet squadrons which were just then receiving the new North American FJ-3 Saber Jets, the navy and Marine Corps version of the F-86.

My interview with the wing assignments officer lasted thirty seconds.

"You married, son?"

"No, sir."

"Sorry. I'm going to have to send you to Edenton."

Right behind me was a tough looking captain who had a ton of ribbons attesting to the fact that he had served a tour in Korea before he went to flight training and wouldn't take that kind of a fast shuffle off anybody.

"You married, Captain?"

"Yes, sir. Two kids, ages six and four."

"Sorry. I'm going to have to send you to Edenton."

Capt. Whit Bakauskis was older than I was, and far more in control of things, and he wasn't about to leave that office until he had been given a full accounting of everything that was important to a man with a wife and two children.

"What are they flying at Edenton?"

"F4U Corsairs."

"Sounds good to me."

It sounded good to me, too. I was listening from the doorway. My heart soared, although I had absolutely no idea where Edenton was. It could have been smack dab in the middle of the Great Dismal Swamp for all I cared. The opportunity to fly the great bent-wing bird was something I had dreamed of ever since I cut the picture of Pappy Boyington out of *Life* and tacked it on my wall, right under Joe Foss. I had flown the Hellcat, and now I was going to fly the Corsair! To hell with Saber Jets! Elation! Joy! Rapture! Life was good!

Edenton, North Carolina, "The Cradle of the Colonies," was a charming old town on the Albemarle Sound, some seventy-five miles north of Cherry Point and about as close to the Great Dismal Swamp as a man could be without getting his feet wet. The town was charming; the Marine Corps auxiliary landing field there in 1954 was not.

The base was one of a thousand airfields built during World War II, and abandoned as soon as the war was over. This one had been reopened—probably just to keep the town of Edenton from claiming some really choice real estate—an air group had been moved in, and no cosmetic repairs had been made.

I got my orders stamped at the Marine Aircraft Group 14 headquarters building—which had two broken windows in the front door alone—drove down the muddy streets to Marine Attack Squadron 225, VMA-225, where I dashed out to the flight line to look at the wonderful hose-nose, bent-wing airplanes I would be lucky enough to fly. To my total dismay, I saw instead twenty-four brand new AD-5s—which are arguably one of the ugliest Skyraider flying machines Donald Douglas ever built.

"What happened to the Corsairs?" I moaned in the personnel office as a clerk processed my orders.

A voice from another desk answered. "Flew the last one out day before yesterday," said Lt. Al Haynes—who would become famous years later as the heroic pilot of United Airlines Flight 232 when he managed to put his DC-10 on the ground at Sioux City, Iowa, without controls, and save a few hundred lives.

"Hell of an air show. You should have seen it!"

A year later, I would miss my second, and last, chance to fly the venerable F4U (*U* stood for the manufacturer, Chance Vought, or Vought-Sikorsky, depending on what year it was). In April of 1955, I checked in at the air station at Quantico, Virginia, to sign up for my flight time while I was going through an infantry training course designed for young, former NAV-CADS who had been selected for regular commissions. I looked lovingly at the beautiful flight line of Corsairs, which were there for all of the Marine pilots in the Washington area to fly.

Unfortunately, I knew how to fly the twin-engined SNB-5 (navy trainer by Beechcraft), and Quantico had a need for Beechcraft pilots to haul colonels and generals around; and while fifty other new regular officers were getting their rocks off in Corsairs on weekends, I drilled holes in the sky, chauffeuring a particularly unpleasant brigadier general around the East Coast so that he could play golf with other generals.

But I learned to fly in VMA-225, and while I never warmed up to the two-seated AD-5, which was truly worthless as a dive bomber, I did come to appreciate the bastard modification when we flew aboard aircraft carriers, some of which were really tiny. Visibility for carrier landings was terrific because the side-by-side cockpit configuration put the pilot a little to the left of the nose; and landing, even on a wee little CV-L like the USS *Saipan*, was a piece of cake.

I have no intention of plugging Rosario Rausa's *Skyraider*, but my picture is in his book. In October of 1954, our squadron, "Two and a Quarter," participated in an amphibious exercise in the Camp Lejeune area, when the Marine Corps air station at New River was still called Peterfield Point Field. Capt. Ken Kopecky, who has been well known in the bus business in California for years, was leading, and we were called upon to make several passes across the beach for the benefit of some photographers. I'm the guy flying in a skid.

From VMA-225 I went to the Marine Corps air station at Miami, Florida—today the civilian field at Opa Locka—where I honed my flying skills as an instrument instructor, flying in the right seat of the Beechcraft-built SNB in VMIT-21, a small, instrument-training squadron.

I volunteered for that assignment because there was a jet group at Miami, MAG-32, and I was absolutely certain that I could wangle my way in after a respectable period of time as an instrument instructor. But the jets all moved up to the new air station at Beaufort, South Carolina, almost as soon as my new wife and I arrived, and I was doomed to flying machines with propellors for several more years.

I managed to escape the boredom of watching capable pilots screw up Charlie patterns and instrument approaches when the Suez crisis of 1956 created a burning need for AD pilots to form an all-Marine carrier air group to go to the Mediterranean Sea and bomb the hell out of whoever it was we were mad at. For a while there, we didn't know whether we would be pissed off at the Egyptians or the British and French, but we had fun flying AD-6s and 7s off the USS *Tarawa*, day and night, until they canceled the war. And then it was back to the grind of watching perfectly good pilots "under the hood" go insane flying ADF approaches into the abandoned airfield that would soon become Homestead Air Force Base. We used the Perrine Homer—which the students hated, but I liked because there was a nudist camp directly under the procedure turn.

All of that multiengine Beechcraft time in my log book was like syphilis in a health record, and when the instrument training squadron was decommissioned later, I was shanghaied into VMR-353 (*R* for transport), where I learned to fly what was absolutely the ugliest airplane in the world, the R4Q Flying Boxcar. This was later renamed the C-119, to match the air force designation.

The R4Q-2s we flew out of Opa Locka—from the same hangar the coast guard uses today—had R-3350 engines, just like the AD Skyraiders, and I was comfortable with them. They were capable of developing 3350 horsepower, one horse per cubic inch displacement. Treated properly, they were the ultimate in reciprocating aircraft engines.

Later on, however, in Iwakuni, Japan, where I joined VMR-253 in October of 1957, I discovered R4Q-1s with R-4360 engines.

These were undoubtedly the most powerful and unreliable power plants ever built, and I learned to hate reciprocating engines with a passion. All those moving parts!

The R-4360, with 4360 cubic inches displacement, was the engine for which Mr. Fairchild's twin boomed monstrosity had been designed in the first place, but the air force's C-124s and B-36s needed all the "corncob" engines in production. And so the later generations of R4Qs and C-119s had come out with the more common, and more reliable, R-3350s bolted onto the mounts.

Just a plug change on that twenty-eight cylinder monstrosity cost more than my salary, and we changed a lot of spark plugs. At one point, every new 4360 we received from overhaul failed in the first ten hours of flight. Five or six Boxcars without engines were stacked up in a corner of the airfield at Iwakuni, where we considered renting them out as substandard housing. The plane was banned from carrying passengers over water, so bad was the engine problem. But the human being is an adaptable creature, and we learned to enjoy the bright side. Cargo we could carry chained down in the back didn't get up and walk around and ask stupid questions and leave a lot of trash lying around. And it never once puked in rough weather.

I once lost an engine just after takeoff out of Iwakuni in an airplane two thousand pounds over max-allowable gross weight. The radio operator defecated in his pants, and I might have, too, but I was too busy nursing the damn thing around to get back to the field.

Right after takeoff the tower called: "Time off, three two, standing by for Kagoshima estimate."

My answer caught him by surprise. "Clear that f——king runway!" I yelled, and probably didn't even need a radio to be heard.

I managed to get about eight hundred feet using full power and water injection on the good engine, and I made a super single-engine landing just before that engine, too, froze in the mounts. I drank a lot of martinis that night.

But it was a great flying experience, and I was able to earn a special instrument rating, long before most pilots my age even thought about it. And I became an expert on just about every airfield in the non-Communist part of Southeast Asia—even a grass strip on the tiny island of Miyako Jima, where I limped in on one engine with a load of liquid oxygen I was trying to get to Ping Tung in southern Taiwan in 1958.

We were getting ready to fight the Chinese Communists for one reason or another then, and that was about the same time an FJ-3 from VMF-323 fired a Sidewinder missile on the flight line at Tainan airfield, causing no end of consternation.

The Chinese Nationalists wanted the new Sidewinder missiles, and Marines secretly flew a bunch in on the wings of some FJs. When external power was plugged into one of them before anyone had safetied all of the switches—*woosh*! The missile took off across the field, bounced off the runway twenty feet behind a landing Chinese C-46 with a camel painted on the tail, then flew upward through the canvas top of a jeep that was racing along the parallel road. Hell of a show! It didn't arm itself, so nothing blew up. But the squadron commander of VMF-323 had to do an artful rug dance on the carpet of one really pissed-off Chinese colonel.

I didn't have to answer for it. I was busy nursing another sick R4Q, further down the flight line, while I waited for my squadron to fly in a new engine.

Our adjutant in VMR-253 in 1958, incidentally, was Capt. Joe Went who went on to earn four stars as assistant commandant, the highest billet an aviator can achieve in the Marine Corps.

I returned to the States at the end of 1958 and was assigned to the group staff in MAG-33 at the Marine Corps air station at El Toro in Southern California. I was absolutely certain I was going to snivel into one of the fighter squadrons there—the F8U Crusader had just arrived, and they were filling the squadrons with lieutenants. But a lieutenant with twenty-five hundred hours didn't have any sympathy points working for him at all, and I was planted in a desk, right beside the personnel officer, to shuffle people and papers for while.

I was able to perform a sleight-of-hand trick and get out of the office by volunteering to be a general's aide. That was not one of my better decisions. Maj. Gen. Sam Jack was one of the greatest guys a brand new captain could work for, and he taught me a lot. But Mrs. Jack and I didn't get along too well. I returned to the wing in less than a year, with enough earned sympathy points to grease myself right into Marine Fighter Squadron 323, which had returned from shooting Sidewinders at Chinese C-46s and was flying Crusaders back in Marine Air Group 33. Being a general's aide had its interesting moments, but I didn't think it was any job for a Marine, and I may have said so once or twice. From that time on, I harbored no desire to rise to lofty, multistarred rank and duck potshots from every politician with an election to win.

The F8U Crusader (*U* now stood for Ling Temco Vought) was a great airplane for its day, and I was just as obnoxious about my exalted position in life as the next Marine fighter pilot. You can always tell a fighter pilot, but you can't tell him much!

Aircraft availability was really sorry in 1960 and 1961. We didn't do very much flying, except when we flew over to our new training base at Yuma, Arizona. We had picked this base up in a swap with the air force. They wanted the navy and Marine base on the Mojave Desert, and gave us Vincent Air Force Base in return. For a week or two every six months, we were able to get in some decent training on the gunnery ranges over the desert, but we didn't accomplish a whole lot at El Toro.

I took a little heat when a lieutenant in a division of four planes I was leading decided to put on a show for some friends of his down at Camp Pendleton during a firepower demonstration, tried a roll at about fifty feet over the stands, and splattered himself all over the countryside. When a pilot died in those days, the flight leader had to take gas, and I was not unhappy when orders for Hawaii arrived in the mail.

I then spent a year and a half in the Air and Naval Gunfire Liaison Company, where I learned to jump out of perfectly good airplanes, and which I discuss in another chapter. Then it was two delightful years in VMF-232, at Kaneohe Bay—again flying Crusaders, which were by then redesignated F-8s in accordance with the Defense Department's edict that all military airplanes be labeled the same way. The F8U-1E had become the F-8B.

There was some great flying to be had in Hawaii. The gunnery range was only thirty miles out to sea north of Kaneohe Bay, and we were able to spray twenty-millimeter cannon shells at tow banners without worrying too much about our fuel supply. Also, we made a lot of carrier landings and enjoyed some competitive air-to-air combat with Air National Guard F-102s from Hickam Field.

Whenever a navy carrier air group came to Hawaii on a mid-Pacific shakedown cruise to prepare for a West-Pac deployment, the carrier would off-load the planes of the air group at NAS Barbers Point and make the deck available to the Marine squadrons there in the islands. Huge ships, like the *Kitty Hawk* and the *Constellation*, would steam southwest all night and turn around at dawn to cruise slowly into the tradewinds toward Oahu during daylight hours. We would fly out to the ship, shoot a bunch of trap landings, and return to Kaneohe Bay. Sometimes, late in the afternoons, we would be making our upwind turns over Waikiki Beach.

The F-8 Crusader was a wonderful airplane to take aboard ship, and the reason was that the wing went up and down. The A-7 of today looks a lot like the Crusader, which means that the plane's design was sound. But the Corsair II's wing is glued to the fuselage, and it doesn't go up and down.

In the forties and fifties, after becoming so famous with the F4U Corsair during World War II, Chance Vought came out with some real losers. There was some funny looking thing that looked like a flying saucer, which they labeled the F5U, and later wished no one had ever seen. And that disaster was followed by the F6U Pirate, and the F7U Cutlass—the latter making it to a few squadrons in the mid-fifties, up the road from us, at NAS Oceana near Norfolk, Virginia. The Cutlass was a good-looking airplane, but turned out to be a loser because it was underpowered and killed so many pilots. The company pretty well staked its future on the F8U Crusader, calling it the "Great Redeemer" after it proved that it could go supersonic without having to go into a dive like the rest of the underpowered slugs the navy and Marine Corps were forced to fly.

The problem with the F7U—aside from the fact that sometimes the nose fuel tank didn't transfer, and the center of gravity imbalance caused the plane to start flipping end over end—was that the angle of attack for landing was so high that the poor pilot had trouble seeing over the nose to find out what the ass end of the carrier looked like. The remarkable "fix" for the F8U Crusader saw a variable-incidence wing, which allowed the fuselage to remain straight and level while the wing attained the high angle of attack all by itself, just by moving a handle in the cockpit.

The incredible visibility made carrier landings a piece of cake. But this same feature made "showtime" formation takeoffs a bit tricky. All of the planes in the formation had to rotate through a major configuration change at the same time, or the whole show looked like something out of a flea circus. That's the reason no one ever saw F-8s take off more than two at a time. After the landing gears were raised simultaneously on a simple head nod, the flight leader nodded his head forward demonstratively as he lowered his wing, and a plane watcher could pretty well tell the experience level of the number two man by how well synchronized the rotation turned out.

We became chummy with the Hawaii Air National Guard, which flew more than any active duty squadron back on the mainland because they were the islands' first line of defense. Some of our dog fights with their F-102s were spectacular, squadron against squadron, with sometimes as many as sixteen airplanes going at it tooth and nail, and creating an overcast of condensation trails over Oahu.

One Friday afternoon, after a great air battle, the Air Guard pilots landed at Kaneohe Bay and tied down their planes for the night, and we all got roaring drunk together at the Marine officers club happy hour, where we got to know one of their young pilots named Don Ho.

In the spring of 1964, I took a two-month sabbatical from the squadron and traveled to Fort Bragg, North Carolina, to attend the army's Special Forces school. First Marine Brigade at Kaneohe had two slots it could fill, and as an aviator I had to suck up to a lot of people to beat out the horde of infantry officers who wanted to go. My wife couldn't understand it any more than she had been able to fathom my going to jump school when I volunteered to form the first airborne unit in 1st ANGLICO. But as some general's wife said a few years later, she was a good sport. And as long as I kept promising to retire the minute I got twenty years under my belt, she kept her mouth shut.

Attending the Special Forces school turned out to be one of my better decisions. I learned a lot about Vietnam during the time I was at Fort Bragg, and within a year that knowledge became more valuable than I ever suspected at the time.

The Hawaii tour ended in October of 1964. I kissed my wife and four children goodbye and left for the 1st Marine Air Wing at Iwakuni, Japan. Having just come out of a squadron, I had no sympathy points coming to me when I checked in, and I was absolutely certain that I was going to be chained to a desk on somebody's staff there in Japan. It never occurred to me that we would go to war in a few months. Nor did I consider just how well trained I had become in areas other than flying.

1965

Let me tell you how the war in Vietnam got started.

Bold talk. A lot of people make handsome livings trying to do just that.

Let me tell you how the war got started, from the myopic viewpoint of a young Marine captain who was there at the beginning. While my eyesight was okay, young warriors tend to look at the world through soda straws. And so my version is a little more narrow in scope than those volumes that gather dust in reference libraries.

During the early 1960s, the Marine Corps personnel system was as stable as clockwork and so predictable that an officer could count on a fourteen-month unaccompanied tour in the Far East every six years. In October of 1964, I reported to 1st Marine Air Wing at Iwakuni, Japan, to start another one of mine. I discovered upon arrival that I had been shanghaied to a planning staff at Camp Hague, Okinawa, to work under my former squadron commander in Hawaii, Lt. Col. Jake Sloan. He was the G-3 (operations) of a curious organization I had never heard of before. It operated under two separate names: Task Force 79, and III Marine Expeditionary Force. Task Force 79 sounds like—and was—the Marine Corps' participation in naval activities. The latter title, III Marine Expeditionary Force, was to be used only if a war started and Marine units ceased to be part of the U.S. Navy's Seventh Fleet.

I had absolutely no experience in plans writing, but that did not seem to be a necessary prerequisite. The Tonkin Gulf flap had just put Vietnam on the map, the Marine Corps was gearing up to do battle, and a long-neglected planning staff was being brought up to strength. Jake Sloan knew that I was literate, had been through the army's Special Warfare school, and bathed regularly. And that apparently was sufficient.

I became the junior officer in G-3 (plans), and set about becoming an expert in translating lofty war plans into practical operational orders—one of which might actually send somebody off to war.

Our entry into Vietnam was code named Operation DROMEDARY, and an explanation of how that label came into being is interesting, if not noteworthy.

It was necessary in 1965 for the Marine Corps to go to war piecemeal. A World War II style invasion was out of the question, not only because it would be too noisy—the South Vietnamese wanted us to save their asses but didn't want people to know about it—but also because adequate shipping to do that simply did not exist. And so we were forced to build up our forces in Vietnam incrementally, unit by unit, often on *rented* ships! Amazing, but true.

Somewhere along the line, the United States had sold a lot of surplus LSTs to Japanese shipping companies, and when we needed them to go to war, we rented them back to haul much of our equipment into Da Nang Harbor. For every USS *Bexar County* tied up in the harbor, there was an LST with the word *Maru* written on it somewhere tied up in the next berth.

Because we had to build up unit by unit, then, it was inevitable that someone on the planning staff would liken the action to the proverbial camel getting its head into the tent. And so, whimsically, the code name Operation CAMEL was assigned.

As junior officer in the plans section, I was assigned the task of preparing a cover sheet for the briefing charts which would be used with greater and greater frequency as D day neared. That should pretty well describe just how important I was in the grand scheme of things.

I sketched out a rough drawing for the young corporal "artist in residence" in graphic arts, and he set about preparing a picture of a camel with its head inside a red-and-white striped Arabian tent, grinning at us through the entrance. We put a moustache on the camel in order that it might resemble the brigadier general who would lead the spearheading 9th Marine Expeditionary Brigade into combat.

An hour later, the corporal sidled up to my desk, asking for help. He had drawn a lot of animals in his young life, he explained, but he hadn't the foggiest notion as to what a Bactrian

camel looked like. Would I, he begged, find for him a picture
of a two-humped camel?

I trekked over to the base library at Camp Hague, which was
not a good one by any standards, and the only camel picture I
could find was one of a single-humped dromedary. In resigna-
tion, I checked the book out, bought a pack of Camel cigarettes
at the exchange, and delivered the prototypes to graphic arts.

The cover sheet was dutifully prepared, and the code name
for the Marine Corps entry into combat in Vietnam was changed
to Operation DROMEDARY. And that's a true story, too. We
couldn't find a picture of a two-humped camel.

For me, the war became imminent during a formal Marine
Corps mess night at the army's Fort Buckner officers club there
in Okinawa, sometime in early February. I cannot recall the
exact date.

The entire Task Force 79/III MEF staff assembled in dress-
blue uniforms to honor traditions and get knee-walking—but
formally—drunk that night. I do not know whose idea it was,
but I must have been in favor of it because I spent the afternoon
there at the club ensuring that everything was correct and according to protocol. I even had someone iron the flags.

It was pretty tame as mess nights went. Gen. Rip Collins,
who was III MEF commander, as well as 3d Marine Division
commander, was in attendance, and that might have had something to do with everyone's behavior. The only real excitement
occurred when Capt. Carl Dubac mistook a slice of carrot
heaped with horseradish for an appetizer and popped it into his
mouth. That was fun, but hardly the stuff great and memorable
mess nights are made of.

Just about the time we were getting to Rip Collins's speech,
and everyone was wishing he'd had the foresight to go to the
bathroom beforehand, someone passed behind us and whispered that an emergency staff conference would be held back at
Camp Hague immediately following the ceremonies. The Viet
Cong had just attacked Americans at Pleiku, and President
Johnson was pissed off.

If the scene had been a Civil War movie, some Confederate
colonel might have swept a southern belle into his arms and
proclaimed that his regiment was to leave at dawn. But as formal
as we were, the only dramatic statement came from Carl Dubac,
who lamented that the damn war was going to f——k up a
perfectly good mess night.

Now, picture the staff conference that began somewhere

around midnight. Picture a dozen or so drunk and half-drunk Marine officers gathered in a crummy Quonset hut, all garbed in dress blues with medals and badges, and planning a war. If anyone ever makes a movie about Marines going to war in Vietnam, he has to include a scene like that because it was absolutely true. It was a scene only Paul Mazlansky could invent for one of his *Police Academy* flicks.

I don't think anyone remembered much of what was said during the conference, but we got the message and began working long hours, seven days a week, until we got the 9th MEB into country.

Let me tell you how the beginning of the Marine Corps buildup in Vietnam ruined a perfectly splendid religious retreat. This also is true. I don't make this stuff up.

All of the officers attached to the 3d Marine Division were required, required mind you, to participate in an ecumenical religious retreat at one of the U.S. military recreational parks of Okinawa over a bone-chilling weekend in February, 1965. I couldn't believe it! I was certain it violated the separation-of-church-and-state code.

Major General Collins, commanding general of the 3d Marine Division, and a wonderful person otherwise, had been charged with the responsibility of "cleaning up" the sin and degradation on the island of Okinawa—as far as Marines were concerned—and a religious retreat must have seemed logical at the time. Besides, it was colder than charity that February, and no one was using the recreation camp, anyway.

I will be honest and state that I did not participate willingly. I do not believe many did. To force every single officer attached to 3d Marine Division into a religious retreat—even those of us who were only attached administratively—was as heavy-handed a stunt as the Marine Corps had seen since they made us all buy overcoats in 1959, and stand inspection in them at the exact same hour, on the exact same day, all over the United States, so that some sneaky aviators would not fly a load of them from base to base and thwart the spirit of the commandant's edict.

The 3d Marine Division chaplain at the time was one of the most dynamic priests the Roman Catholic Church ever produced, and only a religious tiger like Cmdr. John J. O'Connor, later chief of chaplains and now Cardinal O'Connor of New York, could have pulled it off. I must admit that he really did put on a good show.

As long as I live, I shall never forget sitting in a bar at the recreation center, sipping a beer, while Father O'Connor sat in a beach chair on top of the bar and conducted a seminar! Unfortunately, I do not remember what the seminar was about, but I am certain that it must have been inspiring. God knows he was.

About a day into this most unusual and not tremendously uplifting religious experience, the balloon went up, and officers were pulled out for rapid transit back to their units to prepare for war—first by helicopter, then by the truckload.

I suspect Father O'Connor was a bit put out by all of this, but I personally was delighted to get back to Camp Hague where the heaters worked.

I did a lot of writing during that period—op-plan writing, where sentences were constructed in the third person singular, present tense. Because I had been through the Special Forces schools at Fort Bragg and was, therefore, a minor authority on counterinsurgency operations, I was called upon to write something the Marine Corps had never included in any of the thousands of operations plans written over the years—a psychological warfare annex.

Imagine! Marines resorting to psychological warfare! We laughed for a while, and then we were persuaded to believe that the general really was serious, and I began to scribble furiously. Before the day was out, I presented—with great solemnity—my first draft of Annex O, Psychological Warfare.

In addition to all of the usual stuff designed to win the hearts and minds of the people—civic action and the like—I included a paragraph, which to this day I still think was a good idea. I suggested that 3d Marine Division cull from its ranks a lot of mean-looking Marines, all over six feet three, who would keep a three-day growth of beard and stalk ferociously through the Vietnamese villages, thereby impressing the local populace mightily.

The head of G-3, plans, Lt. Col. Bill Lanagan, later to command two different infantry battalions in Vietnam, and later to become a brigadier general, read my annex. He grumbled a few remarks, uncomplimentary to my lineage, and plopped it in the burn basket.

After we moved into country, I discovered that my plan was valid, only for the wrong army.

We moved into living and working spaces once occupied by a French regiment, a group of buildings later to be the 1st Marine Air Wing headquarters area. The building where I was billeted had been French NCO quarters, and I discovered that my line of PSYWAR thinking had been put into practice years earlier by men long accustomed to impressing native colonials in the most subtle ways.

The urinal in the French-built communal bathroom was a troughlike structure, designed not to accommodate ordinary mortals, but rather to present a superman image to the native cleaning ladies who, in turn, would presumably tell all their friends.

The lip of this urinal was not only so high that I had to stand on tip-toes like a small boy but, in addition, it was fully six-inches thick and must have caused those small people to speculate in wonder.

Within a day or two, wooden pallets had been dragged in for us to stand on, and the lip had been chipped away to accommodate reality. I sometimes wonder if our downfall did not begin with that admission of mortality at the very beginning of the war.

This was the same sort of psychological backfire that happened to us in Japan during the 1950s. The Japanese people got to know America through its servicemen, and recognized quickly that while they had been unable to stand up to our hardware, the American men were, in reality, wimps who dressed like girls and talked like girls.

In Japan, only women wore white socks. During the early fifties, it was fashionable for young American men to wear white wool socks, and the sight of our fashionable young servicemen on the streets caused peals of laughter on the part of some young men who were just then thinking about retooling their bicycle factories and maybe competing with America in the automobile business.

More damaging was our speech. The hundreds of thousands of American servicemen who spent time in Japan and Okinawa learned what little Japanese they knew from the only people who would have anything to do with them: waitresses, cleaning ladies, and whores. And in Japan, the difference between male and female speech was considerable. It must have been difficult for Japanese businessmen to take Americans seriously when the former GIs all spoke their limited Japanese like the cute little waitresses in the mess halls.

On 22 February, according to my flight logbook, I delivered to Maj. Gen. Paul Fontana, CG 1st Marine Air Wing in Iwakuni, Japan, the detailed order under which some of the F-4 Phantoms of Marine Air Group 11 would move from Atsugi to Da Nang Air Base.

At a conference in Saigon, Ambassador Maxwell Taylor had stated that he wanted a squadron of Phantoms in Da Nang. For reasons unknown to me, one of our generals didn't think that was a real great idea right about then, and said so; whereupon General Taylor expressed himself more clearly. "There *will* be an F-4 squadron in Da Nang, and I don't much care if the planes are F-4Bs (USMC) or F-4Cs (USAF)."

This, of course, peaked our competitive spirits, and we cranked out an aviation addition to OP PLAN 37, plus an order to go with it, and the typists were still typing as the airplane was being warmed up.

There are a lot of rules about transporting top-secret documents, especially plans for something as momentous as going to war. The courier is supposed to carry a pistol and is to be accompanied by an armed escort. I think handcuffs and briefcases are mentioned in there somewhere. Also, I've been told that you can't fly on any airplane with fewer than four engines.

I knew all that, but I was a hotshot fighter pilot, recently selected for promotion to major, and above rules designed for ordinary mortals. I took two copies of the precious document and put them inside my shirt. I drove over to the Marine Corps airfield at Futemma and grabbed one of the station's twin-engined Beechcrafts, which we used for getting our flight time, and flew up to Iwakuni, using the crew chief as copilot. I think that broke a rule too.

While they refueled my plane at base operations in Iwakuni, I borrowed a jeep and drove over to General Fontana's quarters, where I delivered his go-to-war plan. He, of course, knew exactly what the plan said, and he instructed me to fly on up to Atsugi, where Marine Aircraft Group II was stationed, and hand-deliver the other copy to the group commander.

When I arrived at MAG-11, I stopped first at the group operations office in order that the group S-3 might get a head start on things. This was nothing more than a staff courtesy. The group commander was going to scream for his operations officer as soon as I gave him the go-to-war message, and this allowed the man to have a few minutes lead time. The group had twenty-four hours to have a Phantom squadron ready to deploy in the attack configuration.

This required configuration of the Phantom caused a lot of grief, by the way. You can always tell a fighter pilot, but you can't tell him much. And the last thing he wants to hear is that he's going off to war with bomb racks and stuff hanging off his sleek and precious fighter plane.

Are you ready for this? The group operations officer read the order, handed it back to me, and said, not too pleasantly, "So?"

"That's the go-to-war order, Colonel."

"Don't bullshit me, Captain. If this were real, they'd send someone senior to you!"

A few weeks later, a Marine Phantom squadron, VMFA-513, finally went to war. And when Col. Bob Connaly and the entire air group got to Da Nang a few weeks after that, the disbelieving operations officer wasn't with them.

On Easter Sunday, things hit the fan. I know this because I returned to Okinawa that day from a week's leave in Hawaii with my family. Corporal Rodriguez, who picked me up at Kadena Air Base, told me that the shit had really hit the fan.

That was an interesting leave. I flew to Hawaii on a Marine C-130 with several officers from 1st ANGLICO, air and naval gunfire company, a unit in which I had served with many of these same men, and I was unable to tell them that a few days earlier I had committed the naval gunfire half of their unit to combat and that they would be getting their mount-out orders almost as soon as they got home.

The commander of Seventh Fleet had called for assistance from the Marine Corps in planning the navy's support of our operations in South Vietnam, and I was one of four "experts" who rushed to his flagship, *Oklahoma City*, at Yokosuka, Japan to participate in an all-night conference.

My contribution was miniscule. Marines had no need for AN-GLICO's forward-air-control teams. Similar units were already attached to the infantry units. But there was a need for naval-gunfire support, especially for the army units, which would be operating along the coast, and Seventh Fleet agreed with me that ANGLICO should be called upon to participate.

My leave wasn't supposed to come up until June, a midtour bonus for Marines whose families were in Hawaii; but because we knew we'd be in Da Nang by then, I was allowed to go in mid-April.

What a curious state of events that was, knowing that within a few weeks all of our friends in the 1st Marine Brigade at Kaneohe Bay would be going to war and not being able to tell anybody, not even my wife.

They were in the middle of rehearsing their move, but only a few realized it. Operation SILVER LANCE was designed to move the entire brigade to Camp Pendleton, California. And when it became time to move to Southeast Asia, all they had to do was change the compass headings 180 degrees.

Colonel Dupras moved his 4th Marine Regiment directly into Chu Lai, the Chinese characters for Krulak, General Krulak, who'd named the Marine base south of Da Nang after himself. Col. Smoke Spanjer's Marine Aircraft Group 13 took up temporary quarters in Japan before space was available at Chu Lai. Col. Doug Petty, one of my mentors, would eventually lead MAG-13 into combat and get hollered at because his generators worked and nobody else's did. He had gone out and bought new generators in Japan, and that, apparently, had not been politically correct. Everyone else had American-made generators left over from the Korean War.

The only business acumen I ever showed in my life occurred during this leave, and quite by accident. My wife had decided that three and a half years in Hawaii were just about as much paradise as she could handle, and during my leave, we sold the family station wagon and put the house on the market. It sold quickly, and when the military exodus began and the bottom fell out of the housing market, we were untouched.

Fortunately, I was never accused of being opportunistic in this matter. The downside was that we visited the neighborhood twenty years later and discovered that the house was valued at almost ten times its original cost.

Easter occurred on April 18, and from that day until we moved the headquarters into Da Nang on 9 May, things became predictably busy. Also, OP PLAN 37, Operation DROMEDARY, was overtaken by events. For a few months, everything involving our entrance into Vietnam was lumped together under the pedestrian heading, "The Easter Flap."

By early April, the war plans and op orders had been written and distributed, Task Force 79 ceased to exist, and those of us who were out of a job had been assigned as watch officers in the newly formed III MEF command center.

One night, at maybe two or three in the morning, I was sitting in our newly formed command center at Camp Hague in Okinawa, just a young corporal and I and a lot of message traffic, when *boom*! in stormed the biggest lieutenant I'd seen in a week, and there was no question that he was packing top-secret stuff. He had the briefcase and the handcuffs and an armed guard with some kind of automatic weapon—all the things a courier was supposed to have.

With great ceremony, he produced one of those top-secret, back-channel, burn-before-reading messages that even our closest allies weren't supposed to see, let alone the United States air force.

The lieutenant blustered threatening protests when I glanced at it and handed it to the corporal, but it was a message we were expecting.

It was the shortest go-to-war message in history: "Go. Regards, Krulak."

I picked up the phone and called the chief of staff, and woke Regan Fuller out of a sound sleep.

"Good morning, Colonel. Sorry to wake you, but we just heard from General Krulak."

"Mmph. Okay, Bob goes north, and Dave goes south."

Click!

Pretty cryptic, huh?

Somewhat confused, I climbed into a jeep and drove over to the quarters of the G-3, Lt. Col. Jake Sloan, in order that I might share the mystery.

I woke him up, too. "Good morning, Colonel. Welcome to World War Three. But we aren't going anywhere, unless you can tell me who in the hell Bob and Dave are." My exact words.

Well, Bob was Lt. Col. Bob Jones, 3d Battalion, 4th Marines, and Lt. Col. Dave Clement commanded 2d Battalion, 3d Marines, and Bob went north into Hue/Phu Bai, because his battalion was light on equipment and wouldn't need so many lighters to ferry his stuff up the river. Dave Clement flew into Da Nang and started kicking ass and taking names there.

A few weeks later, an incident occurred, which I include to illustrate just how politicized the war was, even from the beginning. No names. It's too painful.

One of the battalions that had gone into Da Nang with the brigade in March had been given an order that no responsible commander could honor. The battalion commander was ordered to ensure that Marines on patrol did not carry rounds in the chambers of their M-14 rifles.

Can you believe that?

A day or so earlier, there had been an accidental discharge, the result of which had been a dead Marine. Washington did not want American boys getting killed, and one way to ensure against accidental discharges was to keep bullets out of the chambers. People in Washington make decisions like that.

Of course, the battalion commander did not relay that incredible order to the rifle companies. And as fate would have it, there was another accidental discharge. A Marine was hurt, and the battalion commander was relieved of command and shipped to Korea.

I promise you, more careers were ruined in Vietnam than were made.

Let me tell you how the names of our major units got changed.

For years and years, the Marine Corps had moved around the world on expedition. Marine expeditionary units were small and had a Colonel in charge. Expeditionary brigades were bigger, and because the initial incursion into South Vietnam was to be built around the 9th Marine Regiment from Okinawa, it was labeled, logically, 9th Marine Expeditionary Brigade. By adding an air group to the regiment, a brigade was born, which created useful employment for a brigadier general. And for this operation, Brig. Gen. Freddy Karch, moustache and all, was in charge.

The 9th Marine Expeditionary Brigade moved into country in early March, and it was only a matter of time before the 3d Marine Division at Okinawa and 1st Marine Air Wing would follow. Lt. Gen. Victor Krulak, the overall Marine commander in the Pacific area, predicted, accurately, that if 9th MEB was ever committed to combat, the entire III MEF would follow in seventy-five days.

When we moved in for real, in May 1965, it would be as III Marine Expeditionary Force. When May arrived, we began "tac-marking" all of our equipment "III MEF," and marveling at General Krulak's prescience.

Quite by surprise, one day during all of this, a package appeared at our newly formed command center which contained two dozen ashtrays with our new III MEF logo emblazoned thereupon. The arrival of the ashtrays coincided exactly with a pronouncement from on high that the word *Expeditionary* belittled the importance of the Republic of South Vietnam and was, therefore, objectionable to the government of the Republic of South Vietnam. It brought up memories of the French colonialist armies, we were told.

All that artwork for nothing!

We were instructed to change our name to III Marine Amphibious Force, III MAF, and of course 9th MEB became 9th MAB, and to the best of my knowledge, the only objectionable, belittling reference to French colonialist expeditions sneaked into Vietnam on those ashtrays.

I threw the ashtrays out after only a few days in Da Nang, incidentally, and some accused me of giving in to political pressure by doing so. There was a young guy from the State Department working out of a tiny little office right across the hall from our command center as the MAF political advisor, but I promise you that we never discussed the ash trays. The truth of the matter was that they were thin little things, only a quarter-inch deep, and totally disastrous under the ceiling fans of the old French buildings we moved into in Da Nang. Also, most of them had been stolen anyway.

Another story you won't find anywhere else deals with national anthems. We knew ours, but we didn't know theirs.

We were not allowed to fly the American flag for the first three months we were in Da Nang, and the reason was right up there with the reason we couldn't use the word *Expeditionary*. As a result, the division band didn't have to play the national anthem every morning, which probably made them happy. But not being able to fly our flag was a source of real irritation.

My wife was still in Hawaii and could put care packages on the next C-130 passing through Kaneohe Bay. She sent me a small flag, about eight inches long, which I taped to the wall in our command center. Not too many people could enter our command center without being shot or something, and so we didn't have to worry about South Vietnamese nationals having their feelings hurt.

To the best of my knowledge, that tiny flag was the only one displayed in Da Nang during those early days, and a person had to have a security clearance to salute it!

About mid-August, we received word that beginning 1 September, we would be allowed to hoist our colors, and the band director was on my back in an instant. He needed absolute proof that the music he had was for the true South Vietnamese national anthem and not something bogus, like maybe a North Vietnamese fight song!

I grabbed the keys to a jeep and suggested that we drive around the base and ask people, Vietnamese people, and you should have seen the amazed looks on the faces of the ARVN officers when a jeep roared up in a cloud of dust and a middle-aged man jumped out and started singing to them. He must have hummed the music to at least a half dozen ARVN officers before he was satisfied that the Marine Corps would not be embarrassed on 1 September.

The monsoon season began early that year, and the rain at 0800, 1 September 1965, would have solved the drought problems of most states, and some small countries. We endured it happily as the Stars and Stripes was raised for the first time, and the Star Spangled Banner was followed by the correct South Vietnamese anthem.

For the record, there were three flag poles on the small parade field in front of III MAF headquarters. When they were erected in May, we still thought the United Nations flag would be flown, too. That's how naive some of us were.

Further to describe our naivete during those early days in Vietnam, let me tell you about how we got started in the business of civic action and our initial attempts at "winning the hearts and minds of the people."

That very statement resulted in snorts of derision from most of the Marines I knew at the time. Respect, not love, was the desired goal. To them, civic action was a Marine and a candy bar, and anything more was somebody else's business.

The term, civic action, was so foreign to Marines that our new commanding general assigned the task to Civil Affairs, a section of the legal staff that was supposed to pay farmers a few piasters for the occasional pig that was run over by one of our trucks. No one ever claimed that our new CG was very bright.

Maj. Charlie Keever, who was the lawyer in charge of Civil Affairs, ended up doing fantastic things in this area. But when he was first handed the job, he was mightily confused. General Krulak had sent a message from Hawaii requesting a list of things we needed to get the program started, and he was in a hurry because he intended to recruit every church and civic group in America to collect the items and become part of the war effort. General Krulak knew what he was doing.

Major Keever was given the assignment, and he came running to me for the answer—not because I was so brilliant, but because I was the only Marine in the area who had been through the army's Special Forces school and knew what the hell General Krulak was referring to.

He caught me at the bar. We had built a tiny little bar just outside the officers' mess, and for the first time since we moved into Da Nang, we had ice to put in a drink. I was reluctant to leave.

In those early days, when we took casualties, there was no ice. The mess hall's ice maker served as a morgue until the army got a real morgue running, and any time ice was available for officers, it was a banner day.

Rather than run to his office to help him with the list, I pulled out my pocket notepad and began to list everything I could remember from my schooling. Needles, thread, mirrors, soap— basic necessities of life that the struggling Vietnamese villagers had gone without for a long time.

I was able to produce a list of about twenty items, plus the address of the people at Fort Bragg who had been in the business for a few years, and the major ran back to his office to fire off an answer which would be on General Krulak's desk first thing in the morning. And that's how we got started in the business of winning the hearts and minds of the people.

For the record, the list was produced on a genuine notepad and not on a cocktail napkin as was commonly believed at the time.

Father O'Connor, soon to be Monsignor O'Connor, got his own civic action program started through the Catholic Relief Organization, and one of the many donations that came out of his efforts highlighted just how dumb many of us were. The Mattel toy company sent a huge crate of Chatty Cathy dolls for distribution—dolls that were unsuitable for sale in the United States because the string-pull voice mechanisms were defective, and our general was furious because the dolls didn't talk. I was the jerk stupid enough to say, "Who gives a shit? Vietnamese kids don't speak English!" I really wished I hadn't said that.

I didn't like our new commanding general very much. Fortunately, I was so junior that he didn't know who I was, and didn't care, even though our command center was about fifteen feet from his III MAF office.

He was a bully who had made his bones as a hard-nosed infantry commander during World War II, and stars on his collar had not broadened his outlook on warfare. At least once a week, he dropped in on an infantry unit in the field and relieved some hapless company or battalion commander for doing it all wrong, and brought him back to Da Nang in his helicopter. At one point, there were three such people in our barracks building, sitting around with stunned looks on their faces, awaiting transfer to some punitive billet away from the war zone.

Fortunately, the Marine Corps was quick to load the III MAF staff with rising comers on the fast track—truly talented officers, who would all pick up at least one star before they retired. Our war hummed along with reasonable efficiency, in spite of the new commander's curious habit of leadership through intimidation.

A good example was the night the Viet Cong got on the base the first time and blew up a lot of stuff.

It was about one-thirty in the morning of 30 June, and I was in the sweltering command center working on the daily sitrep, the situation report we sent out each morning to all of the major commands around the world, except for the few pages we added for Marine Corps commands that told what really happened. I was called to the phone, and as I stood looking out a window that faced in the general direction of the airfield, I listened impatiently as some colonel back in Hawaii chewed me out for some supply glitch he had discovered.

Suddenly, the sky around the runways lighted up with crashes and booms and sparks and all manner of warlike activity. It was pretty close to the right day for a fireworks display, but hardly the right time or place. There was no question that the enemy had decided to get our attention. It was an impressive show—the first shots ever fired toward me in anger, and my adrenaline count shot right up there with the best of them.

"Excuse me, Colonel," I interrupted, probably not as coolly as I think I did. "I'm going to put one of the clerks on to get the rest of your information. We seem to have a bit of a war going on about us right now."

I handed the receiver to a corporal before the colonel could object and grabbed at EE-8 field telephones right and left and began cranking and calling whoever it was I was supposed to call when somebody started shooting at us. Each time I called, the answering party was already doing whatever it was supposed to be doing, and, predictably, by the time I had called everybody on my list, the fireworks had stopped.

About a half hour later, the commanding general arrived at our headquarters and began to hold court to find out just what had happened and just whom he could blame it on.

He spent the nights on the move in a specially fitted amphibious tractor, and no one ever knew where "Monroe Six" was, and sometimes it took a while for him to get back from his hiding place.

He didn't like to use the word *we*, and for a while there it looked as though a young infantry captain was going to bear the brunt of it all.

The general's immediate problem was the fact that *his* boss, General Krulak, was due to land in three or four hours, and there was a certain look of panic in his eyes as he ranted and raved and pounded his ham-sized fist on his desk so that everyone in the headquarters building would know that it wasn't his fault, and presumably testify to that fact if asked.

Capt. Pat Collins was the commander of the reaction company that responded to the enemy raid, and he arrived straight from combat to make his report. He reeked of fear-sweat and cordite, and had obviously just come from one hell of a firefight. His hands and face were sweaty and black, and it was not grease paint. He tried unsuccessfully to describe the extent of the damage on the air force side of the field.

This was when the general pounded his fist on the desk. "You're a liar, Captain!" His exact words. "My field commanders have assured me that the enemy did *not* get on the base!"

I was standing about two feet behind the captain, and downwind of his sweat and cordite, and I tended to believe the company commander's version.

Just about that time, I was called to the phone to talk to an air force colonel who was in charge of things on their side of the field. He gave me a preliminary damage assessment and cussed a lot. I told him what our general had said about the enemy's not getting on the base.

The colonel's voice was calm. "Well, I'll tell you," he answered. "I'm holding in my left hand an unexploded satchel charge that I personally picked up from under the wing of a C-130. And if I were not holding the telephone in my right hand, I would also be holding an AK-47 banana clip which I found just a few feet away from the satchel charge. I do believe your esteemed general should get his shit together."

You can be certain I did not pass that bit of information on to the esteemed general. In an act of pure cowardice, I whispered it to the chief of staff instead. Then I left the office with Pat Collins, the company commander who had been dismissed unceremoniously and who was in a state of shock and utter disbelief, and still smelling really bad.

General Krulak arrived and calmed everybody down. I watched as he wrote out a three-page message without erasing one word, and which explained the entire episode with such brilliant clarity, and with penmanship so precise, that I relaxed for the first time myself, knowing that he was the man in charge and that our commanding general was just window dressing. Victor Krulak was some kind of superstar, even though he wasn't much over five feet tall, and even if his nickname was "Brute."

That afternoon, I was assigned to an investigative committee to record the enemy raid for posterity. Basically, our initial report was required to state, "With the arrival of the reaction company, the enemy fled," and ignore the fact that they had finished their job and were just leaving. Brigadier General Karch, who headed the committee, sighed and said, "Well, if that's the way the general wants to record history, then so be it."

Fortunately, the published history of the incident altered the verb to reflect reality, and I never did find out if Pat Collins got an apology.

It was a micromanager's war from the beginning, and everyone from the White House on down was on the phone about that incident. They also called about incidents even smaller, and I touch on this to point up the dangers of instant worldwide communications.

One night, an insignificant event that wouldn't even make our daily situation report occurred and sent alarm bells ringing all over the world, even in Washington.

A South Vietnamese patrol boat was rumbling down the Da Nang River about two or three o'clock in the morning when somebody panicked and fired at it from the west bank, thinking it was an enemy boat. A navy ensign on duty at the naval operating base on the east bank saw the fire, assumed for some reason that the Marine base at Marble Mountain was taking 105-millimeter artillery fire from the river, and called for a destroyer to come to the rescue with naval gunfire.

In order to get a destroyer to open up with its five-inch guns, permission had to be granted from General Westmoreland's headquarters in Saigon, and—critical to this episode—those military wizards at MACV were linked to Washington by hot line.

Had the ensign called me before he called Saigon, the incident would have remained just that. Only one round was fired, and no one ever did find out what it was, except that it was definitely not artillery fire. We got the problem under control in about five minutes.

But by calling Saigon, he invited the world—and Washington—into the problem, and it took me an hour to satisfy everyone that it really was a minor incident. It might have taken all day if the watch officers in all of the headquarters had not been personal friends of mine.

By way of good fortune, all of the watch officers, even those in Saigon and at the National Military Command Center in Washington, were Marine contemporaries of mine, and we were able to talk on a first-name basis. They believed what I told them, and we were able to put things to rest quickly. Had I been talking to strangers, however, they would have checked with their superiors, who would have checked with *their* superiors, and the incident might have ended up as a UPI news feature, complete with statements from one really embarrassed ensign.

It wasn't always that easy. I got a call one night from an army colonel in Saigon, asking for the map grid coordinates of a team of Marines operating alone down in the Pleiku area, with only a Vietnamese platoon to protect them.

I wasn't about to give him the air-surveillance radar team's vulnerable position in the clear, and so I told him to hold on a second while I encoded the numbers on one of the "Orphan Annie" code sheets we kept at hand for just this sort of information. Scrambler phones hadn't arrived yet.

He didn't want to hold on. The White House was on the other line, he announced with no small amount of self-importance, and they wanted the coordinates for the president's morning briefing, and he wanted the information right then and there.

I was not tactful. I said things uncomplimentary to bureaucrats and people who were afraid of bureaucrats, and assured him that a six-digit grid coordinate wouldn't even show on the president's map—that the nearest military base would probably suffice, if he couldn't wait thirty seconds longer. While he was getting my name, rank, and serial number and threatening me with all sorts of dire consequences, I finished encoding the information. And when he was through yelling, I read him the shackled message and hung up.

So maybe the new commanding general was justified in being paranoid.

HOW A VERY ORDINARY PERSON GOT TO COMMAND A VERY GOOD SQUADRON

Not much has been written on the subject of middle-level combat command. Generals have written about their armies, admirals have written about their navies, and individuals have written too often about their squads and platoons, where all officers were required to demonstrate at least one character defect. But it is difficult to find factual information on the running of a squadron in combat. Maybe it's because most squadron commanders didn't have as much fun as I did.

In some military services, the squadron was nothing more than a maneuvering unit, and its commander the guy who ensured that all of the rules and regulations were followed. Unit commanders were selected in Washington by screening boards, and the actual command itself was subordinated to the officer's career pattern: an X on the board to help him get promoted.

The Marine Corps looked on command differently. Darwinism was still the law, tactical command was choice duty, and the competition was fierce. Assignment was left to the prerogative of the wing commander, and all Marine Corps headquarters in Washington had to do was ensure that officers with proper credentials were available. It was up to the individual officer to get his squadron.

This inevitably led to the customary complaints from backbiters that "it wasn't *what* you knew but *whom* you knew." While there was a certain amount of validity to the plaint, the system worked both ways. Marine Corps aviation was a small organization, and by the time a pilot reached the rank of lieutenant colonel, he knew a lot of people. More to the point, a lot of people knew him.

It was a rare occasion that a real schmuck got command of a squadron, and if such a person did squeak through simply because he was able to suck up to the right person, he didn't get to keep his command for very long.

PREPARING FOR COMMAND

As youngsters, we were supposed to start preparing for command the day we were commissioned. Maybe before.

When I was a kid, I saw the movie, *The Flying Leathernecks*, at least a dozen times. I knew that Robert Ryan didn't have what it took to be a squadron commander because he didn't have the guts to tell a man to go out and get killed. And I knew that John Wayne, who obviously did have the guts, was able to run that Hellcat squadron with apparent effectiveness simply by being a prick.

Well, I wasn't John Wayne by any means. I was only five feet nine and a half inches tall (to be reduced to five feet eight and three-quarters inches in a few years during an ejection from an F-8 Crusader), and while I was a decent-looking guy, I was slightly nerdy, and really lazy. The movie gave me doubts, but I went to Pensacola anyway. I wanted to fly. My brother was a navy pilot, and I wanted to be one, too.

When I was a young lieutenant, flying out of the old Marine Corps air station at Miami, Florida, I read a conflicting viewpoint on the subject of command leadership, one that negated all the John Wayne movies ever made. Anyone, a *Naval Aviation News* article stated, could be an effective commander if he would follow three simple rules: get a good executive officer; avoid the details; and pay attention to morale.

Wow! I could do that! Adm. George Anderson, the author of those uplifting words, was a naval aviator who had become chief of naval operations, so he must have had some idea of what he was talking about, and I tore the magic paragraph out of the magazine and carried it in my wallet for years until it died of old age.

For eighteen years, I watched dozens of commanding officers do what they saw as their duties, and I took notes. I liked the way this guy talked on the telephone, but I didn't like the way he dressed. That guy wore his uniform well, but had the morals of an alley cat. I liked the way another guy got along with the enlisted Marines, but I thought he was a little heavy-handed with the junior officers. I loved the way Jake Sloan ran a squadron and thought I would probably copy him every time I got the chance, even though he didn't look a thing like John Wayne.

But years later, when I returned from Vietnam in September of 1970, in a hell of a lot better shape than John Wayne came home from his last combat command, incidentally, with his arm all trussed up in that weird cast, I thrilled in the realization that The Duke had been wrong all the time! A squadron commander didn't have to tell a man to go out and get killed. That's what the executive officer was for.

Admiral Anderson had been right all the time, and the notes I had taken along the way were a total waste of time.

And as much as I admired Colonel Sloan, the hard truth of the matter was that a squadron commander could be only one person, and that person was himself.

Also, I added a corollary to Admiral Anderson's doctrine. Not only was it imperative to find a good executive officer to run the day-to-day activities of the squadron, it was equally important to select the maintenance officer with great care. I broke with tradition twice in selecting my maintenance officer, and hurt some peoples' feelings, but I am still convinced that the right maintenance officer is just as important as the right executive officer.

Ninety-five percent of a Marine squadron's enlisted personnel worked in the maintenance department. There were a few clerks in operations and personnel and supply, but everyone else worked under the maintenance officer. It seemed logical to me, then, that the boss of all these people had to be the most dynamic and personable of the available senior officers.

Additionally, I would tell prospective commanders that a Marine squadron can function well without a strong, dynamic sergeant major. A good one is a godsend, but there are so many senior NCOs in maintenance that enlisted leadership is well covered.

What follows, then, is a story of what happened when I took command of Marine Observation Squadron 2. I pass it along to those who aspire to command, in hopes that the anecdotes will be helpful, and I offer it up for those who have been there in hopes that they might get a chuckle from things remembered.

For chronological references, I commanded VMO-2 from 21 January to 15 September 1970. I then took command of Marine Light Helicopter Squadron 267 at Camp Pendleton, California, on 21 October 1970. I retired 1 September 1972 at the age of thirty-nine.

GETTING COMMAND

In the Marine Corps' war in Vietnam, a man was only supposed to be able to command a squadron for six months. Not a bad idea really, when one considers the fact that the CO was under industrial-strength pressure twenty-four hours a day, seven days a week.

In other wars the CO got to take a break. During World War II, a squadron was on the line for a month or so, and then moved back to a rear area for regrouping and retraining. If you count it up, you will find that Pappy Boyington's famous Black Sheep Squadron spent a total of eighty-one days on the line, in actual combat, while he was the commander.

During the Korean war, though, Marine squadrons began staying on the line for long periods of time, and the commanding officers started to show signs of burning out after a while, and rotation after six months became a policy that followed through into the Vietnam War.

I arrived on the scene at the end of September 1969, joined Marine Aircraft Group 16 at Marble Mountain, and was assigned as the group personnel officer, S-1, until the current VMO-2 commander's six months were up.

How did I get there? I laid the groundwork several months earlier. There were no giveaways in the Marine Corps. A man had to work for what he wanted.

Sometime during the spring of that year, I received a telephone call from the lieutenant colonel's monitor in Washington, telling me that I was scheduled to return to Vietnam in September and that I needed three months to retrain in the F-4 Phantom before I left the States. What he wanted to know was where I wanted to do my aircraft transition training—on the East Coast, or the West Coast? My choice. He added, however, that because of my extensive background in air/ground control, I could throw my hat in the ring for OV-10 training. One lieutenant colonel had to be trained in the plane so that a VMO squadron commander would be available around January. And although it would mean sitting behind a desk for a while, and maybe being locked into it and unable to escape, I could take my chances.

I knew that 1st Marine Air Wing was up to its ears in F-4 qualified lieutenant colonels, and that most Phantom squadrons had two of them, with the junior man serving as the executive officer. I wanted to be a squadron commander, and I was pretty junior in rank, so I told him that I didn't care what kind of an airplane I flew as long as it had guns bolted into the front end. At the time, I had never seen an OV-10, except in pictures.

I was lucky enough to win the draw. There were twelve in contention, and I spent the summer with VMO-1 at the Marine Corps air station at New River, North Carolina, learning to fly both the OV-10, and the UH-1E Huey. I wasn't supposed to fly helicopters, but in the Marine Corps a man could do things like that. I didn't get real good at it, though.

To avoid being stuck behind a desk on the wing staff in Vietnam—or worse yet back at the Marine bases in Japan or Okinawa—I had to grease the skids to ensure that I was assigned to Marine Aircraft Group 16 when I arrived overseas. For this, I will be eternally grateful to Col. Doug Petty, who was the senior Marine on the Naval Air Training Command staff at Pensacola. He wrote a letter to the MAG-16 commander, Floyd Fulton, a man I had worked with before, and told him I was coming. A few hours after I got off the plane in Da Nang I was unpacking my B-4 bag in a Quonset hut at the Marble Mountain helicopter base.

Did I get there because I knew people? Sure. Marine Corps aviation is so small a group that it's pretty hard to hang around long enough to be a lieutenant colonel without knowing ninety-five percent of your contemporaries and just about everybody senior to you.

The current VMO-2 commander's six-month tour wasn't up until January, and this gave me three months to prepare. I shuffled papers in the group personnel office, and flew with VMO-2 as the heir apparent, and when the change of command took place in January, I knew the squadron, and the squadron knew me.

TAKING COMMAND

VMO-2 had four pressing problems at the time. The lieutenants were pissed off, the captains were pissed off, the squadron had just been sliced in half, and we had to move to a new base within two weeks.

Let me address the administrative problems first.

Like every squadron in the world, VMO-2 had, over the years, changed airplanes a few times. From World War II until it moved into Da Nang in 1965, the squadron flew light, fixed-wing Bird Dog aircraft, and for about six or seven years the twin-rotored Kaman HOK helicopter. These were gradually replaced by UH-1E Huey helicopters that first year of the war. I say gradually, because in October of 1965, the Viet Cong got onto the newly built base at Marble Mountain and burned all of the Hueys to the ground. They were soon replaced, but for a while there the squadron had to reassemble the Bird Dog planes that had been crated up for shipment home.

The OV-10 joined the squadron a couple of years later, and the squadron operated them alongside the Hueys without difficulty.

When the AH-1G Huey Cobra gunship helicopters arrived in Vietnam, however, they were placed in VMO-2 for reasons known only to the people around at the time, and the UH-1E Hueys were transferred to another squadron.

Those first Cobras were cut-down versions of standard Hueys, quick-fix planes Bell Aerospace cranked out to meet the pressing needs for dedicated helicopter gunships; and while the two planes had a lot in common, the mixing of OV-10s and Huey Cobras was awkward at best.

Those early Cobras were not navy/Marine planes; they were loaners from the army. They had army serial numbers painted on them, and we were required to maintain them by army maintenance procedures, which meant that the squadron had to run two entirely different maintenance operations. The army was still performing hourly checks for instance, a system the navy and Marine Corps had given up years earlier, and all of the paperwork and reporting procedures were different.

On top of that, the Marine Corps' most critical MOS in Vietnam at the time, the scarcest military occupational specialty, was the Huey engine mechanic, and those mechanics were spread too thinly among the squadrons.

As the group personnel officer, I made a rather bold recommendation for the time. I proposed that the Cobras be taken from VMO-2 and put into an existing Huey squadron, where at least we could pool enough mechanics to keep them in the air.

This was done. The gunships were transferred to HML-367, Marine Light Helicopter Squadron 367, and I took command of a truncated squadron that had just lost half its officers and a big chunk of the enlisted Marines. Big morale problems.

The second problem arose as a direct result of the first. Because the squadron was now suddenly a fixed-wing unit for the first time in five years, people began to look at it in a different light—and rather covetously, I might add. The OV-10 had ejection seats, which seemed to make it more acceptable in the eyes of the fixed-wing community, and some people in high places began talking about making VMO-2 part of a fixed-wing air group.

Then, as part of the Marine Corps' gradual pullout from Vietnam, code named KEYSTONE ROBIN, an F-4 Phantom squadron was rotated out of Marine Aircraft Group 11 in January and sent home, leaving an empty hangar and flight line at the crowded Da Nang Air Base. First Marine Air Wing was told to replace the squadron or else lose the space to the air force, and VMO-2 was elected.

A VMO squadron had never been attached to a jet group before. The pilots had an emotional attachment for the helicopter community, and none of us wanted to leave the wonderful beachfront property with surf and sand. More morale problems.

The lieutenants were unhappy, not so much because they were moving to Da Nang, but because they felt unwanted and unloved.

Until the youngsters arrived in September of 1969, the OV-10 pilots had virtually all been second-tour aviators with at least one combat tour in helicopters or jets already under their belts. The arrival of green lieutenants, only three or four months out of the training command, presented the squadron with a bit of a dilemma.

An OV-10 crew, pilot and aerial observer, flew as a single entity, and the only mission that required a wingman was an occasional deep reconnaissance flight that sniffed the Laotian out-of-bounds area for new signs of trail activity.

Lieutenants couldn't be turned loose to control air strikes and to direct various operations by themselves, and so they had been relegated to flying wing on all of the single-plane flights until they had gained enough experience—and of course the lieutenants were certain that day would never come.

Flying the Dash-Two position day after day, on flights where they weren't even needed, had the youngsters spring-loaded to the pissed-off position, and one of them had even taken a new personal call sign. Hostage Dash Two.

On top of this, the experienced pilots were having to fly an excessive number of hours each month to make up for the pilot shortage, and while they never complained, the squadron flight surgeon was making dire threats about gory plane crashes and mental breakdowns.

If the lieutenants were angry, the captains were almost subversive in their unhappiness.

Several months earlier, some OV-10s had taken several hits from ground fire, and in a predictable military solution, somebody in an upper echelon of command passed down an edict that the precious OV-10s would not be flown below one thousand feet. Because it was a direct order, the commanding officer had to live with it, and the hotshot captains were a surly bunch.

It was an ego problem of the first magnitude. There were some five hundred pilots in MAG-16 at that time. That's a *big* air group, and only twenty-five of those pilots had to stay above a thousand feet. Don't you know they caught a lot of flak from the helicopter pilots who spent their days squatting right down on top of the enemy's gun barrels!

The captains had built a party deck behind one of their Quonset huts and had hung a sign that advertised their displeasure. THOUSAND FOOT CLUB, it read. COMBAT PILOTS KEEP OUT!

These were the conditions that existed when I assumed command of the squadron in soggy ceremonies on the flight line that rainy day in January. None of it was the outgoing commander's fault. He had been dealt one ugly blow after another, and the squadron pilots held him responsible.

Rotten deal for him, good deal for the new guy. In the eyes of the squadron, anything I did had to be an improvement.

As soon after the ceremonies as possible, the squadron executive officer, Maj. K. D. Waters, and I had a two-man staff conference to ensure that we were both on the same page. It took about five minutes, and then we met with the assembled squadron officers in the ready room.

First order of business: get the lieutenants in the air. This wasn't too tough. The lieutenants had been flying for three months and were able to perform most tasks, as long as there was an experienced observer in the back seat. Additionally, we ensured that there were always two experienced pilots in the air to cover anything hairy.

My ace in the hole was the fact that I had known the lieutenants for two years, and I was more willing than others to take a chance on them. Not only had I flown with them for three months when we were all at New River, North Carolina, going through our OV-10 training together, I had also known them throughout their flight training.

I had been the executive officer of the Marine Air Detachment at NAS Pensacola when they checked in for flight training, and because there was a backlog of student pilots, they hung around our headquarters for a month or two before slots opened up in preflight.

I got to know them well—some better than they wished I did.

Col. Don Conroy, the colorful man about whom *The Great Santini* was written, was my boss, and together we devoted a great deal of time and effort to finding things for these pool lieutenants to do. A lot of them, for instance, were civil engineers, and they'd designed and helped build a recreation beach on navy property on the Gulf of Mexico. Another group of management majors had invaded the various offices in the training command and provided some valuable updating to systems that hadn't changed since World War II.

Some PE majors went to work in Special Services, and one young man who had a degree in hotel management from Cornell tried to revamp the Mustin Beach officers club's entire system of operations, but was unsuccessful.

I sent plane load after plane load of lieutenants up to Fort Bragg, North Carolina, where the lieutenants got to play soldier for a week or so. The Marine liaison officer there who took care of them went on to become commandant of the Marine Corps, incidentally. P. X. Kelly always was a "doer."

We even sent some thirty young Adonis types to the Miss Universe Pageant to be escorts—but that took a sour turn the morning one of them was caught naked with one of the Misses in the back seat of a car in the hotel parking lot.

Anyway, our lieutenants were in Vietnam now, and they were as ready as they were ever going to be, and the executive officer wanted to get them into the air, so that decision took all of thirty seconds. His announcement brought cheers from the lieutenants, and Skip Roberts tore the Dash-Two patch off his flight suit and replaced it with a proper one. I think he flew under the call sign, Hostage Hotel after that, but I have no idea why.

Solving the captains' problem had taken a little leg work. During my three months in the group personnel office, I spent a lot of time in the wing headquarters. I had the time to wander around the various staffs, buttonholing people to find out if anyone really cared about the thousand-foot rule. Someone in G-3 vaguely remembered that the decision had been made personally by a colonel who had rotated back to the States a month or so before. And no, no one around there really cared.

Second order of business: Rescind the order. After the executive officer announced that the lieutenants would start flying missions the next morning, the captains were all over us like fleas.

"What about the thousand-foot rule?"

"Can't hit anything from up there," I smiled.

Cheers! Smiles! Within thirty minutes of the change of command, both the executive officer and I were heroes.

Rule: When you join a squadron, bring a little joy with you.

BEING ACCEPTED IN COMMAND

Let me tell you a little bit about the executive officer, and then I'll tell you about being tested by the captains.

In the aviation business, the first thing a man was supposed to do when he took over a new job was to train his replacement. This had nothing to do with combat. Eighty percent of pilot fatalities, even during combat, were due to operational accidents.

This was the reason Marine squadron commanders and executive officers shared an office, so that each knew what the other was doing at all times.

Maj. K. D. Waters required no training. He was probably the singularly most qualified pilot in the Marine Corps at the time. He was on his third combat tour, and he knew more about running a squadron than most commanding officers ever would.

He tolerated me because we made a good team. He took care of the details of running the unit, while I flitted around the wing and division, making deals and ensuring that everyone knew us and loved us. He yelled at people who needed yelling at, while I followed behind drying the tears. He was the first to acknowledge that he sometimes exuded the personality of a stucco bathtub.

Following Admiral Anderson's dictum, then, was a piece of cake for me. K. D.—his first name was Kenneth, but I doubt that anyone ever called him that—was smart, efficient, and a terrific stick-and-rudder man in the air, the only pilot the captains acknowledged as their master. He took care of the details, and I worked at keeping everybody happy.

* * *

A new commanding officer must expect to be tested by the captains, just as a new school teacher can count on being tested by a bunch of eighth graders. We males never grow up; we only grow older.

Lieutenants and majors do pretty much as they are told— lieutenants because they don't know any better, and majors because they have become used to it and know they can wear you down eventually anyway. But captains are the hotshots of a squadron, and they tend to be impatient. They think the squadron is theirs, and they resent a new guy.

The hottest prima donna VMO-2 had at the time was a captain who flew under the call sign Hostage Duke. Denny Herbert was good, and he knew it, and it was he who staged the confrontation.

All airfields have course rules, even in combat. They are designed to keep airplanes from running into one another. A pilot approaching a field should be able to come in and land, confident in the knowledge that everyone else is flying by the same rules he is.

Lieutenants fly by the rules because they are afraid not to. Majors and lieutenant colonels fly by the rules because they believe in them. Captains sometimes get wild hairs up their ejection-seat pans and make up their own rules.

At the Marble Mountain Air Facility, which was a wonderful piece of beachfront property, it had long been agreed that fixed-wing aircraft would break over the duty runway at eight hundred feet and turn eastward to a downwind leg over the South China Sea. The runway was only thirty-five hundred feet long, and with mixed helicopter and fixed-wing traffic buzzing around simultaneously, following that simple flight path kept everybody alive.

But the day after I joined the squadron, the forces of evil came into play. The air traffic was light at that point in the afternoon, our hotshot pilot was having a hormonal attack, and a nineteen year old kid in the control tower thought he might like to see an air show, too. Hostage Duke hit the break at fifty feet with as much airspeed as he could generate in an OV-10

He horsed the plane upward in a marvelous wingover maneuver, dumped gear and flaps at the top, and dropped in for a wonderfully smooth landing.

It was a sight worth seeing—which, of course, was the whole problem. I saw it.

I was just walking out of the operations hut as the airplane screamed across the field boundary coming into the break, and I stood there with my mouth hanging open throughout the entire performance. It really was a good show.

I had a fast conversation with myself. I was smart enough to recognize the importance of the upcoming confrontation, but too dumb to think of something really clever to say.

It was show time for the dumpy little lieutenant colonel. If I handled the next five or ten minutes in a mature, professional manner, I might assume mastery over the captains, and with them the entire squadron.

I had about five minutes before the errant Duke postflighted his plane, signed off the yellow sheets in maintenance, and walked across the road to the squadron area. Five minutes to think of something intelligent to say.

The logical solution was to follow the rule book; order him to report to my office at eight o'clock the next morning. That's the rule that covers your butt when you don't know what to do.

But VMO-2 was not an ordinary squadron. There was a lot more riding on this than simply proving that I was the boss.

I sat down on the steps of the supply hut directly across the street from maintenance, made myself as comfortable as my hemorrhoids would let me, and set up my ambush. He had to pass my way, and here I would make my stand.

Soon, the captain crossed the road from the hangar, and our eyes met—determined squints from both of us. I was Gary Cooper in *High Noon*, only about two feet shorter.

The look on the captain's face demanded satisfaction, and I fired the first shot.

"Denny? Did you do that?"

I had caught him by surprise, and the puzzled look on his face said I had winged him.

"Yes, sir." No inflection on the *sir*. Good, he was ready to take it like a man.

"Denny, don't *do* that!"

He stood there, waiting for the other shoe to fall, and I didn't drop it. The look on his face changed from puzzlement to something resembling a golden retriever scratching fleas.

He mumbled something with *sir* on the end and trudged off toward the operations hut and the ready room. I sat there until he had disappeared inside, then got up gingerly and wandered over to maintenance to look official.

* * *

That night in the officers club, I recognized that my gamble had paid off. The captains had met. Perhaps that was when they took down their THOUSAND FOOT CLUB sign and decided to accept me as their squadron commander. They let me buy them drinks and told me how wonderful I was, and Denny Herbert even apologized.

What had taken place at the change-of-command ceremony two days before had been merely the Marine Corps' offer to them. That night they accepted the offer.

And of course, that was the time for me to elbow the Duke to one side and tell him that if he did it again, I'd cut his balls off.

CHANGING AIR GROUPS

We hated to leave MAG-16 and Marble Mountain—mostly MAG-16—and we really missed the people who flew green airplanes. At that time only helicopters and OV-10s were painted green. All the rest were light gray.

The people in MAG-11 were different. They were good, kind, decent human beings, but they were different. Because of the method the Naval Air Training Command used in determining who would fly jets and who would not, most of the jet pilots were engineers and men with analytical minds who did well in the technical ground-school courses. Green airplane drivers were generally people who had majored in English and history and journalism, and we had a sense of humor.

The people in MAG-11, especially the senior officers, took themselves so seriously!

We didn't get along too well at first, and it was mostly my fault. For instance, I allowed the enlisted Marines to black out a huge and really splendid tiger head the former tenants of our hangar, VMFA-542, had painted on the roof, and this was a sacrilege akin to pissing on the grave of a departed loved one. The fighter pilots really hated to see their only fighter squadron replaced by little green airplanes with propellors on the engines, and removing the F-4 squadron's insignia was not a smart move on my part.

While our move was not a long one—Marble Mountain was only about ten or twelve miles east of Da Nang—it was just as hard on the squadron as if we had come from Okinawa. We made the move without missing a single mission, and our Marines toiled long hours setting up shop and running a busy flight line at the same time.

Many of them hadn't slept in twenty-four hours—let alone found time to shave and spruce up their uniforms. At my first group staff conference I requested that the group sergeant major go easy on them until we were properly moved in. Only I did not say it that nicely.

It was then I learned that the group commander was a micromanager who was not accustomed to independent squadron commanders, a point he made very forcefully. I showed bad judgment in smiling while he was yelling, and our relationship went downhill from there.

As fortune would have it, the group commander rotated home about three weeks later. And for me, happiness was an "unobserved" fitness report.

Just before he left though, he almost hit me. My fault again.

There was a floor show in the officers club one night, and I believe he thought I had made a pass at his girlfriend.

VMO-2's table was right beside the group commander's center table, and instead of sitting at the head, the way he dictated squadron commanders ought to, I had taken a seat at the other end, better to see the dancing girls, or whatever was on the stage that night.

As a show of friendship and to say "welcome aboard," the other squadrons of MAG-11 bought VMO-2 bottles of champagne that night. These started at the head of the table and worked their way down to the end. Three nearly empty bottles had come my way so far, and my job became one of draining them to the cheers of the pilots and aerial observers. Silly, I know, but it was fun.

After a while, I rose to go to the bathroom, and as I threaded my way between the chairs of our table and the group commander's, someone handed me another bottle. I assumed it was also nearly empty, and I tipped it up. It was not nearly empty. It was nearly full, and as everyone who has ever tipped up a full bottle of champagne can attest, the air bubbles exploded and burst back out, mostly through my nose.

The group commander's girlfriend was returning from the ladies' room at that precise moment, and a good quantity of the gushing champagne bubbles spewed out of my nose and down the front of her blouse.

Always chivalrous, I whipped out a handkerchief immediately

and proffered it to her—only my eyes were clouded with tears, and I held the hanky too close to her bosom.

The group commander saw what he suspected to be a squadron commander attempting to cop a feel. He leaped to his feet and grabbed my wrist, and I opened my eyes in time to discover that he had failed to see the humor of the situation.

To this day I am certain that his fist was cocked, and I went immediately into a plan-B defensive posture, full of apologies and other signals of groveling. He was a big, strong man, you see, and my defenses were based less on military protocol than they were on self-preservation.

Well, I escaped without having my face rearranged, and the rule I pass on to prospective squadron commanders is a simple one: Take time to check out the personality of a new group commander. It will save you and your squadron a lot of grief.

What I should have done was spend some time visiting the new air group personally before we made the move. Instead, I sent liaison officers over to visit the various sections, and while that made for a smooth move, I should have paid some attention to my own personal acceptance.

One amusing story came out of the move. Capt. Larry Ruymann, a pilot whose collateral ground job was that of flight-line officer, drove over to Da Nang to inspect the F-4 flight line we would be using, and discovered that the protective aircraft revetments were designed for carrier planes and were only thirty-nine feet six inches in width. The OV-10's wing span was forty feet.

Captain Ruymann tried to explain that a serious problem existed, and MAG-11's people couldn't understand why. They were accustomed to A-6s and F-4s with folding wings.

"Can't you just fold the wings?"

"Just once, asshole!" Ruymann snarled in frustration. That didn't help our cause a whole lot.

Life in MAG-11 wasn't a whole lot of fun for a while there, and the air group change-of-command ceremony a couple of days later was one of the more unbelievable things I ever saw in a combat zone. I want to tell you about it in order to stress the fact that just about the time you think you've seen it all, somebody's going to come along and add to your body of knowledge.

Back in the States, parades on airfield tarmacs are a common occurrence. When an air wing gets a new commanding general, or there is cause to stage an awards-and-retirement parade, the squadrons all line up in company-size formations, and after the business at hand is accomplished, the band plays, and the Marines all pass in review. This is a standard military ritual. The spectators enjoy a good parade, and there is always a party afterwards.

Never in my entire life did I see squadron commanders out in front of their units. A gung ho captain always volunteered to do it.

Never in my entire life did I see an air group change-of-command ceremony include a pass-in-review parade. Wing, yes; air group, no. Platoon-size units of Marines who could be spared from each squadron for a half hour or so were formed up, the flag was passed, and everyone went back to work.

And never in my life did I suspect that an air group in combat would shut down operations long enough to stage a pass-in-review parade on the Da Nang flight line, with the wing band playing, and require the squadron commanders to march out in front of their squadrons.

We did all of that in the early spring of 1970. The group base maintenance squadron even put their Pee-Pee pumper into the parade. That was an aircraft defueler tanker truck which had been converted to pump out effluents from the precarious sewage system, and I will say that the MABS commander, Lt. Col. Skip Manning, did clean it up, and it didn't smell too bad at all.

The Pee-Pee pumper notwithstanding, that parade seemed to fly in the face of everything we were in Vietnam to do. A certain amount of self-aggrandizement is okay in moderation, but that was embarrassing.

There was an upside to the ceremony, of course. We got a great new group commander, and Col. Grover "Meat Eyes" Stewart was exactly what MAG-11 needed at that time. He subscribed to Admiral Anderson's doctrine on leadership and allowed the group executive officer to run things.

The group executive officer was Lt. Col J. K. Davis, one of the most able officers the Marine Corps ever had. He went on to earn four stars before he retired as assistant commandant, the highest an aviator can go in the Marine Corps.

The two of them brought harmony to MAG-11, especially to VMO-2.

Meat Eyes had served a tour as an infantry division air officer, and he knew exactly what a VMO squadron was supposed to do. He allowed us to bypass the group and work directly with 1st Marine Division and 1st Marine Air Wing on operational matters, which saved us an enormous amount of time. At the same time, J. K. Davis subscribed to the doctrine that squadron commanders had a God-given right to scream and holler and make unreasonable demands, and the rest of my tour was as pleasant and smooth an experience as combat could be.

No rule here, just a caution: While most air groups are commanded by sensible people, you may draw a guy who doesn't like you. It won't be your fault, and it won't be his. I was lucky. Two of the three group commanders I served under in MAG-11 left VMO-2 alone and allowed us to do our jobs. And best of all, neither of the other two had a girlfriend.

PASSING COMMAND

It's easy to take command. Passing command to someone else and doing it gracefully requires some thought and a lot of will-power.

Permit me to preach for a moment. This is a how-to story, after all, and I know of no other written source that will instruct a man on the art of going against all of his natural macho instincts.

A man's natural ego urges him to depart the squadron as a tough act to follow. He wants to be loved and remembered fondly, and deep down in his heart, he knows that no one can run a squadron as well as he.

This is okay. There is no requirement I know of that says a squadron commander must be a candidate for sainthood. But if he wants to be remembered as a class act and not an ill-bred clod, then he must fight those natural instincts.

Ideally, an outgoing commander tightens the screws as the change-of-command ceremony nears, which allows the new guy to loosen them and begin his reign as a hero. In a peacetime training situation this can be something as simple as an extra formation or two.

A month or so before the old guy is due to depart, he tells the sergeant major to schedule an extra formation each day, maybe just after lunch, when it's least convenient. The new guy comes in, tells the sergeant major to cancel the formation—and presto! He's a good guy. At the same time, the sergeant major scores points with the troops because the new commander tells them that their enlisted leader talked him into it.

When I joined VMO-2, just such an opportunity was presented to me. The former commanding officer had levied some taxing situations on the squadron, and I was able to come along and be a good guy. We were able to solve some morale problems immediately, and after we moved to MAG-11, we were able to do some neat things for the enlisted Marines.

When it came time for me to leave the squadron, another opportunity arose that allowed me to give my relief a chance for brownie points. About six weeks before I was due to rotate home, VMO-2 was ordered to move to a different hangar, at the south end of the flight line at Da Nang. As the Marine Corps reduced its assets in Vietnam, all of the jet squadrons remaining in Vietnam were to be consolidated into one air group, MAG-11, and the hangar we were using had aircraft revetments tailor-made for an A-4 or F-4 squadron.

While the new hangar itself was nicer— there weren't even any rocket holes in the walls, and aircraft revetments were built to fit our forty-foot wing span—no one was happy there, and everyone from the commanding officer down to the most junior enlisted Marine longed to return to the old hangar.

The scheduled move of an A-4 squadron from Chu Lai to Da Nang was canceled two weeks before I left, and a decision was made to move VMO-2 back to the original hangar. I made a request that the squadron not move back to the promised land until after I had left, which was granted, and the new guy got to be the hero who accomplished the miracle.

All this is fine and noble, and not too hard to do. But what happens when the outgoing commander doesn't leave the area? Worse yet, what happens when the outgoing commander moves up to the air group staff as the executive officer and still has some power over the squadron?

I had both experiences. I left Vietnam about six hours after I passed the flag, and there was no way for me to influence anyone in VMO-2. When I relinquished command of HML-267 at Camp Pendleton two years later, however, I moved up into a command position in the new air group we were forming there, and I had to work hard to keep my nose out of the squadron's business. To make matters worse, VMO-2 returned to Camp Pendleton from Vietnam and joined the group. And so I had two squadrons under me, which I had recently commanded and loved. Considering man's natural instincts, I spent a lot of time biting my lower lip and keeping my mouth shut.

This is not easy. No matter who a man is or where he is, there will always be a brownnoser or two who will tell him how much better he was than the new guy is, and how much happier the squadron was when he was the commander. Everyone wants to be loved, and that sort of flattery is hard to ignore. Add that to natural ego, and an ill-bred clod will convince himself that he has to save the squadron from itself before it's too late.

I would love to be able to say that I remained above it all and never once interfered with either of the two squadrons, but I would by lying to you. I was better than most at staying out of squadron business, but I do recall summoning the VMO-2 commander to my office one day, tearing up all of his officers' fitness reports in front of him, and ordering him to learn how to write them before doing it again. I think my motivation came from the grumblings of the junior officers.

If you aspire to be a squadron commander, taking command and passing command are both up to you alone. Nobody can do it for you. What takes place between those two events requires a lot of help, however, and Admiral Anderson's words will carry you through. Get a good executive officer. Don't get bogged down in details. And work your tail off to keep everybody as happy as is possible.

Of course, sometimes you have to play fast and loose with the system.

BENDING THE SYSTEM

Let me tell you some of the ways to make the system work for you. They are devious, but they are not always illegal.

1. HOW TO KEEP VISITING DIGNITARIES AWAY FROM YOUR SQUADRON.

In Da Nang, so easily accessible to visiting military and political dignitaries, a minor problem was one of having to stop what we were doing and spruce up for whatever congressman or general was on a fact-finding or inspection tour, designed to get him either reelected or promoted.

Generally, notification would come down to the squadron the day before a visit. We'd grumble, and an hour or two before the dignitary's arrival, half the kids in the squadron would drop their wrenches and screwdrivers and sweep and straighten up the squadron area.

I'm not saying the squadron area was dirty. But when a general comes to visit, your hangar really ought to look as though you were expecting him.

When we moved the squadron from the remote beachfront property at Marble Mountain to the busy, urban Da Nang Air Base, we found a curious accommodation that went against everything we had ever been taught. Because of the horrendous noise level at Da Nang, our assigned squadron administrative offices were located not in or near the hangar, but rather in the living area some two miles away.

When one considered that ninety-five percent of the enlisted Marines of a squadron were attached to maintenance and, therefore, spent their waking hours in the hangar, locating the CO's office a couple of miles away didn't make a whole lot of sense to us. The executive officer and I instructed the sergeant major to turn some shop space into office space.

An OV-10 squadron has a modest electronic shop requirement compared to that of an A-6 unit with all of its exotic systems, and so ample space was readily available.

The hangar itself wasn't any great shakes. We're not talking Tampa International Airport here; we're talking about a hangar alongside a busy, combat-oriented airfield, which the enemy enjoyed attacking. Basically, it was a standard, corrugated-metal hangar, but over the years it had become so riddled with rocket-blast holes that on a sunny afternoon one could imagine starlike pictures and designs on the walls—if one was really bored.

The office chosen to be the CO/XO/sgt. maj. complex turned out to be the former squadron's hydraulics shop, and those of you who have spent time in hangars know how slimy and dirty hydraulics shops can be.

Another challenge was the fact that the shop area was the last one down, right on the noisy flight line.

Sergeant Major Soliz, who was one of the slickest operators we ever met—and in the Marine Corps you get to meet some legends—asked for a few days in order that he might make some plans. This meant that he had to establish contacts with various clandestine supply enterprises in the Republic of Vietnam, Okinawa, and Iwakuni, Japan.

The sergeant major disappeared for a few days—no one dared ask where—and eventually he asked that Major Waters and I vacate the former hydraulics shop for a week while he subcontracted the work.

We didn't have much in the way of cash flow because our coffee mess had just gotten started and wasn't turning too many dollars yet. (The coffee mess will be subject for later discussion.) As a result, a lot of trading took place, and the sergeant major called in a lot of markers. He had, I think, something juicy on every staff NCO in the entire air wing.

The exec and I moved our place of business into the ready room. This was a mistake about which I must warn future squadron commanders. When you spend a lot of time among the junior officers, they are bound to find out how little office work the commanding officer really does. This is not good.

Other than that, it was a nice vacation from paperwork—at least five Polaroid pictures were taken of me ''resting'' and tacked to bulletin boards—and after a week or so, we were invited to inspect our new offices. They were incredible!

In Marine Corps aviation, the CO and the executive officer shared an office, and the sergeant major's office was separated by only a doorway. The sergeant major had to be able to close himself off so that he could have a young Marine's undivided attention when he wanted to explain something.

In this office, we were separated by a pair of swinging bar doors, the only things we salvaged from the original office spaces. Really good bar doors, too. Just like you see in the western movies.

The offices were soundproofed and pine-paneled. The deck was tiled in red and gray. The air conditioner was recessed, as were the ceiling lights. Closets were built in and specially ventilated to accommodate our flight gear.

Rattan furniture came from an unknown source, and the chinaware had to have come from some ship. The coffee set was in similar good taste.

In fact, the only items that were common to the Marine Corps were the desks and swivel chairs, and they had made the move from Marble Mountain with us.

It was far nicer than the group commander's office. It was nicer than the wing commander's office. I never got to see what the MAF commander's office looked like.

The only shabby thing in the office was the squadron flag, with MARINE OBSERVATION SQUADRON 2 emblazoned under the Marine Corps emblem. Replacements for that official banner had to come from someplace in the United States, so we were stuck with it.

The part of the flag that was torn was along the bottom outside corner, and so when we displayed it, at awards ceremonies and the like, the bearer simply held on to the corner and didn't let anybody see it. At my outgoing change-of-command ceremony, however, where I had to present the flag to my relief, such subterfuge was impossible, and so we borrowed a flag from the squadron next door. To this day I can look at the pictures from that ceremony and read clearly: MARINE ATTACK SQUADRON 225.

What, you may well ask, does all this have to do with warding off visiting dignitaries?

Simple. When congressmen and senators and secretaries of the navy came visiting, the idea was to sell them on the fact that the Marine Corps operated on a shoestring budget and that the taxpayers were getting their money's worth. Never stated overtly, but always implied with all of our guile, was the idea that we were so Spartan, and so mindful of the American taxpayers, that when we said we needed something, we really and truly needed it.

With that in mind, you can understand why VMO-2 was always left off the tour. I performed a few briefing presentations out on the flight line, and one doozy for the secretary of the navy in somebody else's hangar. But never was anyone ushered into our office.

This meant that dignitaries never came near our hangar, either, because we were the last one down the line. That meant that the kids didn't have to go through the biweekly and triweekly, straighten-up-for-company drills.

The kids hailed the sergeant major as a hero for this and, of course, never complained about the opulence of the CO's office.

This is about as close as you can come to having your cake and eating it too.

2. HOW TO MAKE A LOT OF MONEY.

A squadron coffee mess is about as dangerous an enterprise as a squadron commander ever tried to avoid. It was illegal, and every squadron had one. It couldn't be avoided, so you learned to live with it.

Making money was not the problem. How to get rid of it was.

The coffee mess began innocently enough. People working on airplanes needed a coffee break, and so a small corner of the hangar was sectioned off, and a counter was constructed. A coffee urn was set up, and coffee was brought down from the mess hall.

But before long the troops wanted something cold.

Simple enough. The sergeant major found a refrigerator, the officers each chipped in a few dollars, and cases of soft drinks were purchased from the PX.

As I recall, a can of Coca-Cola cost us eleven cents, and we sold it for fifteen in order to be able to buy more.

Two or three cents profit didn't seem like much, but there was absolutely no overhead. We weren't even paying the kid who stood there, pouring and selling. He was the squadron driver, by the way. We wouldn't have wasted a valuable mechanic on the coffee mess.

Pretty soon the troops wanted pretzels and potato chips, and they were purchased and sold at similar bargain prices.

And after a few short months, there were hundreds of dollars in the coffee-mess fund. As I recall, we had about three thousand dollars when I left.

Now, here's where it got really dangerous.

The fleshpots of Thailand were only a few hours away from Da Nang, even in an airplane as slow as the OV-10, and we ran our own R & R program in the city of Udorn, in the northeastern part of the country.

Every three days, a pilot and either an aerial observer or a staff NCO left Da Nang for the U.S. Air Force base there, and that afternoon the plane returned, piloted by a crew that had already spent three days in the Sharon Hotel in downtown Udorn.

This was not totally illegal, but it was highly improper, and presented two problems which required covert measures.

We could not purchase fuel at Udorn, for that would leave a paper trail of gas chits, and sooner or later someone would wonder why VMO-2 was always buying gas a couple of hundred miles away from the war.

We solved this with long-range fuel tanks, and referred to the flights as long-range test flights. Jet squadrons had their own subterfuge. Pilots would be scheduled for late-afternoon training flights, and after a respectable period of time, would decide that the weather at home base was too poor for landing and divert to Udorn or Korat, where they would spend the night. It was legal, but marginally so.

But the second problem was the dangerous one. In Vietnam the only legal tender was MPC, military pay certificates, and it was illegal to have American green money. In Thailand there was no requirement for a controlled currency, and so MPC was worthless.

When an American serviceman left Vietnam, all he had to do was show a copy of his orders to the disbursing office and they would convert his MPC into green dollars. Our trips out of country, however, were clandestine, and we had no orders. Therefore, we had to run our own money exchange.

Before long, the coffee mess fund included hundreds of dollars in green money, which we had collected from people coming into Vietnam legally.

What does one do with the money? It depends on how brave he is.

We found that floor shows in the hangar were nice.

The day crew secured at 1800 when they were relieved by the night crew, and that seemed to be a good time for a party. About five-thirty, we'd set up the charcoal grills, and the lieutenants would come rolling in with about a ton of cold beer in jeep trailers. And at six, some floor show would get up on the stage and start performing.

The stage was a flatbed truck-trailer that always appeared mysteriously, sometimes with bunting, sometimes without, and the floor show was purchased through the local booking agents, just like the USO shows.

The sergeant major ordered me to be ignorant as to the details of these questionable booking transactions, but I doubt if that lack of knowledge would have helped at my court-martial. Someone would have been bound to ask how we paid for them.

Inevitably, the night crew started to complain. They could eat the steaks, but they couldn't drink the beer. The lieutenants had the perfect solution, and soon we began champagne breakfasts for them at 0600 when they were going off duty. Couldn't get a floor show at that hour, though.

Other avenues of disbursement were plaques, cigarette lighters, money clips, squadron patches, and baseball hats.

On the subject of baseball hats, a few readers may recall that the popular television show, "Magnum, P.I." featured baseball hats with "VMO-2, Da Nang" embroidered above the bill with something resembling pilots' wings separating the words.

Ours never looked like that. Ours read:

THE ANGRY TWO
VMO-2

None of us ever found out why the Two was angry, but we didn't change the design either.

Our supply officer did not go on the trips to Thailand. We sent him to Okinawa every few months, ostensibly to coordinate supply problems with our sister squadron, VMO-6, which by 1970 was based at Futemma on that island. During his weeklong "staff visit," he would purchase crates of stuff bearing our squadron logo, and no Marine went home without his share of VMO-2 memorabilia.

Getting orders for him to go to Okinawa was not always easy.

Around the middle of the summer of 1970, a new colonel took over as wing G-1 (personnel) and upset the whole damn apple cart.

I knew him well, having served as his executive officer a few years earlier.

Don Conroy was the colorful man about whom *The Great*

Santini was written, and for some reason he decided to person-alize G-1 and take over the signing of all orders himself. He was one of three men I have worked for in my life who were micro-managers and who believed in ruling by intimidation. I loved the man, but damn he was difficult.

And, yes, everything his son said about him in the book was true. He really could drink a half gallon of coffee without once going to the bathroom.

Just about the time Colonel Conroy had the entire G-1 office absolutely terrorized, I wandered in with a smile on my face and traveling orders for our supply officer in my hand, which required wing endorsement to make them legal.

I was welcomed into his inner sanctum and was stunned to see his desk piled three feet high in sets of orders requiring his personal signature. I kid you not. Three feet! The assistants were waiting for him to admit defeat and allow orders to be signed ''by direction,'' but I knew he was indefatigable and never would.

We had a pleasant chat and a cup of coffee while people waited for him to sign orders, and soon I got around to asking him to sign my set of orders. We had already typed the wing endorse-ment ourselves.

To my chagrin, he decided that my request was a bit high-handed and that he would have to think about it for a while. He gave me a few minutes of lecture time on the subject of respon-sible behavior, even in combat.

I smiled and said, ''Sign the orders.''

''You don't understand,'' he began, and went into more B & B (bombast and bullshit).

I stood up, leaned over his desk, and tapped the orders with my finger. ''Sign the goddamned orders.''

I could hear the two lieutenant colonels in the office gasp.

Colonel Conroy stood up and towered over me. He was a big guy, and I wasn't. He began to launch into a major oration, which included the raising of his right arm over his head, further to emphasize his official declamation.

Splat! He smacked his finger on an overhead fan, which drew blood, and he plopped back down in his chair as fast as he had risen. I figured that was about as subdued as he would ever be for this tour of duty, and I tapped the desk again. ''Sign the orders.''

He did. I thanked him profusely as the office staff scurried around to apply first aid, and then I got the hell out of there.

You can't imagine the measure of respect a simple squadron commander can accrue just by asking the wing G-1 for a favor. I milked this for all it was worth.

3. HOW TO PERVERT THE ENTIRE PERSONNEL SYSTEM.

During the summer months there was a substantial influx of senior officers into 1st Marine Air Wing. This occurred because older officers and staff NCOs had children in school, and war or no war, the Marine Corps tried not to uproot a family during the school year.

We were faced with a lot of inbound majors who were OV-10 qualified, and we knew that most of them would be working their bolts as hard as they could to get into VMO-2.

We had four majors in the squadron already, all of them relatively junior in rank, and the last thing a squadron in combat needed was having to play musical chairs with the senior officers.

Some of the squadrons had as many as ten majors, and some even had two lieutenant colonels. When that happened, morale suffered.

What we needed was a slug of captains, experienced pilots who didn't need impressive job titles on their fitness reports, and there weren't any OV-10 qualified captains on the inbound list.

My problem was simple: how to prove to the wing that we didn't need any more pilots in the squadron and, therefore, had no room for the majors, while at the same time proving to the wing that we were hard up for pilots and needed some captains from the VMO squadron back in Okinawa.

Keeping the majors out was fairly easy and only required a lot of legwork. I had spent a considerable amount of time in the personnel business, and I devoted many hours to finding jobs around the wing for these inbound majors. The results were generally satisfactory. They had good job titles for their fitness reports, and they could fly with the squadron. I believe to this day that I did them a favor.

When the promotion board reviewed their combat records, they would see that while the majors held responsible positions, they were also aggressive enough to fly a respectable combat load, and all but one went on to be colonels and generals. I think I did them a favor.

The one who didn't get ahead was already in terminal rank,

and not only did I have to keep him out of the squadron, I also had to keep him from flying our airplanes. He was not a real great pilot either.

Getting the captains from VMO-6 in Okinawa took a little doing. We had to start a whispering campaign in order to create a demand in Okinawa—a demand that some of the captains in the OV-10 squadron there be allowed to get some combat experience.

Letter writing seemed like a good idea, and suddenly our pilots were writing pleasant little notes to their friends in VMO-6 in which they would drop hints that the flying load in Vietnam was killing them, and that we sure could use some help down here.

That started the Okinawa junior officers screaming. I don't know how effective it is in other services, but some outraged captains can be a persistent force in Marine Corps aviation.

We had a lot of friends who were pilots in the transport squadron, VMGR- 253, based at Futemma also, and we were able to get many of them to deliver the same message to the senior officers. Additionally, our majors dropped similar hints to their friends in Okinawa.

It took about two weeks. I was summoned to the wing one day and asked a simple question: "We know you are pretty well loaded with pilots, but we're getting a lot of pressure from MAG-36 in Okinawa. Do you think that some of their pilots could spend a few months on temporary duty with you so that they can get combat experience?"

I played it straight-faced, and wondered if I shouldn't take up the game of poker.

When I tell these stories, people ask how a squadron commander finds the time to get involved in so many activities and still lead the unit.

The answer is simple. The executive officer runs the squadron administration and the commanding officer doesn't.

It made for a long day, but I was young and healthy. I would generally fly the first launch in the morning, the dawn patrol, and be back on the deck in time for the 0800 staff meeting in the air group headquarters. That gave me most of the morning to wander around like a salesman on his route, making sure that everyone in 1st Marine Air Wing and 1st Marine Division knew who we were.

I would fly my second mission in the afternoon or at night,

and that way I averaged seventy hours a month, which was respectable enough to keep the lieutenants and captains happy.
The lieutenants, after all, made out the flight schedule.

FLIGHT SCHEDULES
AND
THE HUMAN ELEMENT

If an aspiring combat squadron commander anticipates his tour to be a lonely one, I bring glad tidings. The days of the sailing master, out of touch with the world for months at a time, ended long ago, and the prospective hero can rest assured that whenever he has a thorny problem to deal with, he will find himself with more assistance and advice than he really cares for.

Gone are the days when a commander has to play God and decide just whom he must sentence to the perils of death. Ninety percent of a squadron commander's decisions are made for him, and nine more fall under the heading of a crapshoot. The only soul-searching I ever faced came in the form of a requirement from wing or air group headquarters to provide an officer for some staff job. And just as often as not, even that odious task was simplified when someone with only a few months left on his tour volunteered for reasons quite unrelated to any perceived dangers of combat flying.

Take, for example, the flight schedule. Fictional accounts of aerial warfare always seem to dwell on the agonies the squadron commander suffers when he is faced with the gut-wrenching task of deciding whom he will send ''up there'' to do battle.

In fiction, there is always the pilot who has lost his nerve, who can think of nothing but his wife and the baby he has never seen, and who is too ashamed to say so. The commander is advised of this by some well-meaning assistant, and the loneliness-of-command theme is dramatized as he overrides the sympathetic request and orders the young lieutenant into the air.

The truth of the matter is that the lieutenant will have to be a mighty good actor to perch himself upon the horns of that dilemma. In today's Marine Corps—and I am certain the same holds true with the other services—when a pilot doesn't want to fly, he doesn't. If he feels that he is being pressured, the flight surgeon is always there, and in matters dealing with pilots' fitness to fly, that medical officer has power over everybody—the squadron commander, the group commander, the League of Women's Voters, and the SPCA.

Only once did I coerce a pilot into flying, and then I had assistance from the Lieutenants' Protective Association, the only political organization allowed in a Marine squadron.

A few weeks before I joined the squadron, this particular pilot, a young lieutenant who was among those hapless kids who had to fly on someone's wing until the shine wore off their navy wings of gold, had the bad fortune of pranging a plane on landing and doing it at just about the same time the 1st Marine Division was screaming for a young pilot to report to one of the regiments as a forward air controller. The hierarchy of the squadron was collectively pissed off at him, which was understandable, and volunteered his services forthwith.

A few days before the lieutenant's tour was up, he was returned to the squadron, still his parent organization because he had been on temporary duty, and I hated the idea of seeing the poor kid go home without any of the squadron's end-of-tour rituals. I had tried to get him back from the division a couple of times, without success obviously, and while the young man had little love for VMO-2, I was convinced that his grandchildren would enjoy seeing photographs of him being baptized and served champagne.

That's how we told a pilot his flying days in Vietnam were over. We baptized him. Actually, in his case, we damn near drowned him, but I can explain that.

We were still superstitious on the subject of last flights. There was something about taking off on that last mission that sat in the back of every pilot's mind, and our Lieutenants' Protective Association, the LPA, came up with a neat ploy to get around it all. Depending on the need for pilots to fill the flight schedule, a man's flying was terminated before he thought it was going to be—hopefully before he even thought he was ready to shut down his combat tour and start writing his memoirs.

Usually we lied to him and suggested that he could start packing his ditty bag in a couple of days, say, on Thursday. He could then try to figure out just when he would actually stop flying, and the lieutenants had to come up with a clever counter move to catch him by surprise. It could get complicated.

A pilot generally flew two missions a day, and on whatever

day the LPA decided upon as end-of-tour day, the schedule would indeed show two flights. Secretly, another pilot was scheduled for the second flight, so that the departing warrior took off on the first one still thinking that he had another day to go. When the flight schedule ran around the clock, seven days a week, the days ran together. The pilots ended up with short memories and were, therefore, easy to fool.

When the pilot returned from his flight, everyone who wasn't flying lay in wait for him, and in some way or another, one or two people had water at hand for the baptism. Waste baskets and buckets held enough water to soak him properly, and the trick of it all was to catch him off guard—which meant that some office would often get its floor mopped out before it was supposed to.

Polaroid pictures were snapped as rapidly as the camera could spit them out, and the photographs would record both the shocked delight on his face and the squadron commander toasting him as he sipped his first of many glasses of champagne to come.

Within minutes, he was whisked off to the officers club, which was opened for the special occasion, and I repaired to my office to pen out a note to his wife or parents, thanking them for the use of their young warrior and offering pictorial proof positive that he was indeed through flying in Vietnam.

My letter was posted immediately, and because the pilot still had a day or two before he left Da Nang, plus at least a day or two in Okinawa before he made the flight manifest for his trip back to the States, the letter always beat him home. Once, a pilot was delayed for a few days due to some glitch in air transportation, and I got a thank-you note from his father the same day he left.

So, in spite of this particular lieutenant's bitterness, it was decided that he would get that one last flight. And he wasn't too thrilled about going.

I lied to him. I invented a mission that required me to fly up and down the coast and look at stuff, and I told him that part of my high-altitude observation flight would cover the regimental area he had just come from, and that I wanted him to orient me on some of the hills and such. I can't recall every lie I told, but I was convincing enough to get him into the rear cockpit.

It was a boring, two-hour, sight-seeing flight, taking in everything from the DMZ south to Chu Lai, but we landed on schedule, and he was properly doused and plied with alcohol, and sent on his way just like every other VMO-2 pilot that year.

The only person who knew when his last flight took place was this present writer, and so I was prepared for my baptism as I taxied in from the runway. I just didn't know the magnitude of the dunking I would take. In retrospect, it was a lot of fun, but for a few moments I wasn't too happy about it all and wondered if some people were trying to even some score.

I expected to take the brunt of a few buckets of water inside the hangar, probably inside the office I shared with the executive officer, after he had convinced me that I wouldn't be drenched because I was the commanding officer and had to be at some meeting in a few minutes. And so I was somewhat alarmed as I started to climb down from the cockpit and saw the Pee-Pee pumper pull up in front of the plane.

The Pee-Pee pumper was that aircraft defueler truck which the Marine air base squadron had modified to suck the liquid effluents from the group's sewage system and squirt it somewhere else, and the hose operator was on top of the tanker truck with the pressure nozzle pointed right at me.

I knew deep down in my heart that they wouldn't really squirt that crap at a human being, but I will admit to a certain number of misgivings over the times we shot the can gun at the bulldog insignia on the MABS commander's door in the wee hours of the morning when he was trying to sleep.

I played along with the game and scampered theatrically around the steel revetment wall and out of harm's way, and directly into a torrent of water that suddenly streamed from one of the flight line fire truck's pressure hoses. I hadn't been hit with that much water since I parachuted into the Pacific Ocean, and the force of it knocked me on my ass.

The firemen were kind enough to take pity on my prostrate form, and I recovered my composure in time to get my champagne and photo opportunity just like everybody else. The only part of my planning that turned out to be accurate was the part about having to go to a meeting—wet and reeking of alcohol.

The fiction about putting out a flight schedule was just that. The lieutenants put out the flight schedule, and saw to it that everyone got his share of the crappy missions including night standbys, where we had to sleep in the hangar, with our planes all preflighted and ready to go, and were expected overhead the trouble spot fifteen minutes after the phone rang.

Every pilot I ever knew competed for flight time, for combat hours were a sign of manhood, and the Lieutenants' Protective Association saw to it that no one got more than his fair share. The rules stated clearly that no pilot could fly over eighty hours a month without permission from the flight surgeon, and then extensions could be granted only in increments of ten hours. Our flight surgeon, John Carlisle, was the guy who moonlighted at the army hospital at Tien Shau three nights a week because we were such boring patients, and you can be certain that he had no cause to turn down any pilot's request.

I suspect that earlier in the war, when the A-6 pilots were making nightly sorties to Hanoi, some pilots, young and old, blew a secret sigh of relief when they didn't see their names in print, but I never knew a pilot in any squadron to quit.

When I was the group personnel officer in MAG-16, the helicopter group, I recall my assistant convincing me that I had to transfer to the group staff a young lieutenant who had just crashed his third CH-46 due to enemy action. But that's the only case I recall in two tours.

On my first tour in 1965, when I was a commissioned paperweight in the III MAF command center, we needed some junior officers to serve as watch officers. We were convinced that there would be some volunteers from the squadrons as soon as pilots who had never heard a shot fired in anger took their first hits. We were wrong, of course. After a few weeks of my doing double duty and working from three in the morning until eight at night, the chief of staff ordered the wing to send him a senior captain from one of the squadrons, and our command center received one of the most pissed-off pilots I ever met.

He was a remarkably talented officer, and I wrote the most glorious fitness reports on him, and I am certain his career was enhanced by the move. But he held me personally responsible, and I never was able to make friends with him.

Squadron life was a lot of fun. Everybody wanted in, and no one wanted out. But there was a downside; people got hurt.

We lost an aerial observer one day in a bizarre incident that gave us all pause. A pilot had been called upon to assist an infantry platoon as it swept an area not far from Da Nang, and the platoon leader asked him to strafe a spot where he was certain one or two bad guys had holed up.

The pilot made one run, peppering the copse of trees with rockets, then rolled in on a second run with the guns. The four M-60 machine guns chattered as he walked tracer rounds through the target area, and as he pulled up and away, a single AK-47 round penetrated the canopy of the rear cockpit and hit the aerial observer squarely in the head, killing him instantly.

The pilot jammed on full power and raced back to Da Nang as rapidly as the straining OV-10 would fly, and radioed ahead for an ambulance to meet the plane at the end of the runway. The squadron was notified, of course, and a maintenance crew drove out to the runway to secure the airplane.

The rear cockpit was a mess, and the line chief made a decision on the spot that the plane should not be returned to the squadron area until he had cleaned it up. I was grateful to him for that decision.

They removed the ejection seat and scrubbed every inch of the rear cockpit until there were no traces of blood. And then, in the dead of night, they towed the plane back to the hangar. By 0600, they had not only returned the airplane to a pristine condition but changed the number on the nose and tail so that the pilots and aerial observers would not recognize it. I no longer remember the number, either the original or the new one— I think it was fourteen, though—and I never did hear of anyone asking any questions.

COWPOKES

Aerial observers get the short end of the stick when stories are told about Marine observation squadrons, and the present writer has been just as guilty as any other pilot who is easily persuaded to "open the hangar doors" and tell war stories. One of the reasons for this slight is not so much that the guys in the back seats were unworthy of recognition, but rather that aerial observers, AOs, are hard to explain. They are rather an improbable group.

For all practical purposes, aerial observers are artillery and infantry officers attached to a Marine division's G-2 (intelligence), who ride in a VMO squadron's back seats and look at stuff from the air. If one were to look at the arrangement through the eyes of a ground commander, he would be persuaded that an observation squadron exists solely to provide airborne platforms for their aerial observers.

This was indeed the original setup when VMO squadrons came into existence in the early forties. Light aircraft could operate from small dirt strips close to the front lines and be on call for artillery spotting missions and occasional visual reconnaissance flights. The people who climbed into the back seats of those flimsy, vulnerable planes were the "eyes of the division."

In those early days, the forward air controllers who conducted the close air-support missions were pilots attached to the infantry battalions—almost always against their wills—and they plied their trades by laying out brightly colored panels on the ground to mark friendly positions and then talking the bomber pilots onto the targets. Marking targets with smoke rounds was a difficult task, especially when the targets were close in, too close for mortar rounds and too far away for a hand-thrown smoke grenade, and it was inevitable that VMO pilots would begin running air strikes themselves, dropping those smoke grenades on the enemy and trying to get away before they had their tails blown out of the sky.

By the time I got to Vietnam, a lot of us had some pretty strong opinions on the proper utilization of a VMO squadron. My personal crusade was a continual effort to eliminate forward air controllers from the battalions' table of organization. I was convinced that an experienced forward air controller and a talented aerial observer, in an airplane with enough radios, could do the jobs of dozens of ground controllers, thereby saving those valuable pilots for squadron duty, and I hammered away on this subject every time I could get somebody to stand still and listen.

Infantry commanders were hard cases, not easily convinced and always suspicious that I was up to no good. Aviation commanders, always seeking ways to appease ground commanders, agreed with my logic but suspected I was up to something, too—probably because of my constant, often devious harassment of the wing personnel section about my pilot needs.

The aerial observers who came down the hill from division headquarters to fly with VMO-2 did so after completing six-month tours, either as infantry rifle company commanders or as artillery battery commanders. They wiped the mud off their boots and took long, hot showers to rid themselves of the stink of the jungle, and moved into our clean, dry, air-conditioned spaces, and started flying with us. I had very little control over who came and went. They belonged to division G-2, and while it was an administrative anomaly that couldn't possibly be allowed to exist in a proper military establishment, it did work, simply because we in the squadron wanted it to.

In truth, both wing and division wanted to transfer the AOs to VMO-2 completely. It made sense militarily and administratively, but I was the guy who stood in the middle and screamed, "No." The only reason wing wanted the officers transferred administratively was to provide our air group with additional ground officers who could then be assigned collateral duties—the job of provost marshal comes to mind. And while I didn't really give a big rat's ass what the AOs did with their spare time when they were not flying, I felt it was imperative that they retained their dignities as professional infantry and artillery officers. Also, it was one of the few ways I had of sucking up to the AOs and keeping them happy.

And so, at least as long as I commanded the squadron, AOs came and went without benefit of orders. They worked for division G-2, their fitness reports were written by division G-2, and as long as they did their jobs, they enjoyed the best of both worlds.

Rest assured that there were indeed differences of opinions among the pilots and the aerial observers. It wasn't all peaches and cream. Male egos being what they were, occasional disagreements took place, generally in the bar, generally late at night, just about the time a five-and-a-half-foot aviator lieutenant had imbibed enough Dutch courage to convince himself that he could take the six-foot-four-inch former linebacker from Boston College, who was just as drunk as he was and busily insisting that Marine pilots were not the heroes they thought they were. That kind of thing. A few loosened dentures, but nothing of lasting consequence. Besides, they wore sunglasses all the time, and no one ever saw the black eyes anyway.

The pilots were almost all second, and sometimes third, Vietnam tour aviators, who had, over the years, either landed a helicopter or dropped bombs on every square mile of the division's area of responsibility, and the combination of the two men, pilot and observer in one airplane, made up one of the most formidable units of supporting arms any infantry division ever saw in the entire history of warfare. A personal opinion, of course, but one shared by a lot of aerial observers, past and present.

Let me tell a story that might help to explain it all. It all took place south of the Que Son Mountains one afternoon in March of 1970 and involved a rifle company from the 7th Marines that was making its way westward on a standard search-and-destroy mission. Some of the dialogue has been constructed after the fact, but it's not far off the mark.

The Marines on the ground weren't doing as well as one of the platoon sergeants thought they should be.

"Awright, you scurvy ramrods! Spread your butts out across them paddies! Don't be afraid to get your feet wet! Third Squad! Don't bunch up on them dikes! My gray-haired old granny could pick you all off from the five-hundred-yard line!"

Platoon sergeants talk like that. Often they venture into hyperbole.

"Move it, Marine! Dammit! Get off that dike, or I'll unscrew your head and use it for a bowling ball!"

The three platoons of Alpha, 1/7, slogged through steamy, flooded rice fields south of the Que Sons, and pressed westward toward their objective for the day—a low grassy ridge that wandered down out of the high ground to their right. These mountains were not significant to geologists, perhaps, but they were altogether tall enough for the Marines who had to climb them.

The company commander, blond, Teutonic, arrogant, had issued an identical order to his three platoon commanders, but his instructions had left much to the discretion of the three young lieutenants.

Predictably, then, the one hundred and twenty Marines of Alpha Company, 1st Battalion, 7th Marine Regiment, were not spread out well at all.

The sweat-drenched Marines waded slowly, cursing, sloshing, mud sucking at their boots, as they tried without demonstrable success to maintain three separate wedge formations.

Well to the north of the snakelike infantry formation, a pair of Cobra helicopter gunships buzzed the mountain ridges, sniffing at the rocks like matched bird dogs hunting prey among the rocks, while far to the south, barely on the horizon, a formation of army transport helicopters scurried toward its destination.

A twin-tailed, green OV-10 whined high overhead and traced a slow circle over the rifle company. Few Marines bothered to look up.

"Lucky bastards. Hour from now, them flyboys'll be in some air-conditioned bar, suckin' on a cold beer . . . shee-yit!"

No one responded, but one or two looked up for a moment.

In the cooler, bluer air above, I replaced the cap on a brown plastic canteen, and sucked at the cold ice water as I tapped at the stick with my knee to keep the Bronco in a turn. We kept two or three dozen canteens in the freezer of the refrigerator back in our air-conditioned ready room and used the hot sun in the cockpits to melt the ice as we flew. I swallowed, tugged at the collar of my flight suit to allow outside air to cool my chest, and craned my neck as though that would increase the air flow.

We had just completed a truck convoy escort for the 5th Marines, about as boring a mission as existed, and the legalized low-level "flat-hatting" barely made up for the sweat-soaked tedium. A few minutes of nature's own air-conditioning was our only reward, and we learned to enjoy every second of it.

I looked down on Alpha Company, studied the wavering lines, and spoke on the intercom to Lt. Lee Gingras, the aerial observer in the rear cockpit, "Poor bastards. What a miserable way to make a living." I eased back on the stick and trimmed the plane for the turn. "Strange looking formation. You all have a name for that, Lee?"

"Yes, sir. It's called try-to-keep-your-feet-dry. The ARVN invented it.," He raised the dark visor of his helmet. "Good help is hard to find nowadays."

Two thousand feet below, the company commander splashed stoically through the foul-smelling water, close to the formations, and tried to be at once aloof, yet indistinguishable from the lesser mortals entrusted to his command. He detested search-and-destroy missions as much as anyone, but a professional Marine had at least to pretend that he enjoyed the rugged life in the bush.

He thought that humor might help, even though he was not good at it. He gazed skyward and spoke to the radio operator, loud enough for a dozen Marines to hear.

"Corporal, would you be good enough to contact that Hostage bird for me?" The captain had seen a lot of British war movies. "Invite him down into our tedious little war and ask him to inspect our accommodations for tonight."

The radio operator had not seen that particular movie. He stared dumbly. "Sir?"

The captain's face soured. Angrily, he wiped brown sweat from his cheek. "Tell him to get his ass down here and recon that goddamn hill for me! Objective Delta! Jesus!"

"Yes, sir!" That the radio operator understood. Dutifully, he unslung his FM radio, and lagged behind as he tuned in channel 39, the frequency monitored by pilots and aerial observers when in the 7th Marines' area of operations.

"Hostage, Hostage . . . Hostage aircraft south of the Que Sons, this is Black Jack Alpha on Jack Benny, over."

Channel 39 was coded "Jack Benny," a fairly decent joke in 1970 when the comedian was still alive and still lying about his age. Channel 45, on the other hand, was called "Colt Malt Liquor," and another frequency was referred to as "the magic sex act." Not all of the Vietnam humor was good.

Between Alpha Company and its objective, a little to the north and right of the formation, rose a cone-shaped hill of little significance, which barely showed on a 1:50,000 map. The company commander had considered sending out a squad from third platoon to check it out but had rejected the idea after that platoon's lieutenant complained of his Marines' near exhaustion.

Detaching small units had proved to be more trouble than it was worth recently. Besides, no one had seen the enemy all week, and the company commander chose to appease his platoon leader.

He should have sent the squad.

Crouching quietly among the craggy rocks of the cone-shaped hill, two men cradled AK-47 automatic rifles and watched the Marine formation with intense interest. Their weather-faded black clothing attested to a career of ambushes.

Neither of the Viet Cong snipers showed outward signs of emotion, though both churned in anticipation.

They had chosen their ambush site well. They had used it before, and the rifle company, spread out across the rice fields for maximum coverage, would parade before their gunsights, left to right.

The older of the two men studied the airplane above, called the "flying pigsty" because of its unusual silhouette. The OV-10 rolled out of its turn and angled toward the west, and an almost imperceptible trace of relief showed through the sadness of his battle-hardened eyes.

Observation planes overhead put guerrilla fighters in jeopardy, and this new one with the twin tails was an unpredictable threat. It flew too fast to see everything on the ground, but its firepower was awesome. To be detected by the crew of such an airplane was to invite the wrath of the Americans and their deadly bombers.

Only the nearest Americans would pass within killing range, but numbers were not important any more. Marines were busy reducing their numbers in Vietnam, and the snipers wanted to help out as best they could.

Their plan was a simple one, tested over the years: hit as many Americans as possible and depart quickly in the confusion. The primary target, as always, was an officer—any officer—easily spotted in front of a radio operator with the swaying whip antenna.

They had lain there in ambush for twenty-four hours through rain, chill, and blistering heat, waiting for this very opportunity. And now the adrenaline began to flow.

"Roger, Black Jack, this is Hostage Six. Go ahead." Lieutenant Gingras's voice was cold, a practiced, rasping growl that sounded seven feet tall. "We're over your position and have your formation in sight."

"Uhh, Hostage Six, this is Black Jack Alpha. My, uhh, Six requests you scope out the high ground west of our poz. I have the coordinates on my whiz wheel."

The radio operator's stammer was understandable. Too many Sixes. In military parlance the number was synonymous with the title commanding officer.

The aerial observer keyed the intercom. "Okay, Skipper?"

"Sure. We're not going to get any cooler up here." I retarded the power levers, and the plane began a gentle descent into the warm, muggy air. "What high ground is he talking about?"

Gingras answered the radio operator, then me. "Same old finger we've been using for years. Dug in there myself a couple of times when I was with Delta Company. Turn more to the left. See that long, green hill running north and south. Ten o'clock. With all the foxholes and trenches and crap."

"Got it."

"Well, unless they've come up with something original, that's where they're going to spend the night. We can make a few passes and snoop around to keep them happy, but Charlie isn't going to bother them there. He'd rather keep an eye on them and know where they are."

Second Lieutenant Lee Gingras was on his second tour in Vietnam. He had been a sergeant during his first tour and had trudged all over the Marines' area of operations as a squad leader. A few minutes earlier, while we were escorting the truck convoy from An Hoa to Liberty Bridge, he had entertained me with stories of the endless days he had spent guarding the bridge across the Vu Gia River, Liberty Bridge, dropping concussion grenades into the water, both to discourage Viet Cong sappers from planting explosives and to engage in dead-fish-counting contests, and his tales of itinerant pimps and drug dealers were endless.

He had picked up a temporary commission between tours— he would revert to enlisted rank after two years unless he could pick up a warrant officer promotion—and while he was in officer candidate school at Quantico, he signed up for aerial observer training simply because he knew that flying had to be more fun than walking.

It was. He knew the ground below us, and he knew many of the people whom we now watched. And he was not pleased.

* * *

"That company commander ought to have his ass kicked. New guy, probably. If I were running that outfit, I'd have troops out crawling all over that little hill to the northeast. Some people never listen. See it out there? Now, that place can be trouble. I almost got my ass shot off my very first trip to the bush. See it sticking up there with the white rocks? Fantastic fields of fire, and an escape route that's almost perfect. As long as we're going to pull a recon for them, Colonel, we owe it to Black Jack to take a look over there."

"Makes sense." I pushed the microphone switch to transmit, and pissed Lee Gingras off by talking on his FM radio.

"Black Jack, Hostage. No need for the coordinates. We have your high ground in sight, and we're going to sniff around to the north a little bit while we're at it."

At about that same moment the northeast elements of the third platoon waded into the kill zone. Both snipers tensed into firing positions. Their arms coiled around their rifles, cheekbones pressed into scarred wooden stocks as they sighted in on the Marines.

This was to be their reward for the hours and hours of exposure to the elements. Their skin was blistered, their mouths parched. Mosquito bites covered their arms and legs, for they had not dared to slap in the quiet of the night.

Intense rains had chilled their bodies in the early morning hours. Also, the rain had washed some of the blackening off the rifle barrels and sights.

The OV-10 leveled off in its turn and approached the hill from out of the sun. I keyed the intercom. "I'll be damned! Lee, how about turning on the Dynalens and getting a close-up of those rocks of yours. I could swear I saw something flash in the sun."

I added power and banked to a course that would afford the aerial observer an unrestricted view of the cone-shaped hill.

"Already running. I was seeing if I could recognize Alpha Six. Now, if I can zoom this thing in without getting car sick."

The Dynalens was a high-power, gyro-stabilized telescope, light enough to hold in one hand, and on loan from the factory of the same name for combat evaluation.

Lieutenant Gingras trained the monocular scope of the rocks and pressed the zoom button until even the leaves on the scrubby bushes were distinguishable.

He saw the metal.

"Jeez! Gooners! Shoot, Colonel, Shoot!" He mashed his own transmitter switch forward.

"Black Jack! Get your heads down! Snipers to starboard! We're taking them under fire . . . uhh . . . to your north!"

I was enjoying my own adrenaline fix as I jammed on full power and flipped the arming switches to the four M-60 machine guns. I horsed the plane into a shallow firing run and squeezed the trigger on the front of the control stick, hoping to walk the tracer rounds up and into the rocks. My position was horrible and there was time for only a short burst before I had to pull up. None of the bullets found targets.

I climbed for altitude, too busy to curse. My heart pounded with the excitement of the hunt as I flipped the toggle switch to the twenty-millimeter cannon. The bolt slammed home with a thud.

"Goddamn! Fire from the right!" The platoon sergeant was taken by surprise. "Third Squad! Skirmish line into that dike! Move it! SUMBITCH! Hold your fire, now, and keep your goddam heads down!"

The turbo props of the OV-10 snarled and strained for altitude. "They're running like hell for those caves across the stream, Colonel! Over by that big orange rock. See it? You can catch 'em in the stream."

"You've got to be kidding!" I adjusted the gunsight to accommodate both the cannon and the machine guns, and jockeyed for position on the stream. The nose of the airplane was high above the horizon.

"Trust me! They're going to be crossing that stream!"

I rolled the plane on its back until the nose fell through, then rolled upright, wings level in a dive. I set the gunsight pipper on the near side of the stream just as the two guerrillas splashed into the shallow water.

The timing was incredible. I squeezed both triggers and a steady stream of tracer fire raced across the water and danced with the Viet Cong as they tumbled, shattered and bloody, into the rocks on the far side.

"Good shooting, Colonel!"

"Good eyes, Lee." I climbed up and away from the rocks. "How'd you know where they'd be?"

"Like I told you, Skipper. That's where I almost got my ass shot off."

Let me tell you another story about an aerial observer, about a captain named Duffy Daughtery. A lot of aerial observers pulled the sort of stunt I mention here, but Duffy did it with such style.

Duffy was an exact double for the oriental character on the "Hawaii Five-O" television series, an archenemy called Wo-Fat, and just as adventurous. Before he received his temporary commission, he had been a parachute rigger, which hardly qualified him as an infantry expert. But he had parlayed his parachuting experience into a reputation as an expert on Force Reconnaissance matters, and he would go to great lengths to enhance that reputation every chance he got.

He didn't have much use for the OV-10 as a visual reconnaissance platform, and he spent a lot of time flying with the army in their light, Bird Dog planes that flew out of Marble Mountain. Air strikes and artillery missions bored him, and he was convinced that his mission in the war was to sniff out the enemy.

On one occasion, he became convinced that the bad guys were holing up in an area just north of the Que Son Mountains, along the water line of Alligator Lake, and he was determined to get proof, no matter what. He couldn't get it from the back seat of an OV-10, and he couldn't get it from the back seat of an army plane, even though he made the pilot cut his engine at night and glide for a few minutes in an effort to hear some sort of movement. And so he decided to go down there and look for himself.

We didn't even know he was gone. He took two days off, thumbed a helicopter ride to a reconnaissance outpost on top of one of the mountain peaks that overlooked the lake, and sat there with them in an attempt to put his knowledge to work, using recon's detection equipment.

This reconnaissance position was one of my favorites. I can't remember their call sign, but it changed every two or three months anyway, so it's not important. What they had, though, in addition to all of their sensor and detection gear, was a fifty-caliber machine gun, the ammunition for which was belted with nothing but alternating tracer and high explosive rounds. When they marked a target they used that gun any time it would reach the area, and when they told us to follow the dotted line, that was exactly what we saw—a red dotted line, with the target area winking at us. That turned me on for some reason, and I always wanted to go down there and shoot that gun myself. Imagine being able to watch every round you fired from a fifteen-hundred-foot mountain top! Kind of like writing your name in the snow.

Duffy wasn't able to find what he was looking for, so he stole some of their greasepaint and dressed himself up like a swamp creature and climbed down the mountain for a close-up. He had spent almost an entire day and night staring at the same tiny piece of real estate through the most powerful telescopic and electronic devices available and had been unable to spot what he knew, absolutely, to be an enemy staging area.

He spent another day and night slithering along on his belly like a reptile, in and out of every hole and cave in the area, until he finally found what he was looking for.

Unfortunately, the enemy had either noticed that the Americans were showing unusual interest in their staging area and decided to abandon it for a while, or they had just decided to abandon it on general principles, so I cannot report that a great military operation was launched because of his determination. I can report, however, that he smelled really bad when he returned.

Having a well-trained infantry officer as an aerial observer in the back seat could be both good and bad. If the man had only recently been a rifle company commander and we were flying in support of the unit he had just left, over terrain he had walked only weeks earlier, then our assistance could be of tremendous value—an airborne extension of the ground commander with timely suggestions and recommendations. But occasionally, the AO would get carried away and try to run the ground operation himself and cause the earthman to be spring-loaded to the pissed-off position, and then we'd get ugly telephone calls.

Having a well-trained artillery officer in the back seat worked the same way. A man who had come to the squadron after his six months as an artillery battery commander wasn't always that great at helping the infantry with troop deployments, but his efficiency in registering artillery on enemy positions often saved lives in that he could direct the rounds to a target in an unusually short period of time and while the elusive Cong were still shooting at our troops. Also, he had the ability to plot the enemy's egress routes and pursue them with fire as they were beating their hasty retreats.

As fortune would have it, by 1970 there weren't that many pitched battles in the Marine Corps' area of operations, and so most of their expertise was wasted on registering the fire of artillery batteries that had either moved to new positions or screwed a new barrel on a gun.

Probably the most worthless weapons we had were the huge 175mm guns on loan from the army. The barrels were only good

for so many rounds—a hundred or so if memory serves me—
and every time a barrel was changed, one of us had to motor on
out to Elephant Valley and watch for an hour or two as the
cannon-cockers pumped round after round into a winding river
bed with little islets we used as reference points.

We couldn't register them in jungle terrain where they might
possibly do some good, because there were no smoke or white
phosphorous rounds available. The Department of Defense had
decreed that shortcoming, following convoluted logic, which
argued that because the big guns fired the rounds so far out into
Indian country, there would be no one around to observe the
hits anyway; therefore, such a luxury was a waste of money.
The army didn't have the OV-10, and besides, the gun was designed for the big war against the Russians in Europe anyway.
We, of course, blamed the secretary of defense personally, just
as we blamed him for the underpowered engines we had on our
OV-10s because the original engines, for which the planes had
been designed, were made by Pratt and Whitney of Canada, and
he didn't want American defense dollars leaving the country.

Anyway, it took about fifteen rounds to register a new gun
barrel, which took forever because they had to let the barrel cool
off between shots or else it would warp out of shape, or melt,
or something. The registration flights constituted some of the
most boring flying I experienced in all of my thousands of hours
in the air. The artillery officer at least had an academic interest
in what he was doing, but the poor pilot had nothing to do but
position the plane so the AO could see the explosion and correct
the plot, and pray that something urgent would come up and
give him an excuse to leave.

About two-thirds of the AOs were just like Lieutenant Gingras
and Captain Daughtery, temporary officers who were magnificent in the air over the battlefields, wonderful and colorful butterflies released from their enlisted cocoons for a while. They
would have to return to the caterpillar stage when the war was
over, back to the offices and flight equipment shops and electronic shops to resume their less glamorous professions. But for
a few brief months, they were warriors in the true sense of the
word, and ground commanders throughout the Marine Corps
have an obligation to be proud of them.

Occasionally we would see a regular officer among the aerial
observers, but they were rare. Being an aerial observer was not
a good career move. The highest rank that occupation could

ever hope for was that of lieutenant colonel, and I think the Marine Corps had three, maybe four, of those. I only met one in my entire life.

In another chapter I mentioned our efforts to get a color-blind AO into our back seats, and I still insist that the Marine Corps and everybody else needs people with that unique condition, but the only man we were able to find during my time with VMO-2 was a Naval Academy graduate who had to think of his career first and refused to jeopardize it by spending precious combat time away from the mud and mosquitoes.

That was really too bad, too. Color-blind people aren't confused by camouflage, and they were able to see things in the jungle that we ordinary mortals missed.

When I first arrived in Vietnam, my assistant in the MAG-16 personnel office was a former VMO-2 pilot who was color-blind, but not so much that he would flunk his flight physical. Herman Smith had incredible eyeballs and had been personally responsible for two major, and successful, operations just because he was able to see things on the ground that no one else could. He took me out flying a couple of times and tried to teach me some of his tricks, but I was never able to develop his X-ray vision.

One day we spent almost an hour circling a wooded area where there weren't supposed to be any unfriendly people, and he tried to coach me into seeing a hut concealed in a copse of jungle growth.

It was clear as day to him, but try as I might, I couldn't see anything but trees. We blew it away finally, using the bombs from a section of A-4 Skyhawks, which had seen its original mission scrubbed and was looking for a target, but I never did see the huts.

I wrote a lengthy request for color-blind aerial observers and worded it in such a way that, with any luck, it would get back to Washington and become somebody's pet project. About the same time, I also wrote up a lengthy request, tongue in cheek, for an English-speaking Montagnard, on flight orders, who could ride in our back seats and tell us just what the hell we were looking at out in the hills where those semicivilized tribes led their primitive lives. The request for color-blind aerial observers fell on deaf ears, but the insane request for the Montagnard on flight orders got all sorts of attention.

The navy bureau of medicine got into the act on my first request, and when it came to matters dealing with the demanding vision requirements of naval aviation, those bureaucrats had minds like the front end of an LST. But my other venture found its way to Saigon and the desk of a nun who had spent most of her life living in the hills with the Montagnard tribes and convincing those dark, tattooed savages to put away their spears and take up the Christian faith.

I was bombarded with literature about their primitive life styles and the way they farmed the hills, some of which was useful, and for a while there, I was afraid that a Montagnard would actually come walking into the hangar one day and scare the hell out of the pig (about which more later) and the entire maintenance crew, and announce, in English, that he was ready to fly if we could find a place for him to store his spear for a while.

Not everything we did in VMO-2 required the expertise of a trained aerial observer, and they were probably bored to tears on at least half the missions they flew with us. One young lieutenant used the message-drop apparatus to distribute pornography to the Marines on the ground—he was the same fellow who provided the movies for the "Southeast Asia Porn Film Festival" the lieutenants staged in the MAG-11 chapel—and I am certain that AOs bad-mouthed the pilots as often as the pilots complained about them, but they made it all work.

I used to advertise VMO-2 as "the link in the Marine air/ground team," and we were indeed just that. But without well-trained AOs, we'd have been nothing more than a squadron of airborne forward air controllers.

JOSEPH AND
THE GIANT EASTER EGG

Easter Sunday began as Easter mornings should begin that March day in 1970. Rosy-fingered dawn burst forth in all of its glory over the South China Sea, the way Homer decreed that it was supposed to, with pink and red rays soaring skyward and reminding everybody who was old enough what a World War II Japanese battle flag looked like. All over Vietnam, air force, army and navy chaplains were in the middle of their sunrise services, serving communion to anyone who had time to sit still for a few minutes and listen to a sunrise sermon, sip a little wine, and munch a wafer.

Easter was not of great importance that 29th day of March when the aerial observer, Lieutenant Simmons, and I briefed for our "Dawn Patrol" flight. It was still dark outside the hangar, and any thoughts about sunrise wondered only what daylight would permit us to see.

The night before, one of our pilots, Lt. Dave Huffman, had sprung an aerial ambush on a Viet Cong supply effort, and we were on our way out to the Thuong Duc area to take a look at the results.

Dave Huffman had coordinated with a Marine reconnaissance team that was dug into semipermanent positions on a hilltop overlooking the river valley and able to track enemy movement with sensors and night viewing devices. The recon Marines had been able to track groups of Viet Cong porters as they backpacked their loads of ammunition along a riverside trail, but had not been able to get a clear shot at them. Sensors spread out along the trail told the reconnaissance team where the enemy walked and approximately how many there were, but lower hills prevented them from shooting with their own weapons, and priority problems would not permit an artillery battery to be tied up for an hour or two waiting for a fire mission that might never be called.

Lieutenant Huffman, flying the last scheduled mission of the day, Mission 76-Papa, had the fuel and the patience and the curiosity of youth to see if he could pull it off, and so was willing to try an ambush that depended on instant reaction and a one-run attack for success.

Before the sky was completely dark, he had picked three reference points along the trail which would be reasonably visible even if there was no moonlight, and he and the reconnaissance team labeled them A, B, and C for quick identification. The recon Marines depended on their sensors. Dave relied on two large rock formations and a tree that had been hit by something a day or so earlier and was, for reasons still unexplained, still smoldering and glowing dimly, even in daylight.

They gambled that the enemy would stick to the same schedule they had used in the past, and Lieutenant Huffman was prepared to loiter on station for an hour and a half, between eight and nine-thirty. If he was unable to find an unemployed section of bombers to do the job at that awkward hour, his plan B was to swoop down when the sensors said the enemy porters were hoofing it among his reference points and shoot everything he had, guns and rockets, on that one-run opportunity.

As luck would have it, the Direct Air Support Center sent him a section of A-4 Skyhawks that had been launched out of Chu Lai and which had seen its mission canceled before the pilots had expended their ordnance load of two hundred-and-fifty-pound Snake Eye bombs. The A-4 pilots thought an aerial ambush would be a lot of fun, too, and after Lieutenant Huffman briefed the mission and the attack pilots knew exactly where to be, the jets found a tanker and refueled in order to be able to hang around on station for an hour or so.

What we had that night was a bunch of lieutenants making up their own little war as they went along—not always a great idea. Had anyone gone to wing for permission to stage such an operation, the G-3 and G-2 sections would have staffed it to death, or hunkered down into a defensive posture and denied the request on grounds that it was not a sound plan. And perhaps it wasn't, but to the lieutenants it was all perfectly logical. And when Lieutenant Huffman dramatized the story later that night, I could almost see the old Andy Hardy movies, and hear Mickey Rooney telling Judy Garland, "We could put on a show!" And they managed to pull it off.

The enemy porters came plodding down the trail, hauling those incredible loads they were able to put on their backs, and as they triggered the sensors buried in the ground along the trail and the lights started flashing on the reconnaissance team's control panel, Lieutenant Huffman got his A-4s in position to pounce.

Recon counted twelve porters—a guess really—and when they were all trudging between reference points *A* and *C*, Huffman ordered the Skyhawk attack planes to follow him down. He splattered the trail with every one of his white phosphorous rockets and projected a fiery, dotted line for the jets to use as alignment, and the A-4s dumped their Snake Eye, fin-retarded, bombs along the clearly defined target line.

In and out, one run, and the sensors stopped flashing. Some had probably been blown up in the raid, but sensors were expendable. There was one secondary explosion, which meant that a load of ammunition had been hit, and Lieutenant Huffman was one happy fellow in the officers club later on in the evening.

I was buying the beer and the popcorn, and so Dave was happy to tell the story two or three times until the executive officer and I were satisfied that I wasn't going to be called on the carpet in a day or two to perform one of my famous rug dances, explaining to G-3 (operations) why I permitted junior officers to make up their own little wars as they went along.

And so, the results of that action were what we intended to look at that Sunday morning as we briefed in the squadron intelligence office—signs of a successful ambush. The enemy had done it to Marines often enough, and I was looking forward to seeing some of their carnage for a change. Then, after we had made our postaction assessment, we would move on to other areas and look for other signs of enemy activity, and as far as I was concerned, it was just another day in the never-ending war of hide-and-seek and capture the flag.

After briefing the mission, I climbed into my torso harness, complaining to the office walls about the discomfort, and made my way down the hall to flight equipment to pick up fresh survival radios before proceeding on to the line shack to sign out for whatever airplane was scheduled for the mission. My log book says the bureau number of the plane was 155488, but I have no idea what number was painted on the nose of the plane. I flew a lot of my missions in Number 1, 155408, which was personalized with my name painted on the side, but contrary to popular belief we didn't put much stock in personal airplanes the way the navy did. Besides, my name was misspelled, and stayed that way for my entire tour, but I was the only person who ever noticed it.

Lieutenant Simmons and I waddled out onto the flight line, swinging our helmet bags and looking very much like two strangely dressed bowlers on our way to the alleys to roll a few early morning lines. I say waddled, because the torso harnesses were so tight in the crotch that a normal, human gait was impossible. I was always grateful that we didn't have to wear G suits.

The airplane was about halfway down the flight line, partially obscured in angular sunrise shadows created by the high revetment walls, and we were almost in front of the starboard propellor before we saw the giant Easter egg.

It was a wonderment, and I stood and stared in delight for a moment or two. Almost four feet from tip to tip, the giant Easter egg was painted in green and red and blue and had those jagged lines around the middle like the ones we saw when we were kids but were never able to duplicate with our Paas Easter egg coloring kits.

Someone in the squadron knew what day it was, and a person who didn't know better might have suspected that the world's biggest Easter bunny had laid a big one, right there in the front cockpit of a twin-engine, turboprop OV-10A Bronco made by the North American-Rockwell people in Columbus, Ohio.

Rocket pods, shaped pretty much like the tubes in rolls of paper towels, were made in various sizes, and all came with oval nose cones that blew away with the first shot so that fast-moving jets could carry a few of them without a lot of aerodynamic drag to slow them down. The OV-10 was not a fast-moving airplane by any stretch of the imagination, and so our ordnance department generally threw the nose cones away, but in honor of the religious occasion, two had been saved and glued together to form an Easter egg large enough to fill a cockpit.

A small crowd of maintenance and ordnance Marines emerged from out of the revetments to observe the reaction of their steely-eyed squadron commander, and I did not disappoint them. I was easily entertained anyway, and for a few moments the war was forgotten as we all admired the art work. I cannot recall everything that was written on the egg, but I do remember reading Gunnery Sergeant Shroyer's signature comment: "Ho Chi Minh is a fink." I believe there was also a Denver Bronco sticker pasted on the plastic fiber.

We admired the egg collectively for a while and considered the possibility of a squadron Easter egg hunt for a moment, but then rejected the idea when someone suggested that it was a little late to get started on an enterprise of that magnitude, and that even if we had started the night before, Hostage Hog, the squadron mascot, would have found the eggs by now and scarfed them down, shells and all.

We agreed, however, that the giant Easter egg should be relaid in each plane scheduled that morning, and the ordnance crew was delighted to remove it from the cockpit and lug it over to the plane assigned to the next mission, which was to be flown by the squadron maintenance officer, Maj. Joe Roman. On Sunday mornings, the senior officers flew the early missions so that the lieutenants could sleep in.

The aerial observer and I directed our minds back to the business at hand with some reluctance, preflighted the OV-10, strapped ourselves into the ejection seats, and cranked up the engines for what turned out to be a very routine Sunday morning flight.

The enemy was efficient at removing bodies and equipment from battlefields, and so there was not much to look at. It took several passes to ascertain that several Viet Cong had been assisted in their journeys to paradise. Either that, or some large animals had been splattered. Where they had crossed the shallow river before they walked into the ambush was quite clear, but after that the signs disappeared. I hated mysteries, and we spent a half hour or so trying to piece out the trail before we moved on to greener pastures, but we would return to the area again and again over the next two months until the puzzle was solved, and 1st Marine Air Wing mounted one monstrous firebombing raid, which is reported in detail in another chapter.

The rest of the day passed like any other Sunday. We tried to pretend that it was Sunday, but the war kept getting in the way.

I received an Easter card in the mail from the parents of one of the young Marines in the hydraulics shop. They thanked me for watching out for their little boy. That was unusual, but not nearly as strange as the three Mother's Day cards I would receive a month or so later, which were cosigned by the families' parish priests and which designated me the mother pro tem.

It was a quiet day in the sense that not much was going on out in Indian country. Wars are loud, even when nobody is getting hurt. That afternoon, I spent an hour or so sitting atop a revetment wall at the end of the flight line, and munched a can of Cheetos while I watched a couple hundred airplanes take off and land and made myself available to the youngsters. There weren't any crashes. As I said, it was a quiet day.

There were no crises to deal with either. The kid whose parents sent me the Easter card pretended to be embarrassed, and a plane captain visited a while and entertained me with improbable stories of his R & R trip to Australia. I gathered that he had been a virgin before he visited Sydney, but I kept my mouth shut.

It was so quiet that I decided to repair to my quarters and take a nap before dinner, something I was rarely able to do, and as I headed toward my jeep, Maj. Joe Roman trotted up beside me, lugging the giant Easter egg and asking for a ride up to the living area. Damn thing filled the entire back seat.

"It's mine to keep!" he crowed through a smile a yard wide. "Ordnance department put it on my desk with a note saying I could keep it."

"Makes sense. You're the maintenance officer."

The smile faded into mock seriousness. "Oh yeah. That's right." The smile returned. "Hell of a deal!"

That evening, after dinner, I joined the executive officer, Maj. K. D. Waters; the operations officer, Maj. Bob Carlson; and the maintenance officer, Maj. Joseph Roman, in the Marine Air Group 11 officers club for a drink. The lieutenants were having a party of their own that night, a cookout at hut 23-B, and we weren't invited. We looked forward to the rare opportunity of quiet conversation in the club without the children.

We had been asked to the lieutenants' party, of course, but the invitation had been carefully worded so that we would stay away. "There'll be lots of food and beer if you want to stop by," they had said, and that translated into "Please don't come." We were smart enough to stay away from any activity where we would put a damper on the junior officers' main topic of conversation, which we presumed would be the executive officer, Major Waters, because he had recently been giving Lt. Skip Roberts a lot of heat about the length of his moustache. Skip was in his Fu Manchu period about that time.

Joe Roman had become inordinately attached to the giant Easter egg and brought it to the club with him. He held it in his lap the entire time we were in the club, setting it in a chair only long enough to go to the bathroom, and even then, we were all sworn to guard it with our lives.

He wouldn't let go of it, convinced in his exaggerated way that it was so wonderful and such a marvelous thing that someone would steal it if it left our sight even for a minute—and knowing the pilots of MAG-11, he may have been correct. This meant, of course, that we got a lot of curious looks from the pilots of other squadrons. But Lt. Col. Stan Lewis, skipper of VMA-242, treated us to a round of drinks in honor of the splendid art work, and this got Major Roman to thinking. This was always dangerous.

Joe Roman's incredible sense of humor and infectious grin got us through some bad times during that combat tour, and that night there was tacit agreement among us all to allow Joe to lead us down whatever frivolous path his demented mind might choose. If he wanted to play with a giant Easter egg, then so be it. After a few drinks, free and otherwise, he was pretty much in charge of things.

Joe Roman was an interesting man, and we all loved him. He was as short as I was, which endeared him to me the first time we met, and his face matched his name, probably Romano before it was Anglicized.

We first met in the Naval Air Training Command where we were both instructors, between combat tours, at Training Squadron 2, VT-2, at NAS Whiting Field. A captain then, Joe had returned from his first tour in Vietnam a hero, having saved a lot of lives by calling in a dozen or so night air strikes all around his crashed helicopter after being shot down. A rescue would not be possible until daylight, so intense was the enemy's determination to eliminate a CH-46 full of Marines, and Joe was a human dynamo all night long as he tended to the wounded, directed the defensive fire of those Marines who were still able to shoot, and called in air strikes close enough to his tenuous position to keep even the most adventurous NVA troops at bay.

He had been written up for the Navy Cross, the navy and Marine Corps' second highest award for bravery, but somewhere along the chain of command—we were pretty sure it was in Washington—the medal he so richly deserved was downgraded to a Silver Star. He was disappointed, of course, and many of us were purely pissed off that his magnificent display of valor brought only the same medal the army passed out by the hundreds, until it was equated to a senior officer's Good Conduct Medal in that service.

What made Joe so interesting was that at Whiting Field he had been a humorless, straight-faced, all-business personality.

He was a splendid officer, and I liked him, but he wasn't a whole hell of a lot of fun to be around. Even when we engaged in the favorite Marine pastime in the Naval Air Training Command, tweaking the navy's beaks, he was the wet blanket who was forever warning us of the perils of protocol, especially the night after happy hour when we decided to plaster the base commander's staff car with Marine Corps recruiting stickers.

But once he was removed from the responsibilities of being a husband and father and bill payer, his metamorphosis was complete. His Perma-Press smile and delightful humor and a natural flair for diplomacy made his appointment as the squadron maintenance officer a natural choice for me, even though he was the junior major who should have served in a much lower position. The appointment rankled some majors who wanted the prestigious job themselves, but in a combat situation the lineal list of officer seniority is not always the best gauge of those to be placed in the important jobs.

I wouldn't have considered that break with tradition in a squadron back in the States, but in Vietnam, Joe kept the entire maintenance department, ninety-five percent of the squadron, humming along happily, and our aircraft availability was constantly the highest in the 1st Marine Air Wing. Even the members of the ordnance crew liked him, and they were hard to please, and maybe that was the reason he ended up owning the giant Easter egg.

After several drinks, when we were enjoying an apparent respite from crises that Sunday evening, Joe took complete charge of our evening. "I think," he opined, stroking the multicolored glob in his lap the way he might caress a house cat, "that we should take this wonderful Easter egg over to the wing club and see if someone won't give us a prize."

We pondered that proposal for a second or two, nodded our approvals, and jointly agreed that the giant Easter egg was indeed worthy of an award. Bob Carlson, who had flown the Marine Corps' first giant helicopters, H-37s, during an earlier tour, speculated that the wing staff pukes needed a little humor injected into their humdrum paperwork existences. He stood up and shouted, "Let's do it!" and knocked two salty dogs and an ashtray from the table.

Major Waters called the squadron to tell them where we would be, and the five of us, four short guys and a giant Easter egg, marched out of the MAG-11 officers club and drew a few more stares.

We were all approximately the same height, you see, five feet nine inches or less, and this was a source of occasional scorn when things were really dull around the wing. Comments like "When you guys grow up, maybe you'll get to fly jets," and stuff like that. Also, there was scurrilous gossip which impinged on my integrity.

Two months earlier, we had been required to march in a change-of-command parade—I, as the squadron commander, out in front of VMO-2—and I had snarled at the tall, lanky lieutenants who marched directly behind me as platoon leaders when their long legs threatened to climb right up my back.

That night, when the squadron gathered in the club so that I could have the honor of buying their booze, a lot of "short" jokes were inevitable, and it seemed logical at the time for me to make a pronouncement that, hereafter, no officer would be permitted into Marine Observation Squadron 2 if he had the bad fortune of being taller than the squadron commander. That was mildly humorous for the moment, but for the rest of my tour, not one pilot over five foot nine inches of altitude ever checked into the unit, and I am willing to swear under oath that it was pure coincidence, except for one major whom I refused to take under any circumstances, not because of his height, but because he was a terrible pilot and dumb as a hoe and had screwed up everything he had touched in the eight or nine years I had known him. Nothing personal, of course. But people whispered. And because I was known for playing fast and loose with the personnel system anyway, my alcohol-induced proclamation was taken seriously in some quarters.

We piled into my jeep and drove over to the wing compound—the four of us short guys and the massive, jagged-striped lump that looked like Charlie Brown's sweater and caused the sentries at the gates to stare in wonder. I think the sentry at the wing compound phoned ahead to the provost marshal as we pulled away.

We drew a considerable amount of attention as we walked into the 1st Marine Air Wing officers club. This was the gathering place for the higher level staff officers, and they did not go to their well-appointed club dressed in flight suits. We on the squadron level had Vietnamese cleaning ladies who washed and ironed our utility uniforms, too, and polished out boots just as the staff officers did, but the staff officers wore theirs. And so the majors and colonels of that august body backed away from us as we passed, and seemed to look down their noses as though

we were a bad smell. No doubt, the giant Easter egg had something to do with it.

We commandeered a corner of the rich mahogany bar with
simulated leather arm rests and introduced ourselves to the bartender, while Joe Roman tried to talk a stubborn captain out of
his bar stool so that the giant Easter egg could have a place to
sit too.

Failing in that endeavor, Joe decided to brighten things up in
the oh-so-serious club. We marveled in awe as he muscled in
on the table occupied by the wing chief of staff and wing G-3
and another colonel I did not recognize, and asked if they might
be interested in awarding VMO-2 a prize for the best Easter egg
of the season. They weren't, of course, but they were nice about
it. We think Skinny Lamarr, wing G-3, offered Joe a nickel, but
Joe denied it.

A chaplain, who might have sucked up a lot of communion
sherry during the holy day, intercepted Joe on his way back to
the bar and expressed some interest in the giant Easter egg, but
offered no prizes. After a Lenten season and Easter Sunday
among a wing full of heathens, he was willing at least to smile
on pagan rituals, because here, in the bar of all places, he had
found someone who actually knew what day it was.

Staff officers on a Sunday night were not a partying crowd.
We clung together at our corner of the bar and rolled the dice
for drinks, and I lost all three times. No one came over to admire
our egg. We were sober enough to realize that this was about as
far as we were ever going to get with the giant Easter egg in the
wing club, and we put our heads together to decide which club
to visit next. Joe Roman was certain that the helicopter pilots in
MAG-16, over at Marble Mountain, would appreciate what we
had, but that was a long drive and it was getting late. And so
we were just about to pack it in when the bartender handed me
the telephone. "It's for you, Colonel. Sounds important."

It was. Capt. Bill Paulsen had just crashed on the runway.

Yes, the executive officer, operations officer, and maintenance
officer were with me, and yes, we'd be there in just a few minutes.

We headed for the front door at a dead run, which was a
spectacle one did not normally see in the 1st Marine Air Wing
officers club, and of course, everyone in the building that night
knew immediately that Marine Observation Squadron 2 had a
problem. No one else was getting phone calls—and in a combat
zone, *not* getting phone calls constituted a state of serenity. The

chief of staff hadn't budged. Skinny Lamarr only turned around to see what the fuss was about, and the colonel none of us knew kept right on telling his story. As far as 1st Marine Air Wing was concerned, whatever it was that caused the people in the flight suits to bolt out of the club was: (A) a localized problem, and (B) none of their concern.

We rounded the corner of the club building to where I had parked the jeep, and I had the engine running even before I slid onto the red-and-black-striped seat. Jeep locking mechanisms were totally useless, no matter what the provost marshal said, whether on the steering wheel or the gear shift, and so I didn't have to waste a lot of time doing whatever false security a chain and padlock offered. People piled into the jeep as I put it in gear, and I was just starting off when we heard a pitiful shout from behind. "Hey! Wait up, gang!"

Major Waters grabbed my shoulder and urged me to wait as Joe Roman came puffing up, still embracing the giant Easter egg.

"I got stuck in the door!"

"Why didn't you put the egg down? Get in the back!"

"Jeez! I never thought of that. Here. Grab the egg."

We raced off. I ground through the gears as professionally as I could with twenty or thirty cubic feet of giant Easter egg trying to squeeze into the space between the front seats, and our haste convinced the sentry at the gate that we just had to be up to something sinister. Maybe he thought it was a bomb painted to look like an Easter egg. He recognized us as the same nuts who had come through his gate earlier, and so had no reason to stop us, but I suspect he called the provost marshal again.

Over the years, we had all disciplined ourselves not to become emotionally involved in plane crashes, but that didn't make us any less concerned. Bill Paulsen was a good friend and had recently earned the nickname of "Hands" Paulsen, following an incident in the MAG-11 officers club when he dared to "lay hands" about the head and shoulders of the headquarters and maintenance squadron commander—which required K. D. Waters and me to perform amazing lateral arabesques in our rug dances in front of the group executive officer's desk to prove that the squadron commander deserved to be slapped around a little that night, even by a lowly captain. I enjoyed Bill's company, probably because he was the only man in the squadron who was lazier than I was. Tall, blond and Nordic, as his name suggested, he was a reservist back on active duty, and had no aspirations toward greatness. He was an excellent pilot, on his second tour in Vietnam, and all of us in the jeep were concerned about him.

The crash was on runway 34-left, in the vicinity of the passenger terminal, and the exact location was easy to spot as we approached in the dark because of all the fire trucks and flashing lights. There were so many emergency vehicles that we feared the worst.

"Looks bad. God! What do you think?"

"I don't know. You think Bill's okay? I can see the tail. It looks okay."

"How the hell can you crash in the middle of the field? He must have landed wheels up!"

We squealed to a halt—brakes on those Ford jeeps always squealed—and our questions about the fate of Capt. Bill Paulsen were answered almost immediately by Capt. Bill Paulsen himself, who was the first to come over to the jeep and confirm K. D. Waters' suspicions.

"I'm sorry, Skipper." As I said, Bill Paulsen was tall, and he had to stoop to see inside the jeep. "I was trying to avoid landing behind a C-130 that was getting ready to take off on 34-right . . . I've been in that prop wash before . . . and I decided to take it around and make another approach, and so I pulled the gear up . . . and then the tower cleared me to land on 34-left . . . and I forgot to put the gear down."

The aerial observer behind Captain Paulsen wasn't apologetic at all. His reputation wasn't on the line. "You should have seen the sparks! Jeez! I was looking out, and it looked like the Fourth of July. Must have scraped the whole belly off!"

"Asshole!" Captain Paulsen put out his famous hand to quiet the mouthy observer. "That wasn't the belly scraping. We landed on the rocket pods. That was burning white phosphorus you were looking at." He turned back to us. "Thank God we came to a stop right beside the fire truck." He squinted and looked more closely inside the jeep. "What the hell is that?"

K. D. Waters was quick on the uptake. "That's your prize, Bill. You get to keep it until somebody else wins it away from you."

"Aw, c'mon. You wouldn't do that to a guy."

"Wanna bet?" K. D. climbed out of the right seat of the jeep. "Get in and meet your booby prize. I'll stay with the plane."

Major Roman and Major Carlson got out with the executive officer, and Captain Paulsen slid in beside me as the aerial observer squeezed into the back. As I put the jeep in gear, Major

Waters put his hand on Paulsen's shoulder. "And, Bill, that could have happened to any one of us."

I drove across the passenger terminal's tarmac and back to the squadron while Captain Paulsen went through the entire sequence of events again, adding that as he turned to his downwind leg, over the city of Da Nang, a spray of tracer fire aimed in his direction added to his distraction. He shook his head. "Damn, that's embarrassing. He isn't really going to make me carry this thing around, is he? It looks like a giant Easter egg!"

"It's Major Roman's giant Easter egg. I don't think he planned for it to be around after today."

And that pretty well sealed the fate of the giant Easter egg. Within twenty-four hours the airplane was back in the air, and the squadron got away with an incident on the record instead of an accident. The double nose cone with the stripes that looked like Charlie Brown's sweater disappeared forever.

The rocket pods absorbed most of the damage, and once the sponsons on the bottom of the fuselage had been replaced, the plane was ready to fly again. Maintenance hours required to repair the damage were fewer than seventy-five, though maybe the maintenance department lied a little, and without an accident since a lieutenant pranged a plane on landing back at Marble Mountain, the squadron eventually won the coveted chief of naval operations safety award.

In accordance with the traditions of the season, the giant Easter egg was mysteriously resurrected, to some place other than Marine Observation Squadron 2. I saw it sitting in a chair in the ready room the next day, but then it disappeared, and I chose never to ask where it went—although I suspect someone laid hands upon it out behind the ordnance shack.

EJECT!

Jumping out of an airplane under controlled conditions is exciting and a lot of fun. Jumping out of an airplane when you have not planned on it is exciting, but it sure isn't much fun. It's an adventure, one you'll never forget, but I never met a man who enjoyed it.

Let me tell you some quick-ejection and bail-out stories, which will lead me into one of the great dramas of my tour as a squadron commander.

Both involved the same Marine F-4 Phantom pilot and took place within the space of a month. I was a witness to both of them, although I didn't find out it was the same pilot until he buttonholed me at the Chu Lai officers club one afternoon and told me about it.

The first ejection was a dazzling air show that entertained the entire Da Nang Air Base. One hot, sunny day, I had just climbed down from my plane after a mission, and I was walking toward our hangar with Major Waters, who had met me at planeside with some pressing business. I have no idea what the business might have been, but I'll never forget the episode that interrupted it.

As we walked and talked about the squadron business, I looked to the north and was startled to see two white parachutes floating downward over the Da Nang harbor. No big thing, but not an everyday occurrence either. They were survival chutes and not the brown T-10s used by Force Recon or the red-and-white chutes used to recover drones.

"K. D.!" I shouted, pointing. "Look at *that*!"

Major Waters looked up and pointed over my shoulder toward the runway. "The hell with that! Look *there*!"

At an altitude of about fifty feet and perfectly aligned with the runway, flew a flaming F-4 Phantom. Instead of canopies and pilots, we could see only the steel poles which seconds before had held ejection seats in place, and around the tail and wing roots, flames licked as though they were rolling around logs in a fireplace.

I didn't think flames would do that. The airflow over an airplane traveling at 150 knots should have blown the flames backwards, but lick they did, and shot a few holes in age-old theories about putting a plane in a dive to blow out engine fires.

This was probably the most fascinating thing we would see all day, and we raced toward the runway, along with just about every Marine who was out of doors at the time, before the fiery Phantom disappeared behind the tall revetments that protected parked planes on the ground from enemy rockets.

The plane flew on to the south, straight as an arrow, and eventually ran into enough turbulence to upset the trim of the controls and cause it to crash.

No big thing. There were a couple of crashes a day at Da Nang, and this one was just a little more out of the ordinary. The jet had taken some hits and was making an emergency approach into Da Nang because the pilot didn't think he could make it to his home base at Chu Lai, a couple of provinces to the south. Had such an event occurred at an air station in the States it would have made the front page of the local paper, but in Da Nang it provided only a few hours of "did-you-see" conversation.

A couple of weeks later, in the middle of the night, I flew out of the west end of the Que Son Mountains, to Landing Zone Ryder, about forty miles south-southwest of Da Nang, to control what was called a Blackboard Exercise, in which the troops on the ground underwent an imaginary attack and called on 1st Marine Air Wing to beat off the imaginary enemy assault.

The terrain around Landing Zone Ryder dicated that any sort of attack in force would have to come from the south where the land sloped away, and we were going to put on the night firepower show there. To the north and west were sheer drops into Antenna Valley, and the eastern slope was not only steep, but under our guns at LZ Ross as well.

We at VMO-2 knew about the exercise in advance, and I had scheduled my takeoff to allow me to arrive in the area just as the Marines at LZ Ryder put out their scheduled cry for help. Apparently, not everyone in the wing got the word about such a training exercise, and the pilots who sat on the hot pad at Chu Lai thought they were launching on a true emergency situation when they were scrambled so late at night.

The F-4 Phantoms arrived with loads of napalm, and so I had to work out an air strike solution that would accommodate those weapons. I dropped a log flare about halfway down the hill to establish a reference marker. I chose a northeasterly run-in heading in order to allow the planes to pull up and be able to see the lights of Da Nang in the distance. It was a dark, dark night, and disorientation on pull-up was far more critical than rising terrain in front of the bomber pilot. There are two situations in which a pilot will sell his soul for some reference lights: during a night catapult shot from a carrier, and pulling off a target after a night bombing run.

We set up a flight pattern over the target exactly like the patterns we used for night air strikes back in the States in the desert training areas around the Marine Corps air station at Yuma, Arizona. The only difference was that the planes would turn off their lights when they rolled into their attack runs.

I found out later that the F-4 crews thought I was pretty much of a pussy for being so painstakingly meticulous when clearly there was an emergency situation on the ground below, and he couldn't understand why I wanted him to put his napalm on the log flare that had been burning there for two or three minutes.

The lead plane rolled into his run and turned out his lights, and from then on there was no way I could tell anything about his lineup or his altitude, which was the reason I wanted him to drop on the flare, which was well away from any friendlies. He called "Wings level," and I cleared him to drop.

The napalm tanks hit the ground and erupted predictably. The next time you see film of napalm hitting flat terrain, watch for the fuse that generally takes off in front of the fireball and flies straight ahead for a second before it burns itself out. That was exactly what I saw on the drop.

Instead of burning itself out and disappearing, however, the "fuze" kept growing and growing, until it was unmistakably the Phantom itself. The jet had hit the ground along with the napalm tanks, and was one incredible torch that flew up and over the Marines at Landing Zone Ryder.

I don't know if the flames licked that time. I was dumbfounded for an instant, and watched in horror as the airborne holocaust splattered into Antenna Valley to the north.

It was one of those horror shows for which there is never a

happy ending, let alone a viable rescue solution. The Marines at Ryder announced that they had seen no parachutes, but they set about getting together a group of volunteers who were willing to climb down the steep hill. I got on the radio and tried to drum up a helicopter rescue package, but met with no success.

The air force Jolly Green Giant rescue apparatus wouldn't launch because the crash was not out of country, and it was going to be a while before we could get Marine helicopters into the area. All in all, it was a bad scene. I felt absolutely helpless and frustrated and guilt ridden. I sent the wingman home, of course. But there was nothing I could do except fly around in circles and cuss a lot until I ran out of gas and had to go home.

Just about the time the Ryder Marines were about to descend into the valley of death, I was electrified by a radio transmission: "Hostage Six, this is Lovebug Two Two Six Alpha. I'm up and okay!"

This was followed by a second transmission from Lovebug 226 Bravo, the backseat airman, with the same message. They had ejected after all! And done so in time to avoid landing in the plane's fireball. It was true deliverance from what appeared to be certain death and one of the most exciting moments of my life.

We rewrote the book on our night-air-strike procedures the very next day. I added a second plane to the night-standby package, one loaded with nothing but flare pods. No one ever objected to the change, and I hope the new procedures are still in use, because I got damn sick and tired of pilots flying into the ground on night bombing missions.

Our flares were ten times brighter than the flares carried by the Basketball, the C-117 that remained airborne all night to provide flares for the ground units that requested them; and when it was time for the bombers to commence their runs, we lit up the sky to the point that we could use daylight bombing procedures.

We could only maintain that amount of illumination for about fifteen minutes, but an air strike seldom required more.

If that evening's drama was exciting for me, it was pretty exciting for the F-4 crew, too, and I'm certain they're still telling the story today. While the ground strike wasn't a planned maneuver, the pilots survived because they were well trained for just such an eventuality. They were in superb physical condition, which made their climb up that steep hill a lot simpler. They knew their equipment and they were well drilled in ejection-and-survival procedures.

EVASION & ESCAPE

The name of one of the principal figures in this story is fictionalized, not because he did anything wrong, but because he didn't do something correctly, and I don't want to embarrass his children.

I will call him Major Jones. It's a common name, and we never had a pilot in VMO-2 by that name while I was a member of the squadron.

One of the first things a student pilot is taught in flight training is how to survive in the event of a crash or an ejection, and survival training continues throughout the pilot's career. Or at least it's supposed to. Physical conditioning and the techniques of staying alive are as important as being able to fly the airplane itself, and the military pilot who allows himself to grow soft of body and stale in his survival skills is doing a gross disservice to himself, his family, and his country. Replacing an airplane is easy; replacing an experienced pilot is not.

But survival training is not a whole lot of fun. It is a rare person who will willingly give up his comfortable existence for a week or so in order to plunge into somebody's jungle to practice the art of playing Tarzan. Even rarer is the man who willingly goes off to an evasion-and-escape school and allows himself to undergo the brutality of a mock prison camp.

Survival, evasion and escape, all of this is vital. And yet, the pilot who avoids these schools is exactly the pilot who needs it the most. He is the senior officer, the man who is physically beyond his prime and who has forgotten much of what he had been taught when he was young.

When quotas for survival training schools come down to the squadron level, the first thing the commanding officer does is look around to see who can be most easily spared. Never in my life did I see the CO or any of the senior officers volunteer to leave the unit just to practice staying alive. Junior officers, especially the lieutenants in unimportant jobs, received all of this valuable training, and as soon as they were senior enough to avoid it, they did. Not all, but most.

Col. Al Pommerenck, MAG-11's group commander toward the end of my tour, was just about the oldest colonel in the Corps before he made brigadier general. But he kept himself in tremendous physical condition, and when he was forced to eject over Laos, he ended up carrying his observer on his back for several miles before being rescued—an observer who was half his age.

When I was a captain in VMF-232 at Kaneohe Bay in Hawaii, the squadron had an aggressive safety-and-survival program, and as much as we grumbled and complained, every three months we went out into the bay, jumped off the back of a motorboat in a parachute harness, and practiced the art of being picked up by a helicopter. Because all of our flying was done over water, this training made sense. In August of 1964, when I had the occasion to eject from a burning airplane, forty miles out to sea, the experience made survival and rescue a piece of cake.

I swallowed half the Pacific Ocean before I scootched myself into my life raft, and I got seasick bobbing around in nine-foot swells for an hour, and I puked all over the inside of the air/sea rescue helicopter when the crew chief offered me a cigarette. But I had practiced the important stuff, and afterwards I became a strong supporter of survival training. Until I became more senior and supposedly had more important things to do.

When I got to Vietnam, I was sent back to the Philippines within a week of my arrival to attend the navy's jungle escape and survival training course in the Cubi Point/Subic Bay area. No pilot was allowed to fly in Vietnam without attending this course, and there is no question that many lives were saved because of it. But this three-day course was the only jungle survival training I received in my entire life.

It wasn't the Marine Corps' fault; it was mine. I was too busy to waste my valuable time on something so plebeian, and I flew almost six hundred hours of combat time without any real preparation for staying alive in some of the most inhospitable terrain Southeast Asia had to offer.

And ninety percent of the senior officers who flew in Vietnam were just as guilty as I was. I didn't get shot down. Most didn't, but many of those who did have the misfortune to play Rambo for a while did not survive the experience.

An argument rages about the fitness of women to fly in combat. To me, a healthy woman is a lot more valuable to a squadron than an out-of-shape major. Until, of course, she becomes senior and too busy to train and exercise.

Maj. James D. Jones was a staff wizard, an administrator of the first magnitude who had a bright future in the Marine Corps. He came to Vietnam after a three-year tour at Headquarters, Marine Corps in Washington, where he had made a name for himself in the personnel business. When his tour in Vietnam was over, he would report to another high-level staff, and his steady advancement was assured.

He went through OV-10 training at the same time I did, but upon arrival at 1st Marine Air Wing, his administrative talents were put to use immediately in the wing Personnel section. The Marine Corps was in the middle of withdrawing from Vietnam, and because Major Jones had been a key player in drawing up the plans in Washington, he was, in effect, the mastermind of Operation KEYSTONE ROBIN, code name for the withdrawal of about half of the Marine Corps assets in country.

But it was a rare aviator who wanted to spend his entire combat tour behind a desk. "What did you do in the war, Daddy?" "I was a commissioned paperweight, Son. Now, shut up and do your homework!"

No, our egos were too strong for that. Hormonal attacks occurred in men in their mid-thirties too, and after about seven months of badgering and scheming, Major Jones finally had his way. KEYSTONE ROBIN was just about completed, and he wangled his way into VMO-2.

He was a nice guy, and he had lost a lot of the weight he had picked up sitting behind a desk in Washington, but I wasn't too thrilled about his joining the squadron. He was senior to Major K. D. Waters, which meant that he was going to bump K. D. out of the executive officer's slot. All good things have to come to an end sometime, but I didn't want it to happen on my watch.

K. D. was pissed, and decided to take a position in the air group operations office rather than step back to a lesser job in the squadron and bump somebody else. I am certain he blamed me for letting it happen. But I had no choice in the matter, and

Major Jones must have felt deeply the animosity the squadron felt for his being there.

As I said, he was a nice person—but he wasn't K. D. Waters. The wing commander owed him one for all of the brilliant work he had done, and if combat-squadron time was what he wanted, that was what he was going to get.

Late one morning toward the end of April, I was getting ready to go flying on a standard, Mission 76 reconnaissance flight. Captain Selleck and I were in the intelligence office, an annex to the air-conditioned ready room where most of our preflight briefing took place, and we watched Major Jones and his flight brief for a deep reconnaissance mission that would cover a sector on the Laotian border.

Captain Selleck was the assigned aerial observer for my flight, and the only thing we had scheduled was a convoy escort. Neither of us was too interested in such an activity, but if the ground Marine Corps was going to run a truck convoy from the 5th Marines' area at An Hoa to Da Nang, it needed air support for the trip as far as Liberty Bridge, after which the roads were pretty safe and well patrolled.

While Selleck drew a whiz-wheel encoding device from the intelligence clerk, I joined Major Jones; his aerial observer, Capt. Chuck Hatch; and his wingman for the flight, Lt. Peter Colt, in front of the huge wall map that covered the entire tactical area of operations.

"How's it going? Got it all figured out?"

Jones turned. "Morning, Skipper. Yeah, I think we've got everything under control. G-2 wants us to take it in sections, so this trip we're going to cover this sector here." He pointed to an area on the Laotian border that was blocked in red grease pencil.

I leaned toward the map and examined the block. "Don't get lost out there."

Jones grinned. "No, sir. We won't. We figure that Peter can keep a lock on to the Da Nang TACAN if he stays high enough."

"Right, Colonel. I'll fly navigator and shotgun both." Peter Colt, blond and slight of build, went through the motions of firing a shotgun. Deep probes into the hinterland were among the very few missions VMO-2 flew in two-plane sections; safety in numbers being the primary consideration. While Major Jones and Captain Hatch searched for trail activity, Lieutenant Colt would lurk overhead, ready to roll in on anyone who took a pot shot.

Captain Selleck had his code wheel, and put an end to our conversation. "I'm all ready when you are, Colonel."

"Let's do it, then. You all have fun, now, Jim." I spoke over my shoulder as Selleck and I started for the door.

"We'll do our best, Skipper." Major Jones turned back to the map.

"Major, suppose we follow this river to the valley." Hatch traced a route to the outlined area. "Then we can run due south to that ring of hills. See how they form a semicircle there? We can use that as our reference point for the whole sector."

Lieutenant Colt measured the radial and distance with a string and with the compass rose pasted on the map around the Da Nang airfield. "Looks like about two-five-zero and fifty-seven miles." He cocked his head to one side as he inspected his calculations.

Major Jones copied the figures on his knee board. "All that country sure looks the same. We're going to fly high out there, and we're going to stay high until we're sure we have the right spot."

"Sounds good to me." Captain Hatch wrote the radial and distance on his knee board too.

The two OV-10s took off right behind me, and by the time I got to Hill 55, fifteen miles southwest of Da Nang, they were way above me and heading west as I churned through the hot, sticky air at low altitude, headed for An Hoa and the dusty truck convoy. I would have preferred trading places with Major Jones at that moment, but he wanted to get involved with all of the squadron missions, and I wasn't about to stick him with the boring flights while I went out and had fun.

Major Jones leveled off at eight thousand feet, where the air was cool and the TACAN held steady. He flew a course that would intercept the two-five-zero degree radial, and adjusted his power. The engine temperature and pressures were good, and he trimmed the controls until the Bronco flew hands-off.

Peter Colt had taken his new Japanese camera along, and he maneuvered around Jones's plane, changing positions and camera angles as he shot picture after picture.

They flew over the "Tennis Courts" plateau and encountered updraft turbulence just as Colt was taking a close-up, with both hands off the controls. He narrowly avoided a midair collision and dropped the camera in his lap when he grabbed the controls.

He put the camera away and settled down in a loose trail position on Jones's right wing. He'd never try that again.

They flew past the first ridges of mountains, and a layer of clouds stretched out in front of the two planes. Jones descended slowly, gently, to stay beneath them, and soon he had reached four thousand feet. Within minutes, the mountains between them and Da Nang masked the TACAN station and the needle swung uselessly.

"So much for my navigating," Colt transmitted.

Both Jones and Hatch traced their progress on the map. There was a thunderstorm directly in front of them, and Jones turned right to fly around it.

Soon they were well away from the river, and Jones skirted the circumference of the rain trying to get back to the visual navigation aids. He searched the jungle below, straining to see the river through the downpour.

Neither Jones nor Hatch knew that the thunderstorm sat directly in the center of the valley they had selected for their turning point. The maps were so inaccurate in this remote area that the flyers were certain that the valley was three miles further on.

Jones found the river again, finally, and continued on to the west, unaware that the was flying past the valley and well into Laos.

"There's the valley. Dead ahead." He transmitted so that both Hatch, in the backseat, and Colt, behind him, could hear.

Hatch checked and rechecked his map with the valley below. They did not look the same, but he knew how inaccurate the original French road maps had been, and he guessed it was the right one.

Jones turned left and looked for the ring of hills to the south. The valley ended in a round bowl, remnants of an ancient volcano. It wasn't exactly a ring of hills, but maybe the French hadn't been too good on contour lines either.

They flew over the bowl-shaped mountain and orbited once while they rechecked their maps with the terrain. The weather was much better here, and the sun punched down through gaping holes in the cloud cover. It was green and beautiful below, and Hatch pictured a large, western ranch with cattle roaming in the lush valley.

"Okay," Hatch said. "Fly due south from here and work your way back and forth, moving to the east. I'm not too sure of this terrain, though. These maps are really rotten."

"Going down to the deck," Jones transmitted. Then on the

intercom, "We're almost in the airway that crosses Laos. Ought to be safe enough."

"Got you covered, pardner." Colt mocked a western drawl from his shotgun position above.

Jones descended to an altitude where he could see the detail of the terrain and flew to the south. Together, he and Hatch searched for clues of enemy activity, but saw none. The enemy wasn't giving anything away out here. They reversed course in a tight left turn so that their fields of vision would overlap the ground they just covered.

It was a standard navy search pattern, developed by patrol pilots fifty years before, and had they been closer to home, Jones might have performed a wingover in the turn, just as crop dusters did when they were bored.

Jones reversed direction again as he drew abreast of their reference point, the volcanic bowl.

"Lots of nothing out here."

"Yeah, but it sure is pretty." Jones continued his southern track, and the hills and streams whizzed by underneath.

They crossed a ridgeline, and a new valley stretched out before them. The valley was oriented east and west and should have been prominent on the map. Hatch studied the chart and could not place it.

"This doesn't look right, Major. Let's turn back." Major Jones agreed, and banked into a gentle left turn that carried them just over the far edge of the gently rolling valley.

Suddenly Jones saw a road. He blinked his eyes and looked again as he flew over a gravel highway, wide enough for traffic to pass in both directions in some spots, and winding eastward along the southern slope of the ridgeline.

"Good Lord, Chuck! Look!"

"I see it! Let's get the hell out of here!"

"Get your camera!"

"I've got it, Major. I've got it."

Jones continued his turn, and the OV-10 returned to the ridgeline. He lined the plane up on an angle to the road, and Hatch sighted in with his camera.

"We'll get these shots while we're down here. Then I'll climb up higher so we can orient it all."

Hatch still thought getting the hell out of Laos was a better idea, but these were going to be pretty good pictures, too.

The plane passed close to the road. Suddenly there was a crashing *thud*! The OV-10 was jolted severely. Hatch's helmet was ripped off his head as a thirty-seven-millimeter shell tore into the left wing root and exploded, splattering hot metal everywhere and throwing the plane wildly.

Flames shot out of the left engine as it quit and died abruptly. Both Jones and Hatch felt totally engulfed in flames, and the horrendous noise without the helmet made Hatch fear for his life instantly.

"I'm hit!" Jones shouted into the microphone, panic rising in his voice.

Lieutenant Colt received the message simultaneous to his seeing the flames himself. He watched in horror, not knowing what to do.

Jones was frightened, probably more frightened than he had ever been in his life. Flames licked all around. He sensed that the enemy fire had come from the high ground near the road, and he turned frantically to the left to get away from it, into the dead engine. The stricken plane was already in a violent yaw to the left, and the searing flames enveloped the cockpit. The OV-10 started down, barely clearing the ridge, and into the valley.

"Get out!" Jones screamed, gasping for air and not keying the intercom. He had no control over the stalled plane, and he grabbed the yellow-and-black-striped ejection-seat handle between his legs. He straightened his back and held his head upright as he jerked the firing handle.

Hatch reached for his firing handle and was astonished when his seat charge exploded, hurtling him upwards as the top of the seat smashed through the canopy. The back seat was designed to go first in the firing sequence. Then Jones shot up and out of the fireball.

In an instant, both airmen hung suspended in their parachute straps and watched the burning plane smash into the valley only a hundred feet below and off to the east in an open clearing.

It took only a few seconds for the parachutes to reach the ground, but to both men it seemed long enough for the entire North Vietnamese Army to sight in on them.

Hatch landed to the east of Jones and closer to the high ground. His feet hit the hard earth, and he released the quick-disconnect fasteners that held the parachute straps to his torso harness. He gathered the white parachute together in a bundle and ran into a small cane field that lay untended between the wreckage and the hills.

The cane field drew him like a magnet and provided a small amount of confidence. He had once been lost in a sugarcane field on a training exercise, where it had taken him an hour to thrash his way out, and he knew immediately how well he would be concealed now.

Jones was not so fortunate, and crunched down into a low tree. He came to an abrupt stop, and bounced twice as the branches sagged under his weight. His boots were only a few feet off the ground.

He released the quick-disconnects and dropped to his feet, running as best he could with the seat pan still attached by the lower buckles. The pain in his ankles also made running difficult. He stopped long enough to release the left buckle and pulled the seat pan around under his right arm.

Adrenaline pumped through his body. He took off his helmet and threw it away to the other side of the tree that had ensnared his parachute canopy, then started running again into the brush that grew uphill from the trees. He hoped that the discarded helmet would indicate an eastward direction of travel of any search party the enemy might send out.

Hatch threaded his way through the cane, trying not to break any of the stalks, and when he could no longer see the surrounding terrain clearly, he started digging a hole to bury his parachute.

He was thirsty. He could not believe how thirsty he was. His breath came in asthmatic gasps, and his hands trembled as he clawed the soft earth around the cane. The hole grew larger, and he decided to bury himself with the parachute.

"Mayday! Mayday!" Peter Colt cried out on the UHF guard channel. "This is Hostage Colt! Crash, crash, crash . . . on the two-four-five degree radial . . . fifty-seven miles off channel seventy-seven!"

Colt had climbed for altitude, and the Da Nang TACAN came in clearly.

"Mayday, Mayday," he sobbed. Would anyone hear his distress call this far away? He tried desperately to think of something he himself could do, and tears rolled down over his face.

A microphone clicked with a metallic sound, and a deep voice boomed with hollow resonance.

"Hostage Colt? This is King." The *ng* fairly rang. "Understand you have a Mayday on the two-four-five at fifty-seven off channel seventy-seven?"

"R-roger, King." Colt brightened at the immediate response.

"My wingman was hit by ground fire. There were two good chutes."

"Okay, Hostage Colt, you are the on-scene commander at this time." The voice was clear and deliberate. Peter Colt would later tell me that King's transmitter was so loud it would make even his tinny voice sound like the Wizard of Oz. "Orbit east to the crash and remain above ten thousand. Attempt to contact the crew. We will have help to you shortly."

King was the call sign for the elaborate and highly effective air force rescue system control plane. When pilots were down in enemy territory, King assumed control of virtually everything that could fly. Squadrons of Jolly Green Giant CH-53 helicopters and A-1 Skyraiders existed solely to support the rescue efforts.

Colt leveled off at eleven thousand feet and called, "Hostage Nan? This is Hostage Colt, over. Please come up, Nan!"

Major Jones was disappointed with his hiding place. A few branches and leaves. That was it. Yet he did not dare run. There was clearing all around him, and he would surely be seen. The adrenaline charge subsided, and his whole body trembled.

He could see the white of his parachute in the trees. That could be good or bad. The enemy could see the chute, but so could the rescue airplanes. The enemy had seen him land in the trees anyway, so maybe that wasn't a big thing. And he had thrown his helmet in the opposite direction from that in which he ran. Someone mentioned that in jungle survival school, and he hoped it would work.

What else had they taught him? It was so long ago! He was happy he had lost all of the extra weight he had picked up over the years, but he wished he were in better shape. God! He was so tired! His ankle hadn't started to hurt yet.

He looked around, this time without panic. It was quiet. No one was shooting at him. He had left no footprints on the hard ground. There were large rocks behind the thicket, and he crawled toward them slowly. If he could wedge himself in between those two big ones with the branches covering the tops, he might hide nicely.

He was surprised at how thirsty he had become. They had reminded him of this in survival school too, and he promised himself a drink the moment he was safely hidden.

Discipline. That was the key to survival. Panic and die, they had said. Or get captured. He wasn't sure which was worse.

Water discipline was all-important. He had two pints in his

seat pan and two small plastic bottles in his survival vest. He would ration himself severely.

Captain Hatch was uneasy in his shallow grave, but satisfied that he had chosen the best of the available hiding places. If he lay flat on his back, only the tip of his nose was above ground level, and he had widened the trench near his right shoulder to conceal the seat pan which contained so many things that would keep him going.

He unzipped the left pocket of his survival vest and took out a white plastic water bottle. He wanted to drain it, but forced himself to stop after two sips. He screwed the top back on carefully and set it beside the seat pan.

He was calm now, although his hands still trembled. From the same pocket of the survival vest he drew his snub-nosed .38 revolver and checked it out. The pistol was loaded with purple-tipped tracer bullets, and he could not decide whether to reload with regular ball ammunition or with the new flare bullets he had been issued only a few weeks earlier. He decided to stick with tracers. With those he could signal or shoot to kill.

Why, he wondered had he stopped carrying his .45? He was an infantry officer, and the .45 was his T/O weapon. And now here he was where he really could use a powerful weapon. All he had to defend himself with was a dinky, aviation-issue snub-nosed .38 with a barrel so short it wouldn't hit anything even if it stood still and grinned at him.

He put the pistol back in its holster and zipped the vest pocket halfway, in case he needed the pistol in a hurry. He took out one of the small radios. He was glad that Flight Equipment had insisted on taking the radios back after each flight. He knew the batteries were fresh and that the radios worked. Switching from beeper to voice, he pulled the antenna up and keyed the transmit button.

"Hello up there! This is Hostage Nan Bravo on guard!"

In a survival situation, Alpha designated the front seat, Bravo the rear.

Lieutenant Colt was electrified at the sound of Chuck Hatch's voice. "Roger, Nan Bravo! Read you loud and clear!"

"Just wanted to let you know I'm okay." Captain Hatch was impressed at how calm his own voice sounded.

Major Jones had just turned on his radio, having successfully maneuvered his frame into the rocks. He heard Hatch's second transmission and joined the conversation, hoping he hadn't missed anything important.

"This is Nan Alpha. I'm all right too."

Colt did not know what to say. "Roger, Nan Alpha and Bravo. You stay put now, and we'll have you out of there in no time at all." It sounded pretty stupid even as he said it, but he could think of nothing better.

Meanwhile, back in the Da Nang area, the truck convoy arrived at Liberty Bridge intact, and I was through with the escort duty. The dust had settled back on the red-dirt road that connected the 5th Marine Regiment with civilization, and no ambush had been attempted, although we thought we had seen a drug deal going down near the bridge. I put full power to the engines and started a climb for altitude and cool air, hoping for a few minutes respite. I took a long drink from my canteen and wiped away the sweat with a chamois cloth.

"Hostage Six?" The radio interrupted as I climbed over the hills. "Hostage Six, this is Da Nang DASC, over."

"Roger, DASC. Hostage Six up."

"Hostage Six, we just got a call. Hostage Nan is down."

"Down? I was momentarily confused. Down where? Down was a nebulous term. It meant a lot of things.

"Where, DASC? Down where?" I looked back at the small airstrip at An Hoa, fully expecting to see an OV-10 on the runway. There were only helicopters there.

"King reports the two-four-five degree radial at fifty-seven."

A shot of electricity stung me. "My God! Did you hear that?"

"Yes, sir!" Captain Selleck opened his map. The radial and distance put Hostage Nan in Laos, and he unfolded the map all the way.

I mentally computed a course that would intercept the 245 degree radial of the Da Nang TACAN and left the full-power setting on the engines.

"Roger, DASC. Understand two-four-five at fifty-seven. I'm on my way. Would you call the squadron and tell them where I'm going?"

I wasn't certain just what I'd do next. I climbed out to the west and pictured the box outlined on the wall map in intelligence. I wished I had studied it more carefully.

"Take up a heading of two-six-zero, Colonel." There was anxiety in Selleck's voice. "As best I can figure, they're down on the Laotian border where it turns southeast." He handed the map up to me, folded to the area of the crash.

"You fly it." I took the map, and while Captain Selleck flew,

I studied it. I recognized the border area and knew it was way south of where Jones should have been.

"How do you suppose they got way down there?"

"Beats hell out of me. Look! There go the Sandys! Three o'clock high.'

I looked up to the right. A flight of A-1 Skyraiders flew past in a southwesterly direction, and the sight of them erased all uncertainty as to what was going on.

The prop-driven A-1s, once navy and Marine dive-bombers, had been taken out of mothballs by the air force for duty in Vietnam. The Spads—so nicknamed to reflect their antiquity—were there to lay down bombs and rockets to suppress the enemy while the Jolly Green Giant helicopters swooped in for the pickup.

That's what I hoped would happen—and soon. I searched the sky for the helicopters, but could not see any.

From his high orbit, Peter Colt looked down on the crash site. The highway that caused all of the trouble in the first place snaked into South Vietnam from Laos and disappeared into the jungle almost exactly where it touched the border. This was the first time he had seen the "other war," the Ho Chi Minh trail that attracted so much attention and bombing, and he was confused. How, he wondered, could a highway like this exist? In VOM-2's war, the enemy moved on hidden trails, and it was a grim game of "keepsies" hide-and-seek. Here, only sixty miles from Da Nang, was an open highway defended by enemy gunners. The entire U.S. Air Force, and sometimes the navy and Marine Corps, were there to keep the road neutralized, and still the enemy was there.

Jones and Hatch had stumbled onto the road by accident and had been shot down making the fatal error of going back for a second look. The enemy had probably been as surprised as the airmen—surprised that anyone would fly over their guns at such a low altitude.

Colt shook his head in bewilderment and moved his orbit farther to the east, wondering just how high up the gunners could reach. He saw the flight of A-1s approaching from the northeast and called them on guard channel.

"Sandy?" He did not know anything else to call them. "Sandy? This is Hostage Colt, over."

There was no answer and the A-1s droned past him. Then Colt heard a familiar voice—mine.

"This is Hostage Six arriving on scene."

"Hostage Six? This is Colt. I'm orbiting east of the crash at eleven thousand."

"Roger, Colt. I'll be there in a minute. You okay?"

A new voice interrupted before Colt could transmit. "Hostage Six, this is Covey."

"Roger, Covey. Go ahead."

"Hostage, I'm headed your way. Stay out of the area until I get there."

Covey was the call sign of the air force controllers, the airborne forward air controllers who patrolled this part of the war. They flew OV-10s like VMO-2's, but painted gray instead of green, and performed reconnaissance missions and controlled air strikes on the enemy traffic that moved down through Laos. Covey knew this territory; we were interlopers. I was a pro in my own ball park, but out here I was a minor leaguer and quick to agree with Covey's instructions.

"Okay, Covey!" The booming voice of King resounded. "You've got Cobra One Five and Gunfighter Two Three headed your way."

I recognized the call signs of the air force F-4 squadrons based at Da Nang, and started taking notes. Already there were four A-1 Skyraiders, four F-4 Phantoms, and an OV-10 control plane involved in the rescue. Pretty quick reaction.

From his hiding place on the ground below, Hatch was both frightened and relieved at the same time. He could hear the unintelligible shouts from the North Vietnamese patrols, and knew they were searching for him and for Major Jones, but he could hear the sounds of more and more aircraft overhead, too. The addition of the jet noises to the putter of the A-1 reciprocating engines and the familiar OV-10 whines made him feel better, and he turned on his survival radio. He heard Covey talking to me, and that made him feel better.

"Hostage Six? This is Hostage Nan Bravo. How're we doing up there?"

Hearing Chuck Hatch's voice sent a shiver through me, but before I could answer, the powerful transmitter of the King controller boomed:

"Hostage Nan? This is King. Stay on the air until we have your position, then come up every half hour on the quarter hour. This will conserve your batteries. Do you understand?"

"This is Nan Bravo. Roger, I understand."

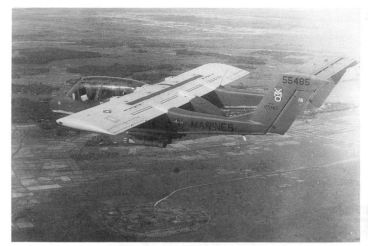

OV-10 Bronco with Marble Mountain in the background.

UH-1E at Camp Pendleton. HML-267 markings.

A4 Skyhawk on takeoff run at Chu Lai. VMA-211 markings.

F4 Phantom (VMFA-542) and A6 Intruder (VMA (AW) 242).

The writer at the height of his boxing career, pictured with the Naval Academy's legendary boxing coach, Spike Webb.

The writer in 1970, VMO-2, Danang.

Before and after shots. The writer the day after taking command and the night before relinquishing command.

The writer passing the flag to Major Carl Olson. Name spelled correctly in time for the ceremony; flag held tightly so that no one could see that we used another squadron's flag because ours was torn.

The writer, short of stature, photographed with his visiting brother-in-law, army colonel Charles Green.

Hostage Hog with her guardian, Corporal Bartz.

The writer briefing Force Reconnaissance Marines before a training jump over Red Beach.

Every squadron had a calling card. This was ours.

Captain Chuck Hatch, who evaded enemy patrols after being shot down in Laos.

The writer receiving his end-of-tour baptism.

A "sweep shot" of Danang Air Base, taken from the rear cockpit camera mount. This 180 degree camera allowed us to pin-point sensor drops.

Daisy-cutter fuses being screwed into bomb noses on VMA-242's flight line. The extended fuse caused the bomb to detonate above the ground.

Loading rockets into an OV-10.

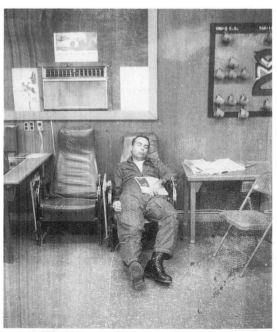

VMO-2's cold, steely-eyed commander in the squadron ready room.

"Nan Alpha. Roger, I understand."

"Okay, Nan," King continued, "the time is now one seven after the hour."

Hatch listened to the instructions from his shallow grave. He could see the planes clearly when they flew overhead, and he felt reassured. He transmitted his acknowledgment.

"Hostage Nan? This is Covey. Do not tell me where you are unless we start to come too close with our ordnance. If you see the helicopters coming, get on the radio for instructions."

Not all of this made sense to Hatch, but he had to assume Covey knew what he was talking about. He wondered how far away Major Jones was. If only the two of them could get together. They couldn't be too far apart.

Up above, I turned toward Lieutenant Colt and commenced a slow rendezvous as the both of us watched the "other war" unfold. The Covey controller fired a white phosphorous rocket from an altitude I considered too high for any kind of accuracy, but his verbal description to the F-4 bombers was vivid, and I made a mental note to include colors in my future target descriptions. The dirt road he wanted them to hit really did look purple.

The F-4s dropped their ordnance from what I also thought was too great an altitude, but they dropped Rockeye canisters, which blew apart in the air and rained hundreds of bomblets on what I presumed was an enemy gun position.

"I'm hit! Gunfighter Two Three is hit! I'm heading for Da Nang!"

I looked up. High above the hilly terrain I could see black puffs of antiaircraft fire, and one deadly cloud was directly behind an F-4, which I estimated to be at fifteen thousand feet.

"I'm joining on you, Two Three," said the wingman.

"Okay. Doesn't seem to be so bad right now. No fire. I can still control it. Covey, I'm headed home. I'll dump my ordnance in the Zulu impact area."

"Roger, Gunfighter. We'll nail that gun for you."

I pulled up on Colt's wing and watched the F-4s limp off to the east and wondered just where the Zulu impact area was. This was not going to be a routine rescue, and it would be a long afternoon.

"Okay, Sandy," Covey called to the A-1 Skyraiders, which had been orbiting miles to the south. "Let's go to Tac Two, and monitor guard. King? I'm going to take those guns out now. We'll be working on Tac Two frequency."

"Roger, Covey," King answered. "Cleared to switch to your tactical frequency."

I had not the foggiest idea of what Tac Two was, and I was furious. I had been snubbed before, but this one took the cake. There was not the slightest question, however, that the rescue effort was the exclusive domain of the United States Air Force. I looked at my fuel gauge. Four hundred and fifty pounds. I didn't have much choice in the matter anyway.

"Colt? Six. What state?"

"Five hundred pounds."

"Okay, I've got the lead. Let's head home."

I turned to the east and watched Colt slide into a parade wing position. "Hostage Nan? This is Six, over."

"Go ahead, Six. Nan Alpha." Jones sounded dejected.

"We're running low on fuel and have to go home now. The pros have taken charge, and Covey and King have things under control. Looks like they're going to get you out pretty quick. Keep your heads down, and we'll have a cold beer waiting for you when you get back."

"Roger, Skipper."

We flew back to Da Nang, and Peter Colt maintained a constant parade position the entire time. We saw the CH-53 Jolly Green Giant helicopters pass beneath us, headed for the crash, and by the time we landed, our engines just about sucking on fumes, I felt a little bit better about things. Jones and Hatch might be out before I could drive over to the air force side of the field to meet them.

But there was one hell of a lot to be done, and the first thing on my agenda after this was over was to pay a visit to the Covey OV-10 squadron. The air force and the Marine Corps might have shown great interservice cooperation in some areas, but there was a definite breakdown in communications as far as intelligence was concerned. VMO-2 had been sent to the border to find out what the air force already knew. I was furious, not only with myself, but at the entire bureaucratic system.

I told Captain Selleck that I thought it was a dumb goddamn way to run a war, and I was scowling as I turned off the taxiway and into the squadron flight line.

From the cane field, Captain Hatch could see the A-1s setting up a pattern above him, and he clawed more of the dirt out from under his body as far down as his arms would reach. He piled the earth around himself, as though a three-inch parapet would protect him from any bomb fragments, and he wiggled his back deeper into the earth.

Then he heard the sounds he had been waiting for. He could not see, but the noises of the CH-53 engines and rotor blades were distinctive. The Jolly Greens had arrived.

Major Waters joined me, and we drove around the airfield perimeter as fast as we dared, then turned in at the air force compound near the control tower. We pulled up in front of a hangar that was decorated with a mural of a green giant, twenty feet high.

We found our way to the squadron operations center by following a trail of huge, green feet painted on the cement. A slight major sat at a desk in the center of the long office and faced a lighted status board. He held a cup of coffee in both hands and stared intently at the board.

I introduced myself and asked how things were going. The major did not get up. He turned slowly in his chair and fixed his eyes on me. "Not so good," he said without expression. "Two Sandy's just got shot down, and one of our paramedics was killed pulling the pilots out." The bitterness in his voice said it was all my fault.

"They got them out?" My face lit up.

"They got the Sandy pilots out. Couldn't get to your boys. Gooners peppered hell out of one of our helicopters."

My dejection was interrupted when an older man entered the office from the other end. The major rose and stared toward him. "What did they say, Colonel?"

The new arrival, whom I assumed was the squadron commander, had a worried look on his face. "We'll try again at seventeen thirty. Get the 'B' crew ready for a 1645 takeoff."

The lieutenant colonel turned out to be the squadron operations officer, and he was as amazed as I was angry over the lack of communications between us. After a short conversation and a bad cup of coffee, it was decided that Major Waters would stay, and I would return to the squadron where there were a lot of unhappy faces.

On the way back around the field, I considered grabbing a plane and flying back out to watch the next rescue effort, but decided against it. Grandstand play. I belonged in the ready room.

And they were there to meet me—all who weren't flying. I told the pilots what I knew, and somehow the mood of the pilots improved. By the time I left and drove over to group headquarters, the pilots were thinking up ways to fine Hatch and Jones for leaving the country without permission.

At five-fifteen, Captain Hatch turned on his survival radio and wondered how long the batteries would last. There were two more radios—the other in his vest pocket and the one in his seat pan beside him, and he hoped he would not be there long enough to test the life of all three. He listened for Major Jones.

"Nan Alpha, up and okay."

He heard Jones and spoke up as soon as King acknowledged Jones's call. "Nan Bravo up and okay."

"Roger, Nan Alpha and Bravo. Okay, you two just sit tight now."

Hatch waited for more, but none was forthcoming. Sit tight? What the hell did that mean? Maybe they were about to try again.

He had been elated the time before when he saw one of the Jolly Greens start in, right for him. But then the two A-1s got hit. *Bam!* *Bam!* Just like in a shooting gallery. He couldn't blame the helicopter pilot for going after the Sandy pilots. Still . . .

And where the hell was Major Jones anyway? He began to worry about the new executive officer, so soft from all those years sitting behind a desk. Hatch was an infantry officer who had completed a six-month tour as a rifle company commander before changing into clean clothes and joining the aerial observer team at VMO-2. He could handle himself in the bush pretty well, except for that damn snub-nosed .38 pistol that wasn't good for anything except signaling with the tracers and flares.

He hoped Jones would keep cool and not panic. What would he do if a patrol came near? Would he keep his head down, or would he lose it and try to shoot it out?

He looked at his watch. Twenty past five. He tried to figure the time difference between Vietnam and the States, and thought about what he might be doing right about now if he were there.

At five twenty-five, he heard the sounds of jets and props in the eastern sky. Here came the cavalry charge! He could sit tight another few minutes.

He looked over his survival equipment and decided to take the seat pan with him when he ran for the helicopter. No sense in leaving all that stuff for the enemy, especially the radio. They had enough of our radios anyway.

* * *

He wondered where the helicopter would touch down and how many seconds it would take to run the distance. Should he zig-zag or run in a straight line? He supposed that if a helicopter could land, there shouldn't be any bullets to dodge.

"Covey? This is Bravo One," called the pilot of the lead Jolly Green giant helicopter. "Let's do it!"

"Roger, Bravo One. Sandy? Covey is rolling in for the mark!"

The gray OV-10 pushed into a dive and fired a white phosphorous rocket into a clump of trees up on the graded road where it turned to the east.

Hatch could see the twin-tailed plane fire the rocket, and he heard the small crack of an explosion as the Covey plane pulled away to the east.

Then he heard the whine of an A-1 as it picked up speed in its steep bombing run. Through the tops of the slender reeds of cane he saw the Skyraider release four bombs and pull up and away, its powerful engine straining at full power.

We're in business, he told himself. About five minutes of this, and he'd be climbing aboard a helicopter.

The bombs went off with a crash, the explosions echoing with a deep rasp throughout the valley as the second A-1 rolled into a dive. Hatch could feel the beat of six massive helicopter rotor blades approaching from the east, and he took a firm grip on the seat pan. He would leave only the parachute behind.

More bombs, and the ground shook, and a third A-1 rolled in. A single bomb fell. That would be the smoke bomb that would put out a dense, white cloud and establish a smoke screen.

Hatch had worked with these four-plane flights on practice missions around Da Nang, and he knew that the fourth pilot would fly in low and rake the enemy with twenty millimeter as the helicopter whirred in at treetop level for the pickup.

He heard the softer explosion of the smoke bomb and the whine of the number four A-1. He could not see it, but he knew that this was the key run. He strained to hear the helicopter, and soon detected the distinctive buzzing of the CH-53 behind the firing of the A-1 cannons.

"Here we go!" He cried half aloud as the buzzing grew into a whirring roar over his left shoulder. He bolted into a crouch, and the dirt fell away, back into the hole. His legs tensed like a sprinter ready to dash.

He could see the brown-green-and-black camouflaged helicopter as its nose started to rise for the landing. He could barely restrain himself. He would wait until the plane was five feet off the ground before he ran.

Suddenly the helicopter rocked crazily as pieces of fuselage flew away. Huge holes the sizes of baseballs opened up as the plane was stitched with fifty-caliber machine-gun fire. It rolled wildly to the left, away from Hatch, and he could see that the massive rotor blades were about to chop into the ground.

The pilot pulled hard on the collective, and black smoke belched from the exhaust stacks as the shattered helicopter strained and heaved under the power surge. Only the sloping terrain falling away from under the blades prevented the plane from crashing, and the pilot regained control, flying southeast into the valley.

The lead A-1 was in another run, and Hatch could see it clearly from his upright position. They were not giving up. The second helicopter could make it if the Sandy could take out that fifty.

The bombs fell from the wing racks of the A-1, and instantly, the dive-bomber was engulfed in black smoke as flames erupted from the fuel tanks. He watched in horror as the pilot pulled back on the controls and turned south, the flames growing until the plane was a fireball.

"Get out! Get out!" Hatch shouted, forgetting his own predicament. A black dot fell away from the inferno and blossomed as the parachute canopy opened.

The Bravo Two helicopter raced toward the parachute. It landed almost simultaneously with the pilot, the heavy rotor wash blowing the parachute away as the pilot scrambled into the side door. It was airborne within seconds, disappearing from Hatch's view.

"Oh my God, no!" He grabbed at his survival radio, nearly tearing the canvas vest as he pulled the zipper open. He wrenched the antenna out and turned the radio on.

Not a sound. Just the static of dead air. "Damn!" He cursed out loud. He unzipped the right pocket and took out the other radio. He was more careful this time. Maybe he had broken the first one.

He worked the telescoping antenna up carefully and turned on the switch. Still nothing. He keyed the transmit button.

"Major? You okay?"

"Yeah. I'm all right."

"Did you expose yourself?"

"Yeah, but I don't think anyone saw me."

"Hostage Nan? This is King!" The booming, hollow voice rang clearly. "We're going to have to wait and try it again in the morning. Sorry, but it'll be dark before we could get back to you tonight."

Neither Hatch nor Jones answered. Hatch felt nauseated, so deep was his despair.

King continued, "Come up on the radio every hour on the quarter hour. We'll stay with you all night and be back to get you in the morning. If you sit tight, everything will turn out okay." Then, seemingly as an afterthought, "Call if you get in trouble. We'll be listening.'

Tears welled in Hatch's eyes as he looked down at his hole. He put the radio back in his vest and zipped the pocket closed. Then he dropped to his knees and scooped the loose dirt out.

That night, in the wing G-3 office, I heard one of the more attention grabbing statements of my little war.

" . . . and if they don't get them out this time, they're going in with gas."

I looked up at the wing operations officer in astonishment. "They're going in with what? What are you talking about?"

"Oh . . . Well, I won't go into all of the details . . . pretty highly classified stuff . . . but if the rescue effort tomorrow morning doesn't work, they're not going to screw around. They've lost three A-1s and two paramedics so far, and they don't want to lose any more.

"The A-1s will drop gas canisters throughout the area and coldcock everybody around. Then paramedics will go in, wearing gas masks obviously, and pick up the pilots. It won't kill anyone, but they'll be pretty sick for a day or so. Hell of a way to be rescued, but it may be the only way."

I was stunned. I thought I knew pretty much everything that was going on in the war, but I had never heard of this. It was logical, though.

After a while, sworn to secrecy, and having been warned three times not to fly out there that night, I drove down to the hangar to spread what cheer I could and to ensure that I was scheduled for the 76-Alpha, dawn patrol.

The night standby crew had been launched on a Blackboard exercise, and I was satisfied that everything was running normally in spite of the emotional tension we all felt.

Blackboard which I referred to in the previous ejection story, was nothing more than a night firepower demonstration. About once a week, one of the regiments requested the mission, ostensibly to show any would-be attackers the futility of testing the Marine defenses. A-4s and F-4s loaded with napalm dropped their firebombs all around the regimental perimeter, and Cobra gunships hosed down the barbed wire with their Gatling guns.

All of this, coupled with artillery fire and interlocking bands of machine-gun fire, made a spectacular show in the dark. A rapid firing SUU-11 Gatling gun, firing tracers at the ground at night, looked just like a garden hose splattering bright red water on the driveway.

I returned to my quarters and went to bed early. My alarm clock was set for 0430.

While I ate an early breakfast in our steamy hot mess hall, Captain Hatch shivered. There was mist in the predawn air, and his flight suit was as damp as the earth on top of him. He turned his hand and looked at his watch. The luminous dial showed a few minutes past five, and he thought the sky was beginning to brighten.

He put his tongue between his teeth to keep them from chattering. Every sound was magnified in the dense stillness.

All night long, he'd heard the wheezing and chugging of tractors, bulldozers probably, repairing the road. He thought it strange that the enemy engineers would continue their work and ignore the jets overhead. He did not know that the vehicles never moved over five miles per hour, and so were not detectable on the sophisticated moving-target indicators of the jets above.

Hatch convinced himself that the uninterrupted work meant that the enemy had given up the search, thinking that the helicopters had made a successful pickup. There had been no patrols. He heard voices shouting once or twice, but always far away. Interesting how far the human voice could carry.

But the construction sounds had stopped now, and Hatch supposed that they had parked the heavy equipment under concealment. He would remember to tell the intelligence people about this when he got back—that the vehicles did not move far from the road when they stopped work. He wondered what else he could report.

He heard a faint and rasping scrape of a handsaw ripping into a board in the distance and heard the bark of a dog muffled in the mist. The dog and the saw sounded the same.

Dogs! His heart began to pound. My God! They're coming

after us with dogs! Of course the Gooners would not search at night. They were waiting for daylight!

Suddenly he was abnormally thirsty again, and he fairly sobbed with fear as he drained the second bottle of water. The sky began to lighten into a dull gray, and he could see tiny bits of moisture swimming in the air with his heaving breath.

The sun rose, and Hatch could hear shouts as a squad leader ordered his patrol about. He could not understand the commands, but from his own experience he had a pretty good idea.

The sounds grew closer, and soon he could hear the crackling and rattling of bushes being searched. His heart raced, and he concentrated on lying still and breathing evenly. He closed his eyes in an effort to conceal himself as the patrol neared the cane field.

There were no dogs. He had imagined that, but he could hear the voices. They were there, right next to the cane. He could feel the footsteps and hear the little clinks of their equipment.

He opened his eyes, squinting, and could see the shadows. No heroics, he decided. He would lie still and hope the enemy missed him. If discovered, he would surrender. There were at least a dozen shadows, and his snub-nosed .38 only held five rounds. He would play the odds.

He almost cried out in alarm when he heard the snap of a cane reed. Then the sounds, the footfalls and the jingles, faded away.

His heart thumped like a trip-hammer, and his body went limp with sudden relief. He wondered if Major Jones had heard the patrol, or whether it was even headed his way.

Where the hell was the major anyway? Ten times during the night he had started to go out and look for him, but each time he had permitted discipline—and fear—to restrain him.

The patrol was gone now. Perhaps they were as frightened as he was and had given it up. Certainly they were no braver than Marines. They had made their patrol, and quit as soon as they could without looking bad.

It was six o'clock, and the mist was disappearing, swallowed up in the sunlight. He would come up on the radio at six fifteen. Surely King would have something to tell them then. There was a faint sound of an OV-10, an unmistakable sound. Help was on the way!

It was I, and I wasn't able to be of much help at ten thousand feet. "They should come up on the air at six fifteen," I said to Captain Selleck on the intercom. "I'll stay out of the area, on this side of the border. God, I hope they made it through the night."

"You want the Jolly Green's tactical frequency? We have all that stuff this morning."

"No. Not yet, anyway. I had to promise that I'd stay out of the way. I'm just going to listen in on the guard channel to hear if they're still healthy."

"Roger that."

The OV-10 droned westward, high above the green mountains and valleys. Mist veiled the river valleys like fine cotton candy, and I understood why the rescue effort had been scheduled for 0730 instead of dawn. It was pointless to try until the ground was clear.

"Six-fifteen, Colonel."

I looked at the clock on the instrument panel and watched the second hand tick around, wondering what I would do if Jones and Hatch did not come up on the air. I rechecked the radio receiver to make sure the selector switch was on guard. The valley leading eastward from the crash site hove into view above the mist. Why didn't King come up on the air?

"Hostage Nan? This is King. How do you read me?"

The suddenness of the transmission was startling.

"Nan Alpha up."

"Nan Bravo up."

My heartbeat doubled. They made it through the night!

"Good morning, Nan." King went on. "Continue to sit tight. Are you both all right? Any injuries?"

"Alpha's okay, except I think I sprained my ankle."

"Bravo's okay."

They did not sound happy, but I was pleased with their radio discipline. I suspected that I would have had far more to say under similar circumstances.

Satisfied that the situation was as secure as it could be, I hung around a few minutes more, then turned back to VMO-2's war, to perform some of the chores assigned to my early morning reconnaissance flight.

Hatch wiped the dirt from his cheek and felt his stubble of beard. He decided that an hour under a hot shower would be one of the first things on his agenda when he got back. Funny. He had gone for days in the field without a bath and never felt as dirty as he did right now after only one night. Living with the air wing had certainly corrupted him.

From the way Major Jones had told King he was okay, Hatch sensed that the patrol had not gone near him. The enemy really had quit.

Above, he could see the silhouette of an OV-10. No way to tell whether it was gray or green, air force or Marine. Besides, from below, Marine planes were gray too. He decided it was an air force Covey controller.

Nothing to do but sit and wait. He felt hunger pangs. He had not eaten since yesterday morning. Strange how the human body could ignore such things. Not only had he not felt hunger, he had never even had the urge to urinate. Sweated it all out, probably.

He opened the seat pan and found a chocolate bar. It was dry and hard, but he ate it all and washed it down with water from the big plastic bottle he found in the seat-shaped box.

Suddenly—three sharp cracks! Pistol fire!

An electric shock stung his hair, and his tongue tasted metallic.

Then, a short stutter of automatic rifle fire! His breath came in heaves, and his skin drew up tight.

What the hell was that? He lay there, tense, his eyes huge in wonderment. It sounded like a .38 pistol. Small, not like the bang of a .45. And only pilots carried .38s.

Did the patrol stumble on Jones's hiding place? Did Jones panic and shoot—only to be cut down by an AK-47? He was nauseated and rolled over to vomit.

His skin tingled, clammy with a cold sweat, and he spit out the rest of the chocolate, still dry in his mouth. He stood up to see, and his legs were so weak he could hardly keep his balance.

Nothing. He wasn't sure where Jones was hiding, but the shots came from the direction of the trees where the parachute still clung to the branches. The reeds of cane blocked his view of the ground, and he could detect no movement.

If Jones had only been there in that cane field with him! He sobbed and dropped back into his hole.

He lay there, his mind empty of thought. Then he heard the sounds of jets streaking across the sky, and he sat up. It wasn't just a flight of planes passing overhead. There were a lot of planes. He looked up, shading his eyes from the sun. Two . . . no, three flights. And they were low, leaving black exhaust trails in the heavier atmosphere.

One flight separated as the wingman took interval on his

leader. Both planes started down, and Hatch saw clearly that they were F-4s. The lead plane rolled its wings level.

At that distance, the F-4 seemed to be headed right for him, and he dropped back, face down. He covered the back of his neck with his hands, and the earth shook from the impact of the bombs.

He dared not look up. Explosions and jet screams were all around him. He drew the survival radio out of his vest and set it beside his face, inching the antenna out with his fingers. He turned it on and wedged the speaker under his ear.

The explosions kept coming, some near, some farther to the north and west. How many airplanes did they put on this strike? The noise and concussions were frightening.

Hatch thought he heard a voice, but he wasn't certain.

"I say again, Hostage Nan," the voice insisted, "are you ready?"

"This is Nan Bravo! Yes, sir, I'm ready!" He rolled over on his back and held the radio in an upright position.

"Nan, this is King. Do you read me?"

"This is Nan Bravo! I'm ready!"

That was dumb, Hatch scolded himself. The whole thing could have been blown because he was trying to bury his head like an ostrich.

"Roger, Bravo. Nan Alpha? This is King. Do you read me?"

There was no answer. Two more calls and no response.

Oh, God!" Hatch cried aloud. Until that moment, he had hoped that the pistol shots and the AK-47 fire had been imagined. But Jones did not answer.

He heard the propellor-driven A-1s add their sounds to the screams of the jets, and soon he felt the pressure beats of rotor blades.

He stood up and looked to the east. There it was! The big CH-53, with its refueling probe lunging forward from under the camouflaged nose like a rapier, raced in. He watched the nose come up as the helicopter slowed, and black puffs of exhaust smoke punctuated power changes.

Closer and closer it came. Hatch judged the plane's flight path and selected a spot where he thought it would land.

Now! He crashed through the cane and set out on a dead run down the slope of the hill.

He saw the door gunner point at him from behind a fifty-caliber machine gun, and the helicopter turned toward him as it closed with the ground.

But just as the wheels were inches off the ground the plane turned away. Hatch thought for an instant that it would fly away again as it had done yesterday, and he tried to make his legs go faster. The wheels touched the ground, and Hatch saw the open tail ramp yawning at him. The pilot had turned to give him room to run aboard.

His feet hit the metal of the tail ramp, and his tired legs buckled under the G forces as the pilot pulled up on the collective and the helicopter rose quickly into the air, like a fast elevator.

He crawled forward on his stomach until he was well into the cargo compartment, then stopped and lay there gasping, his lungs begging for air as he gripped a seat pole tightly. The helicopter darkened inside as the ramp closed behind him.

He was afraid to open his eyes, and he buried his face in his arms. The roar of the engines was deafening.

He felt the plane turn sharply. Then the engines became quieter, and he felt himself descending. They were going down!

He looked up at the crewmen in front. They did not appear to be in fear of crashing. The door gunner was pointing, and cupped his lip microphone with his free hand, masking his mouth from the high-pitched screams of the two jet engines.

Major Jones! Hatch felt a surge of elation. They're going in after Jones!

The helicopter's descent slowed, and the engine noises grew louder as the pilot added power to cushion the landing. The back of the plane opened as the ramp lowered to a flat position.

The wheels hit with a jolt and a figure clutching a parachute ran quickly aboard, grinning broadly.

It was not Major Jones. Hatch was pressed down into the deck of the helicopter as the pilot added full power and climbed sharply out of the valley.

It wasn't Jones! It was a young air force pilot in a bluish-gray flight suit with silver first lieutenant bars sewn to the shoulders. Another plane must have been shot down.

Hatch lay there staring at the young pilot who had been forced down onto a seat by the G force. Hatch hated him for not being Major Jones, but he felt a strange camaraderie in spite of his disappointment. He did not know the man. His hair was too long, and a sweaty curl was plastered against his forehead. He had never seen the man before, but they were brothers-in-arms.

The air force pilot stared back at Hatch, half smiling, and Hatch realized how ridiculous he must have looked there on the floor. He released his grip on the seat pole, picked himself up,

and dropped back on the row of seats. He found the ends of the
lap belts and buckled himself in.

He forced a smile and made a slight waving motion with his
hand, and he felt like a complete idiot.

Major Waters and I drove into the parking area beside the
hangar with the Green Giant mural as a flight of three A-1 Skyraiders flew over the runway and broke to take interval for landing. Neither of us noticed then that the fourth plane was missing.

I still couldn't understand why they were only able to get the
aerial observer out. After all, I had heard Major Jones talking
on the radio only two hours earlier, and he sounded pretty healthy
then.

We spoke with the squadron operations officer as soon as we
arrived, and it was then that I discovered that the pickup that
morning had been almost as dangerous as the previous tries.
The operations officer pointed out to us the three-plane flight of
A-1s in the landing pattern and explained that the fourth pilot
was a passenger on the CH-53 with Chuck Hatch, and it was at
that moment that reality sank in.

K. D. Waters and I stood there, waiting for the CH-53 to
arrive, as a crowd gathered. A young air force lieutenant came
out of the hangar carrying a bottle of champagne and two paper
cups.

"We always celebrate when we snatch a pilot. It's become a
tradition," someone explained to us.

I wondered what they had to celebrate. This was as costly a
pickup as any I had ever heard of. I could not recall the exact
number of A-1s that had been shot down, and two Jolly Green
Giant paramedics had been hit, one killed.

I spoke quietly to Major Waters. "We sure caused them a lot
of grief."

K. D.'s answer put everything back into perspective. "Bullshit!" he hissed out of the side of his mouth. "That's their job."

The buzz of the helicopters taxiing in from the runway spared
me from pursuing that conversation. Airmen and pilots moved
toward the revetments as a taxi director beckoned the lead plane
in. The giant helicopter rolled to a stop, and the noises dimin-
ished rapidly as the pilots cut the engines.

A young air force pilot, still clutching his parachute, ran out
of the side door and into the waiting arms of his friends.

I worked my way through the crowd and climbed up into the

helicopter. Captain Hatch stood there, smiling faintly, not knowing what to say. I didn't know what to say either.

For the briefest instant, a terrible thought had crossed my mind just as I was climbing up to the door. Twenty years later I still cringe at the memory, and the sight of the side of the helicopter flashes in my mind when it happens.

I did not know Captain Hatch very well, and Major Jones was my friend. For an instant my mind cried out, "We got back the wrong guy!" I have regretted that thought ever since.

"Thank God you're back, Chuck!" I moved toward him, arms outstretched, and we embraced without embarrassment.

"I'm sorry we got lost, Colonel. I think Major Jones is dead."

I had no answer for that. I pulled away and, with a hand on his shoulder, steered him toward the door. "Your public awaits." I forced a smile.

Hatch climbed down out of the side door and met the crowd of well-wishers who shook his hand and clapped him on the back. A group of Marines had followed us in the aerial observers' jeep.

The Jolly Green Giant operations officer fastened a colorful pin to Hatch's flight suit that would forever be his badge of recognition as a flyer who had been rescued under combat conditions.

"Hey, thanks!" Hatch took a cup of champagne. "You pulled me out of the bush, and *you* give *me* champagne?"

"No problem," the operations officer laughed. "You're going to buy us a whole case of the stuff!"

"That's fair, by God!" Hatch laughed too.

I joined them and was happy for the moment that Captain Hatch was in such good spirits. A blue field-ambulance drove up. The operations officer spoke to Hatch.

"I hate to tear you away from all this, but the ambulance is here to take you to the dispensary. We pulled you out, so our doctors get to look at you first."

Hatch walked with him to the back of the ambulance, and Major Waters and I followed. "I'll follow you in the jeep," K. D. said, reading my mind.

I climbed into the ambulance behind Hatch and sat down on a side bench facing him. The air force A-1 pilot climbed in and sat down next to the exhausted aerial observer and turned to the major who assisted him.

"I'll be ready to fly again tomorrow, Major. Really!"

"Like hell you will!" The major turned to me. "This is the third time he's been shot down in six weeks!" He shut the door.

I was stunned. The ambulance lurched off toward the dispensary, and I asked dumbly, "Three times in six weeks?"

"Right!" The lieutenant smiled smugly. Then his face turned serious. "The only trouble is, they've got a rule. Three times, and they send you out of country. And I've only been here four months."

I looked at Hatch. Neither of us had an answer for that one.

The exultation of the homecoming wore off quickly in the confines of the stuffy ambulance, and Hatch's face grew long. The lack of sleep and the stubble of beard made him look years older.

"I heard pistol shots, and then automatic-rifle fire. Sounded like an AK-47."

"Jones?"

"Yes, sir. Just before they came to pick us up. I can't swear to it, you understand. We were pretty far apart."

"But you believe he's dead?"

"Yes, sir." Tears came to Hatch's eyes as he answered, and he heaved a single sob.

The ambulance drove the short distance to the dispensary, and backed into the emergency entrance. An air force medic held the door, and we followed a flight surgeon inside. The young air force lieutenant walked with a spring in his step. Hatch plodded slowly, his head bowed, weeping softly.

Chuck Hatch was back in the cockpit in a day or two, and after a week, we managed to piece the story together from his experience and from Peter Colt's observations. I may have embellished the story somewhat, but what I have just told you is as accurate an account as I can give.

Major Jones's remains were recovered about five years later, but for a while we weren't so sure he was dead.

That night after the rescue, the VMO-2 senior officers and I sequestered ourselves from the rest of the squadron in Major Waters's hut. The loss of Major Jones and the recovery of Captain Hatch triggered mixed emotions among the junior officers, and we thought it best to leave them alone.

We were critiquing the command-interface problems regarding the sharing of intelligence and communications information, when there was a knock on the door.

The group adjutant, a tiny administrative officer with an unusually close haircut, opened the door, then stood at attention in the entrance. "Colonel? The group commander sends his compliments and wishes to see the colonel right away."

"At this hour? Where?"

"He's down at VMCJ-1."

I looked at Major Waters, and he held out his hands, palms up. He didn't know why either.

"Be right there." I put my drink and cigar down on the bar. "Come and go with me, K. D."

We drove the two miles to VMCJ-1, the composite photo and electronics countermeasures squadron, located next door to the group headquarters building.

We entered and were directed to a trailer van out back. Inside the ECM van, we found Colonel Pommerenck standing behind a technician who controlled a large console of mysterious lights and switches. Above the console a magnetic tape whirred on its reels, and the technician listened to the static. Neither Major Waters nor I had ever been invited into VMCJ's electronic inner sanctum before.

"Hi, Mike . . . K. D.!" Pommerenck waved us closer. "We have a tape I want you to hear."

The Marine at the console ran the tape back, then started it forward and turned up the volume. We listened to the static, and Pommerenck cleared up some of the mystery.

"Now, the receiver that picked up the sound on this tape was beamed in the general direction of where your pilots went down. The tape was made this evening."

"Where did you get it?"

"That's none of your business, is it?"

I was surprised at the sharp rebuke, but Colonel Pommerenck was so intent on what the tape might reveal that I doubt that he was even thinking about social amenities. A faint voice seemed to scratch through the gravelly interference, and no one could make out the words.

"Run it again," Pommerenck ordered.

We listened to the tape five or six times. There was some kind of a voice, but we couldn't make any sense out of it. I think we were hearing something we wanted to hear.

After a while, K. D. and I left and returned to the living area, more confused than ever. We remembered a Huey pilot who had walked out of the jungle nineteen days after being shot down and given up for the dead—long after his parents had already held memorial services. And I recalled making a death call on a young girl in Pensacola, whose husband showed up a month later in a POW camp, making antiwar statements to the press.

So, for a few days, we secretly harbored some hope. But as the days wore on and the electronics countermeasures were unable to gather any more information, we had to put it behind us.

End of story. But you can be certain that we who were older began to put emphasis on physical conditioning and survival training. When I joined Marine Light Helicopter Squadron 267 at Camp Pendleton in October, the first thing I drew from special services was a pair of sneakers and a jock strap.

HOSTAGE HOG

China Beach was a real place. There wasn't any hospital there, as a popular network television show suggested; the army hospital was further up the beach at Tien Shau, which was near Monkey Mountain, where there used to be a huge population of tall black-and-white monkeys that stood upright and walked like people.

Maybe they were apes. The poor devils stood four feet tall when they walked, and in the dark, it was pretty hard for a sentry to tell the difference between the apes and the Viet Cong infiltrators, who didn't stand much taller. And . . . Well, it wasn't a pretty story.

No, there wasn't a hospital at China Beach. What was there was a USO recreation center, with lots of dedicated young women who worked hard at providing in-country R & R for battle-weary soldiers and Marines. And maybe that was the story the original script for the television series wanted to tell, but it was changed to a hospital with doctors and nurses because viewers who might buy the concept of a hospital would probably think that a recreation center was really a whorehouse located on some really great beachfront property with whispering pine trees, hot showers, and cold beer.

On the Fourth of July, 1970, VMO-2's supply section visited China Beach. They piled into a huge six-by-six truck and motored over to the recreation center for a day of fun in the sun, to relax from the seven-day-a-week grind of combat and to celebrate the end of the fiscal year—which probably doesn't sound like a great cause for celebration, but our aggressive supply officer, who made it through the end-of-the-year auditing without anybody catching on, thought it was. And the commanding of-

ficer agreed with him. And so the department took the day off
to breathe a sigh of relief and drink a lot of beer.

Lest a prospective squadron commander think that his combat
tour will be all fun and games and air medals, let me point out
one of the hard, cruel realities of the Marine Corps. Your ster-
ling combat record won't be worth doodly squat if you're not
on real, intimate speaking terms with your supply officer—or if
your fiscal management takes a header.

Valor and leadership and big-time medals will make your
uniform look pretty and impress second lieutenants and get your
name in the hometown newspapers, but it takes more than that
to get your name on a promotion list. The CO of a squadron a
couple of hangars down from us blew his career completely one
day when his supply people decided to hide some excess electronics parts from an inspection team and—are you ready for
this?—wrapped the goods in plastic and buried them! We
couldn't believe it. Now, we're not talking criminal activity here,
just a little hoarding so that the aircraft availability might be
enhanced one rainy day. The commanding officer didn't even
know about it—at least that was what we believed at the time—
but that didn't save his ass one bit, and he was relieved of his
command immediately. One more combat commander to bite
the dust and retire about ten years sooner than he had planned.

So, we were celebrating making it through the fiscal year
without going to jail or anything, and I joined the supply department celebrants around noon when the party was already in
progress.

One of the special recreational activities the USO people
staged that day was a greased-pig contest. That wasn't the highlight of the day of course, but it took place directly in front of
the picnic table Capt. Jim Berry and his supply accomplices
occupied, and the amount of beer the Marines had consumed
by contest time made pig fanciers out of every one of them.
Except for an embarrassing incident that involved one of our
Marines climbing a tree and taking pictures of the inside of the
woman's latrine, the idea of pig ownership became an obsession
which would have lasting consequences for all of us.

Greased-pig-catching contests can be a lot of fun and a source
of good-natured humiliation for all but the drunkest participants. But the main ingredient of that fun is a requirement that
the pig be swift of foot and possessed of a certain amount of
agility. As fate would have it, the only animal the USO girls
could find for the event was possessed of neither, and we in

VMO-2 found ourselves with ringside seats for a debacle so pitiful that Captain Berry swiped a towel from around Corporal Bartz's neck and threw it into the arena.

The poor little pig couldn't have been more than a month old, not much larger than a dachshund, and with its swayed back and well-stuffed belly that dragged in the sand, there wasn't much of a contest. Greased down with a couple of quarts of Crisco, and released, the pitiful creature took no more than three steps before it nestled into the cozy warm sand, just as the first contestant took a mighty leap and overshot the target by about six feet.

The rodeo officials tried again and again to coax the pig into running, but running was a feat the potbellied porker had not yet even considered, let alone mastered, and the entertainment was abandoned right there in front of our boys, the most talented group of thieves, scalawags, and poachers ever to wear Marine uniforms.

Commanding officers are not supposed to stay long at social events such as this, and so, after making effusive apologies to the USO people about the oafish behavior of our disgraced paparazzo cameraman and promising swift punishment up to and including psychiatric evaluation, I left the party and returned to Da Nang, to spend the rest of the day tending to squadron business. While it was indeed the Fourth of July, for VMO-2 it was just another working day of flying and playing around with great fireworks.

That night I was seated in the officers club with a group from the squadron, engaged in my usual club activity which somehow always turned out to be paying for most of the drinks, when I was approached by Captain Berry who wore one of those serious, we've-got-a-problem looks on his sunburned face. With him was the squadron flight surgeon, John Carlisle, who appeared to be all business, too, and I suffered a cold rush to the heart as I braced for the bad news.

Captain Berry had some papers in his hand—always a bad sign. They pulled chairs over to the table, boxing me in so that I couldn't escape.

Jim Berry was all business. "Skipper, you won't believe it. You just won't believe it."

Oh, Lordy! The cold rush went all the way down to my toes. "What won't I believe, Jim?"

"The pig, Skipper! It followed us home. Jumped right up into the truck and followed us home. Can we keep it? Huh? Huh?"

Now, the back end of a six-by-six truck stands about five feet off the ground. I had, of course, seen the animal in question, and so I allowed my sphincter to release its death grip on the chair cushion. Bailing the supply officer out of trouble with the MPs would be a piece of cake compared to some of the rug dances I had already performed in his behalf. And, besides, both he and the flight surgeon were laughing their asses off as they watched the color return to my face.

The paperwork he carried was a requisition form for pig food! Doctor Carlisle, whose professional authority in porcine matters came from having dated a veterinary medicine student in college, had joined the intrigue by using his good offices to declare the pig pregnant and therefore eligible for pig food under some arcane civic action ruling that allowed us to nurture the beast in return for our donating a portion of each litter to whatever the Vietnamese called their local 4-H club.

With a stroke of a pen, Marine Observation Squadron owned a pig. Worse, we owned a pig legally, which implied all manner of obligations and responsibilities. And so I set about immediately doing what a lazy squadron commander does best—delegating authority and as much of that onerous responsibility as was humanly possible.

Doctor Carlisle had been correct in one part of his examination; the pig was female. I can't imagine how horrible and disgusting the animal would have been had it been a male. And the subject of her having baby pigs never did come up, for there wasn't another pig within miles of the Da Nang flight line—although the people in a refueling outfit not far from our hangar did have as their mascot a dim-witted little yellow dog that was constantly hanging around and sniffing our little girl and trying to mount her when no one was looking.

Funny thing about Asian dogs and pigs: the dogs have curly tails, and the pigs have straight ones, which they wag a lot. I suspect that might have been what confused the little yellow dog.

Hostage Hog, for that was the name the supply department gave her, and no one ever said that supply men were funny guys, grew and grew. But not on pig food. She turned up her nose at the government issue Purina the first time she tasted macaroni and cheese, and I made it a point never to ask just how the mess hall managed to produce so much of it.

Macaroni and cheese and hard-boiled eggs. Each morning at 0600, she stood at the bus stop, waiting for the gray school bus with the grenade screen in the windows to disgorge the first load of day-crew maintenance men, wagged that damn tail for all she was worth, and homed in immediately on Corporal Bartz, who always carried a tub of macaroni and cheese to work. The hard-boiled eggs were appetizers, and Bartz allowed other Marines to curry favor with those, although no one ever got her to sit up and beg. Pretty soon she got big enough to take a man down with a knee-crunching body block when he teased her.

She grew into a full-sized animal with the damndest coloring anyone ever saw on a hog. Visitors to the squadron accused us of hiring Earl Scheib to give her one of his $39.95 paint jobs, so much like our airplanes did she appear. When a sudden rain shower caught her outdoors and washed off two or three layers of mud, the gray-green of her head, back, and tail was uncomfortably close to our OV-10 paint job, and the white beneath that Marine green matched the bottoms of the planes exactly.

Mud was a big part of our little darling's life. Mud was plentiful in Vietnam, but not on a paved flight line. And so the supply department, augmented with people who knew how to saw wood and drive nails, built a hog wallow on the east side of the hangar, where it was shady in the afternoon.

The larger she grew, the more mud she used up. Before long, the entire hangar was mud colored to a level of about two feet where she rubbed against the corrugated metal in a continual back-scratching that sounded pretty much like a small boy running a stick along a picket fence.

She spent most of her time inside the hangar and out of the sun, and away from the Vietnamese garbage collectors who were not averse to a little pig-napping. At first, she saved herself from ending up as pork chops and bacon by learning how to squeal real loud.

One morning in late July, when Hostage Hog was still quite small, an incident occurred that gave everyone something to talk about for days.

I had just returned from flying, and was walking toward the squadron area from the flight line, when there occurred an eruption of humanity from within the hangar that looked to me to be a fire drill of some sort. People were pouring out of the metal building as though something inside was either on fire or smelling really bad. I started running, too, if only to find out what was going on. As I got to the hangar, I was caught up in a second wave of running, screaming, threatening, highly pissed-off Marines, who explained it all to me in grunts and snarls.

"They're stealing the goddamn pig!"

"Who?" I was wearing a torso harness, and it was hard for me to keep up.

"The f——king gooners!"

"What?" A torso harness really bites into the crotch.

"Garbage men! Stealing our pig!"

"Where?" Apparently there was a connection between my crotch and my brain.

We rounded the corner of the hangar, and there in front of us was a picture of confrontation right out of the Detroit auto workers' strikes in the 1930s. About a hundred Marines surrounded a creaky, beat-up old stake truck. It was probably a World War II Dodge of some sort, but it was hard to tell through the dents and lumps and rust and crust and a blue paint job that Earl Scheib might have charged $19.95 for in 1950. If it didn't look exactly like some sort of a serious union problem, then it might have been an Eastern European auto show. One Marine, who had jumped up on the running board to take the key out of the ignition, was hopping around on one foot, holding his other leg, because he had barked his shin when the running board collapsed, and cursing because there wasn't any key or any place to put a key. As far as he was concerned, and he hoped to tell the world, that wasn't fair.

The two Vietnamese inside the cab of the truck didn't look really happy either, which was certainly understandable. If they spoke any English at all, they knew that they had already been tried and convicted—not only of pig-napping but also of the Mann Act, the Intolerable Act, the Smoot-Hawley Act, and a host of other un-American acts.

Most of the Marines pointed to the business end of the truck, shouting, shaking their fists, and as I neared the growing violence of confrontation I heard distinct, but muffled piggy squeals filtering through the piles of fetid garbage.

The Marines were livid. "Give us back our pig!"

"No pig! No pig!"

"Goddamn it! Get out of that f——king truck and get our pig!"

Those terrified little people weren't about to get out of that truck, and I couldn't blame them one bit—although I would gladly have ripped their faces off. They sat frozen, both trying to occupy the exact center of the seat, and I shouted an order which in any other situation would have incited a riot.

"Get the pig!"

Not tremendously inspiring, I'll admit. Within seconds I

thought of "Over the top, men!" and "Bring home the bacon!" and a whole bunch of other stuff that wouldn't have worked either. But the crack, lean, mean, and well-trained Marines of Marine Observation Squadron 2 showed incredible discipline and restraint and refrained from hooliganism and acts of violence, mainly because no one wanted to be the guy to jump into the back of that filthy, stinking garbage truck.

More squeals, and Corporal Bartz, God bless him, scaled the side of the truck in an instant and vaulted over the top with the grace of a gazelle and plunged headlong into the middle of some really world-class stink.

Like a man possessed, he thrashed through boxes and cans of used C rations and coffee grounds and slimy stuff, all congealed by heat and flies and maggots. We cheered him on, careful to dodge the occasional slop that oozed through the slats, and in an instant Bartz was climbing back up the shaky siding, a wriggling pig under his arm, and a huge piece of brown wrapping paper stuck to his shoulder that lent a momentary aura of caped-crusader heroism.

We cheered and shouted our praises of adulation. All glory, laud, and honor! Hail the conquering hero!

We wanted to take Corporal Bartz into our arms, to hug him, to embrace him . . . But of course, none of us wanted to get near him.

We cheered from a safe distance as the Marines on the flight-line crew hosed them both down, man and beast, and without our even noticing, the garbage truck chugged away to the A-6 squadron next door to see what delights VMA-225 had to offer.

The dilapidated stake truck continued to make its rounds each morning as the garbage contractors made their daily pickups and intelligence surveys of aircraft availability and target assignments, and VMO-2's Marines watched them like hawks. Within weeks our pig was too heavy for the small garbagemen to lift. A few weeks after that she was too heavy for Corporal Bartz to lift, and after a while, we stopped worrying about her disappearing and began cussing her presence.

One of the problems of delegating authority is that sometimes nobody knows who's in charge. This worked to the advantage of both the squadron and Hostage Hog herself. One night, returning from a mission around midnight, I tripped over her in the darkened hallway which lead from the flight line to the ready room. I cursed, as I was prone to do—remember, I was the guy who was put on report by the radio battalion for using the big *F* word as an adverb—and the duty officer chided me with a gentle warning that I ought not let the night crew hear me bad-mouthing the sergeant major's pig.

The very next day, I overheard the sergeant major himself reprimanding a young Marine for a similar outburst of anger, warning him about bad-mouthing the commanding officer's pig. Soon I began to understand how horrendous corporate irresponsibility, like death from insulation fibers, could erupt out of some simple, innocent project like wanting to keep everybody warm and making a buck on the deal. But as long as nobody owned her, everybody owned her, and that was the value of Hostage Hog. Deep down we all knew she belonged to Corporal Bartz and the supply department. But as long as everyone pretended to ownership, then she was truly a squadron mascot.

She was also a very large animal, and because she tracked so much mud into the hangar, the supply department scrounged up door mats for all of the office doors so that we would not carry her dirt further inside. These mats she found very much to her liking, and upon them she took long naps. Really long naps. Siestas. Comatose conditions.

The office doors all opened outward into the hangar bay, for fire regulations are enforced in combat too, and it was a given that when she was sleeping in front of your office, you better not have to go to the bathroom real bad. It took two people pushing on a door to move her, and her outraged squeals on awakening caused the entire maintenance crew to drop their wrenches and screw drivers and come running, accusing innocent people of animal abuse and other crimes against nature.

Hostage Hog acquired a taste for beer. Beer and hard-boiled eggs, sometimes mixed together. That was party fare, and at our monthly, hangar floor show and beer parties, she was encouraged by the day crew to get roaring drunk—which of course caused her to lose control of her bladder because she wasn't housebroken. Because she was nothing more than a four-legged alimentary system with ears and a tail, the night crew had to spend a lot of time cleaning up after her, generally after slipping in it.

When the lieutenants began to stage champagne breakfasts at six in the morning for the night crew, those long-suffering Marines seized upon the opportunity to retaliate, and introduced Hostage Hog to the delights of the bubbly. The results of that really bad drunk, plus the steak and fried eggs she consumed in prodigious amounts, left an aura of used pigsty throughout the hangar bay for days.

A snockered hog was a sight to behold, especially when she was wearing a squadron baseball cap. But after all, that was the whole point of keeping a mascot in the first place.

She was unique. She wore sound suppressors on her ears without shaking them off, and she could keep a baseball hat on for at least an hour without losing it. Paper clips and Scotch tape helped there, and once a guy tried a stapler, but she started bitching after the third staple.

She was ours. No one else had a mascot like her, and she helped the squadron through some of the hard times just by being there.

Moral of the story: When you get your squadron in combat, hope to God you can come up with a mascot that truly belongs to everyone. You can't dictate it. It just has to happen. And when it does, you have another suture holding things together on those horrible days.

Of course, wars have a way of ending, and VMO-2's war ended before Hostage Hog did. No one would let the squadron take the beast home with them, and so a custody problem of considerable magnitude arose. Finally, the thorny issue was settled by the supply department.

The squadron had for years supported a German orphanage over on the beach near Marble Mountain, and that's where the hog ended up, with fervent promises that she would forever be a brood sow and have lots and lots of green and white piglets and make the orphanage rich. How it all turned out is anyone's guess. As long as there was no supply of beer or champagne available, she couldn't disgrace herself, and so we all hope she lived a long and fruitful life.

Of course, knowing the German taste for sausage . . . .

MEDALS

Did you ever see a guy with seventy-five Air Medals? I have. Damndest thing I ever did see. He may not have won a prize from the Guiness book, but he sure grabbed my attention and caused a lot of people to do a double take.

He was a huge, strapping lieutenant, a Huey Cobra pilot, who checked into my squadron at Camp Pendleton after returning from Vietnam in 1971 or '72. He was so tall that we ordinary mortals stood eyeball to hero badges with him, and the metal numbers 75 were pretty hard to miss.

We had a lot of well-seasoned combat helicopter pilots in the squadron, men who had amassed twenty or thirty strike-flight Air Medals over two tours in Vietnam, but none of us had ever seen seventy-five.

A strike-flight Air Medal was awarded administratively for every twenty documented combat missions, a carryover from World War II when it took a long time to live through twenty missions. That meant that the lieutenant, whose name I have forgotten, flew fifteen hundred missions!

I asked him how he accomplished such a feat in one tour. His answer was to the point. "I flew a lot."

The personal decoration was the most baffling contradiction I ever encountered in all my years in the Marine Corps. Everyone wanted one, but very few admitted to it. People would lie and cheat to get one, and then pretend that it wasn't important.

The communal bathroom in the MAG-11 pilots' living area boasted a graffiti board over the urinals which was truly entertaining. Clever bon mots included Latin phrases and poetic commentary, not the least of which was an up-to-date paraphrasing:

174

Was there ever a man with soul so dead
Who never in his life hath said
"I ought to get a DFC for this!"

For those who might one day command a squadron in combat,
I present some thoughts on the subject. Believe me when I tell
you that medals are important. How you handle the subject can
determine how successful you are as a commander.

Lieutenants and captains didn't present a problem. They
wanted enough Air Medals to prove that they had participated
in the manly art of war, and if they were lucky enough to earn
Distinguished Flying Crosses in their first tours, then so much
the better.

Senior officers presented a lot of problems. Not only did they
covet medals more than junior officers, they also had the clout
to bully their way into getting them.

Let me tell you about an episode that involved a senior officer.
The villain will be referred to as "Colonel X."

I was out flying late one afternoon, during the monsoon season, when I got a call to hurry on over to an area in the western
Que Son Mountains where a rifle company had run into some
stiff opposition, in Antenna Valley for those who are familiar
with the topography.

It was a standard close-air-support situation, and as the aerial
observer in my backseat talked with the company commander,
I called for fixed-wing bombers with snake and nape (fin-
retarded Snake Eye bombs and napalm).

The DASC, Direct Air Support Center, scrambled two F-4s
off the hot pad down at Chu Lai, and it was only a few minutes
before they were overhead, and we were ready to go to work.

The flight leader and I recognized each other's voices as well
as call signs, and I was comfortable with the fact that he was
one of the most experienced F-4 pilots in the Marine Corps.

I set up the bombing pattern roughly west to east, which called
for a sharp pullout to avoid the high ground to the east. It also
required the F-4s to play with some puffy little clouds as they
rolled into their runs. The sun was below the horizon, but that
was because of mountains rather than the hour.

The F-4s dropped their napalm on their first runs, then made
two bombing runs apiece. I worked from a position north of the
bombing pattern, raking the target area behind the jets with
machine-gun fire to suppress any small-arms fire directed at the
bombers.

When we were finished, the company commander thanked us for our help. I told the flight leader how wonderful he was and cleared him to depart the area, then settled down in a lazy orbit to keep the infantry Marines company as they moved out toward the position where they would dig in for the night.

The F-4 flight leader sounded quite chipper on the radio and apparently felt playful, because after the jets had joined up in formation, they roared by within feet of my lighter plane and tossed us around in their jet wash. This must have been accompanied by a little chitchat, cute on his part and reproving on mine, but I do not recall what it might have entailed.

Eventually the rifle company commander called and assured us that everything was okay with them. They had reached their objective and didn't need us any longer. I left the area and flew back to base.

End of mission. End of story. However . . .

A few days later I got a telephone call from Colonel X down at Chu Lai. My jaw dropped in amazement as he described a hazardous mission I could not recall, and he asked for a write-up from me to authenticate the awards recommendation he was preparing. According to him, the mission I just described to you was worth a Silver Star at least, and he intended to go "all out on this one."

One of the F-4s had taken a hit, which he was pretty sure was enemy small-arms fire, and that, coupled with darkness and bad weather, provided all of the ingredients for a hero badge.

I protested the weather and darkness, but kept my mouth shut on the subject of small-arms fire. To have suggested that one of the planes might have flown through its own bomb blast seemed counterproductive at the moment.

He sent a copy of his award's recommendation up to me, and I appended a rather lukewarm endorsement. The aerial observer who had been with me that day couldn't even remember the air strike, it was so commonplace. All I did, in reality, was verify that the mission did take place and that the bombing and napalm results were excellent.

A few days after all of that, I was again working with the same rifle company, this time in the flat ground east of the Que Sons, and after things had quieted down, the company commander came up on the radio to discuss the air strike in question. He too had received a copy of the award's recommendation and had been asked to add his endorsement.

He couldn't get excited about it either, and he asked me what I thought he should do. After all, it was a senior officer.

My exact answer: "Forget it. It's a fairy tale."

He thought so, too.

Colonel X never got his Silver Star, to the best of my knowledge, but I wonder what would have happened if the air controller pilot had been an impressionable junior officer. Worse yet, what if Colonel X had been one of the wheels in our own air group?

A lieutenant colonel on the air group staff can exert a lot of pressure on a squadron, especially when he is a big name star in Marine Corps aviation, and I suspect he would have received his Silver Star, or maybe a Distinguished Flying Cross.

This incident bothered me. It came at a time when the junior officers were livid over similar shenanigans on the part of a former commanding officer of another VMO squadron, and I was determined to do something about it.

The former VMO commander was a man I had known for years and a man I regarded as a pillar of honor and propriety. If he, as a squadron commander, had really bullied his squadron officers into questionable "creative writing," then I had to come up with something foolproof. Morale among the junior officers was critical to a successful squadron.

I didn't know quite how to handle it, and this is why I'm writing about it now. The next time we go to war for an extended period of time, everyone who remembers how screwed up the awards system can get will be either retired or dead.

I was lucky. Our squadron executive officer was one of the most experienced combat pilots around. K. D. Waters was on his third combat tour, and already a legend in his own right, and he knew exactly how to handle it. He had just been too polite to bring it up because he didn't know where I stood on the subject.

As the squadron executive officer, he sat on the air-group awards board which processed all of the recommendations that came up from the squadrons and sent them on to wing, recommending either approval or disapproval.

When VMO-2 had been attached to MAG-16, the helicopter group, the awards board had been a busy function. More pure heroism took place in a week in MAG-16 than any fixed-wing group would see in two or three years. In MAG-11 in 1970, with the A-6 squadrons no longer flying to Hanoi, things were pretty tame.

Major Waters had recently attended a meeting which devoted a great deal of time to discussing a recommendation for the Distinguished Flying Cross for an A-6 pilot, a major, who had—are you ready—knocked out a bulldozer one night on the Ho Chi Minh trail.

Major Waters was furious, but the recommendation was approved anyway in a six-to-one vote. He was as ready as I was to rewrite the book.

Our maintenance officer, Maj. Joe Roman, had himself been awarded a Silver Star for an incident during his first Vietnam tour when he was flying CH-46s, and which I mentioned in an earlier chapter. He had been shot down at night, way out in Indian country, and spent the many hours of darkness defending his passengers and crew from repeated enemy assaults. While the healthy and mobile infantry Marines aboard maintained a perimeter defense, Joe called artillery fire and air strikes on his own position until daylight when help finally arrived.

Joe was written up for a Navy Cross, but it was downgraded to a Silver Star. We included Joe on our blue ribbon panel and went to work on the problem.

The policy to be established had to be simple enough for everybody to understand, and altruistic enough so that a new commanding officer would think twice before changing it. With these and other thoughts in mind, the meeting to establish an awards policy within VMO-2 took less than a half hour.

1. No field grade officer—major and above—could be written up for an award higher than a strike-flight Air Medal until he had left the squadron.
2. No VMO-2 commanding officer could be written up for an award higher than a strike-flight Air Medal until he had left Vietnam and gone home.

This satisfied the company grade officers.

If a squadron commander is career oriented and thinks of his command only as a stepping stone to stardom, he had better be especially wary in this area. Junior officers have a way of becoming senior officers, and they talk. And the people they talk to include senior officers who become general officers and sit on promotion boards.

Whenever pilots gathered, either in the officers club in Da Nang or Marble Mountain or at a more relaxed social gathering anywhere in the United States, the subject eventually turned to medals: who got them and who didn't, how they got them and whether or not they deserved them.

Every year there are hundreds of military reunions all over the United States, and at every one, after the formal business has been attended to and the cups have been filled a couple of times, the subject turns to heroism.

Attend a Marine aviation reunion and hang around a while. You'll hear some great stories, for that's what reunions are all about. But you will also hear bitterness, sometimes fifty years after the fact, over someone who got a medal he didn't deserve.

Having said this, let me emphasize that there were a lot of senior officers who flew helicopters and won big-time medals fair and square.

During my second tour in Vietnam, I saw helicopter squadron commanders win Navy Crosses and Silver Stars, and they flat earned them. For instance:

Walt Ledbetter was the CO of HMM-263, flying CH-46s. He was a big teddy bear of a man, fearless, and so popular with his squadron that never once did I hear him called Colonel Bed-wetter.

Early one morning, an incident occurred when he was leading a flight of four CH-46s on a Kingfisher operation.

The purpose of Kingfisher operations was to locate bad guys at dawn when they were headed home after a night of skullduggery, swoop down right on top of them, and unleash a platoon of Marines.

With the element of surprise in our favor, the operations had so far been mighty successful.

The "package" consisted of the CH-46s with Cobra escort, one OV-10, and a Huey slick, which coordinated the mission.

From bits and pieces of intelligence, four or five specific points in a general area would be targeted as zones where the enemy had been known to pass on their way back to their bases. The target areas were numbered, and the OV-10 would race over them at high speed as soon as there was enough daylight to see any movement on the ground.

When movement or activity was detected, the OV-10 pilot had only to call out the target number. The CH-46s, loaded with a platoon of Marines and already moving rapidly toward the general area, would turn toward the designated target and land.

On this particular morning, the Kingfisher raid flushed a sizable group of the enemy. The Marines were in hot pursuit when the fleeing Viet Cong ran into a forgotten minefield.

This was an embarrassment. A few years earlier, Washington had decreed that Da Nang would be insulated from enemy encroachment by a ring of impenetrable minefields. Derisively called the "McNamara Line," the defensive measure was singularly ineffective and, unfortunately, forgotten. With Marines serving twelve-month tours in Vietnam, there was no one around after two years who remembered the mines.

The enemy knew where the mines were, and the Marines did not. Suddenly there were some dead and wounded Marines.

Not only was Walt the squadron commander, he was also the flight leader on the mission, and his performance was magnificent. He ordered the other helicopters away from the minefield and landed there himself—three times. A young Marine lance corporal got out of the helicopter three times to drag in the dead and wounded. Walt Ledbetter got a Navy Cross, and the lance corporal got the Medal of Honor.

In the aviation business, the squadron commander generally led all of the truly difficult missions. He didn't stay in the rear and direct people to leap in with both feet. He leapt first. As a result, some senior officers did receive some big medals, often posthumously, and I never heard anyone complain about Walt Ledbetter.

The only medal we ever played around with in VMO-2 was the strike-flight Air Medal. I guess we considered it to be more or less like the army's Combat Infantry Badge. It said you had been there and had not spent your entire tour sitting on your duff in Saigon, or in Okinawa, or the Philippines.

Case in point: A poor, hapless navy ensign, fresh out of the training command, who had the bad fortune of being assigned to the naval air station at Cubi Point in the Philippines for his first tour.

Almost as soon as a new pilot checked into VMO-2, he was sent back to the Philippines for jungle survival training, and it was there that some of our new pilots met the ensign. They took pity on him, and so did we. And so we arranged for him to come to Da Nang for a few days.

I don't remember how long he stayed, a week or so, but he spent almost the entire time in the air, sitting in the backseat of every mission that didn't require a qualified aerial observer. We got him his twenty missions and his Air Medal, and sent him back to the Philippines with a modicum of pride.

Technically, I suppose we were toying with the system, but I'd do it again in a minute.

We did the same thing for our squadron flight surgeon, except that we were very careful about which missions he flew. We didn't want him to get hurt. He was one of two doctors in the Da Nang area who were certified to perform vasectomies, and his services were sought constantly by older, family men.

Also, it was legal for flight surgeons to fly; they just weren't supposed to fly combat missions.

The only flagrant violation of a flight surgeon's flying took place down at Chu Lai. The medical officer in question shall remain nameless, but he was a former Marine pilot whom we all knew, and who had gone to medical school after he was released from active duty ten years earlier.

As a navy flight surgeon, he managed to get himself stationed at Chu Lai with the Marine Corps and attached to an A-4 Sky-hawk squadron. He flew dozens of illegal combat missions, and we all supported it. I doubt if he ever got in trouble for it.

Air Medals were easy. Purple Hearts, on the other hand, were not a whole lot of fun. Most pilots received Purple Hearts post-humously, and there aren't too many funny stories to tell about them.

Between Vietnam tours, I spent two years in the Naval Air Training Command at Pensacola. Half that time, I was a flight instructor, teaching aerobatics in the T-28, and that was a lot of fun. The other half I spent as the executive officer of the Marine headquarters there, and that wasn't.

The only nice thing about the administrative job was that I had a parking spot right across the street from the navy exchange. That doesn't seem to be much, but junior majors took their perks where they could find them.

What made the tour so unpleasant was that I spent an inordinate amount of time burying Marines. If a Marine from the Florida Panhandle was killed, I was the guy who told his wife or his parents, and at one time I was convinced that ninety percent of the Marines killed during the Tet offensive in 1968 came from western Florida.

Not true, of course, but I became an expert at delivering folded flags at funerals, and to this day I have to fight back tears when I hear Taps played.

But there can be a lighter side to any subject if you work at it.

The Purple Heart recipient in this story will remain nameless, mainly because he's a prominent general right now, and I wouldn't want to cause him any embarrassment. I'll call him "Major Y," simply because I called another guy "Colonel X."

Major Y arrived in Vietnam, OV-10 qualified, but did not join the squadron. He was a brand-new major and wanted a career-enhancing staff job, so he flew with us and partied with us, but did his administration work on the group staff where he could gain recognition.

In addition to flying with us, he also flew MAG-11's two-seated A-4 Skyhawk jets, performing tactical air-control missions out of country, over Laos mostly.

After a flight one afternoon, I was met at planeside by our executive officer, Major Waters. When the exec is waiting for you on the flight line you can be damn sure that the news is not good, and the look on K. D. Waters's face confirmed it.

Major Y had been hit. No, he was not dead, but he had taken a round in the cockpit, and the backseat pilot had brought the plane home.

Word had it that Major Y had been taken to the naval support activity hospital, maybe even flown out to the hospital ship, but no one was sure. The squadron pilots were pretty upset because the major was one of the "good guys." K. D. and I agreed that whatever I was going to do that afternoon would have to wait until I found out where he was and got over there on the double to see him.

I hurried through the postflight paperwork, then jumped into my jeep and raced to the living area to change out of my stinking flight suit and into a uniform. I had to be able to show my rank if I was going to bully my way through hospital bureaucracy.

As I drove, my brain was rummaging through the options available as a starting point in my search for our fallen comrade, and my mind was not on the road. I pulled to a stop in the parking area across the dirt road from the Quonset huts just in time to miss hitting Major Y!

He was in PE gear, sneakers and all, running along the dirt road! Running! Sweating! All that athletic stuff!

"Hey!" I yelled. "What the hell are you doing? You were supposed to have been shot!"

Major Y stopped and came over to the jeep smiling. "I was."

"Where?"

He lifted the right leg of his running shorts, and I saw a Band-Aid. It wasn't even a big Band-Aid.

"Right here. The armor plating and the seat slowed the bullet down."

"Stitches?"

"Two."

"Damn! We were worried about you. I was on my way to the hospital to hold your hand!"

About a year or so later, I saw Major Y again. I was the CO of HML-267, a Huey and OV-10 squadron at Camp Pendleton, California, and my wife and I were getting dressed to go to a squadron party at the officers club when the phone rang. Maj. John Morris, our maintenance officer, called, stating that Major Y was passing through town, and he asked if it would be okay for him to come to our party?

I agreed enthusiastically, and all of us who had been in Vietnam together enjoyed seeing him again. As I said, he was one of the good guys.

At some point during the evening, Major Y and I were standing alone, and curiosity got the better of me. We were all wearing civilian clothes, and there was no other way to find out except ask.

"Some of us are dying of curiosity. Did you get a Purple Heart for that Band-Aid job you took flying over Laos that day?"

Major Y turned purple, or at least burnt orange, and grinned in embarrassment. "Yeah."

No big thing as Purple Heart stories went. After all, most stories about live pilots wearing the medal dealt with minor wounds, and if the stories were repeated at all, it was because the insignificance of the wound appeared miraculous when compared to the severity of the trauma.

A former flight student of mine at Whiting Field was flying in the left, copilot's, seat in a Huey gunship one day when bullets were whizzing about the western Arizona Territory just north of Antenna Valley. The battle raged, and the Huey gave as good as it got until Lieutenant Keck's head flew back, and he let out a muted yell as he clutched his face. Large quantities of blood poured through his fingers. Then he went limp, his hands fell to his lap, and blood dripped down over his "bullet-bouncer" vest and pooled in his lap.

The pilot wasted no time breaking off the engagement and wheeling about toward the nearest battalion aid station, with the tachometer on the red line—which meant that he might have gotten about a hundred and ten knots out of the overloaded helicopter, and then only if he had a tail wind in a dive.

As he slowed the UH-1E and rotated for landing, Lieutenant

Keck regained consciousness, reached back to his bleeding fore-head, and with a thumb and forefinger extracted the bullet that shot him. "Damn!" he said, adjusting his lip mike and speaking normally over the intercom. "That really hurt!" Chalk up another "save" for armor plating.

At the other extreme were pilots who died truly heroic deaths and never received Purple Hearts. One of the statistical curiosities of aerial combat was the fact that the death rate in a war did not escalate remarkably over that of peace-time training. Most pilot deaths during combat, then, occurred from operational accidents, not DEA, direct enemy action; and one of the requirements for a Purple Heart was that a wound had to be suffered as a result of direct enemy action. As a result, many helicopter pilots gave their lives and demonstrated heroic disregard for personal safety and were awarded big-time medals for their efforts—posthumously of course—but even though their heroism took place in the heat of combat, no Purple Heart was awarded, simply because the deaths occurred as a result of a crash.

We didn't think that was fair, by the way. We in VMO-2 were of the opinion that the giving of one's life for his country deserved a Purple Heart even though there was no blood drawn immediately prior to the point of impact. Hell, in Korea my brother got a Purple Heart for the burns he suffered when he was shot down. But, then, that was the navy.

And a reader might not believe it today, but the simple statement "killed in action" was, on occasion, important enough to a bereaved widow to cause a helluva big stink: "killed in action" as opposed to "died of wounds." Try this one on.

An enemy rocket landed in a tent occupied by the senior officers of a helicopter squadron. The pilot in question was very badly wounded, but not dead, and the flight surgeon did what he could, then got him on a Da Nang-bound helicopter immediately in hopes of saving his life.

As fortune would have it, the helicopter, flying out over the water and out of range of any enemy gunfire, experienced some mishap and crashed into the sea in the middle of the night with total loss of life.

There was no body to return to Pensacola, and I staged a truly epic memorial service in the main chapel, complete with band and drum rolls and an honor guard of twenty Marine officers in addition to the five who delivered the folded flag, all of them in dress blues as the drums beat a dirge that sounded like something out of *A Tale of Two Cities*. I thought I was going to be accused of staging some pagan ritual, but the widow instead was furious for a reason I was quite unprepared for: The official notification said he died of wounds, and that was not a glorious way to die.

We were able to bring the widow's unhappiness to an end with a few phone calls. The squadron flight surgeon was contacted, and he simply lied and put an end to the whole stink. He amended the death report to state that in his professional opinion the pilot was dead when he was loaded aboard the helicopter for the trip to Da Nang. That simple statement changed the status from "died of wounds" to "killed in action" and everybody went on about their lives.

People got hurt flying in Vietnam, no question about it. But most pilots, fixed-wing pilots especially, received Purple Hearts either for small wounds, or posthumously. If it didn't kill the pilot, he probably walked away from it, as in the case of Ted "Nine Fingers" Robinson who, after taking a round in the cockpit, flew his helicopter directly out to the hospital ship where he was convinced the surgeons could sew the end of his finger back on. They couldn't, and Ted has had trouble playing the saxophone ever since.

If you plan to be a squadron commander, you need to know these things, like how to get a Purple Heart for yourself when the wound was nothing more than a Band-Aid job. Major Y was honest and had to take some gentle ribbing from his friends. But there's a sneaky way of getting one . . . presuming that you really did get dinged.

All you do is ensure that the flight surgeon notates DEA, direct enemy action, in your medical record when he patches you up. You, the cold, steely-eyed commander go on about your business and demonstrate to your squadron that you are above taking a Purple Heart for something so insignificant because that medal was designed by George Washington for men who made true sacrifices. Then, after you have returned to the United States and are in a new organization, probably in a staff billet, you find the opportunity in some conversation to mention that, come to think of it, you did take a hit and that, yes, you were pretty sure it was listed in your health record as DEA. And some junior officer, trying to suck up to you, will carry the ball for you and get you your medal—all over your magnanimous protests, of course.

I never got hurt, but one day when I was lying on an operating table, my back all covered with blood and bandages as a corpsman did a really bad job of removing a growth that was being chafed by the torso harness straps, I was asked if I wanted them to add DEA to the entry in my health record. At the time, I assumed that the corpsman who assisted and made the notes didn't know I was only having a wart removed, but by the time I retired and had become a bit cynical on the subject, I suspected that similar hanky-panky had occurred before.

A question which is often asked involves the Medal of Honor and how many Marine pilots won them in Vietnam.

The answer is one, just one, and I want to take a moment to tell you about it. Not only is it a neat war story, it also contains some unanswered political intrigue.

I got to know Steve Pless pretty well before he was killed in a tragic accident in Pensacola in 1969. He told me the story at least three times, drunk and sober, and I am going to give you two versions of it. One is the official version, and one is his. Neither differs as to his personal actions and heroism, but the circumstances of the people whom he rescued have been clouded in bureaucratic mystery. In fact, the last account I read had him rescuing other Marines instead of army personnel.

Politics got involved here, and in order to understand the awkward situation you have to know that the army had a penchant for pinning a medal on a soldier as soon after the award-winning incident as was possible.

Early in the war, during my first tour, when I was a commissioned paperweight in III MAF headquarters, a young army officer, who was an advisor to a Vietnamese unit, had acquitted himself well when the unit was overrun by a Viet Cong night attack.

At 0800 the next morning, I received a telephone call from Saigon asking me if we had a Silver Star available. General Westmoreland was on his way up to Da Nang to decorate the lieutenant, and they were fresh out.

As luck would have it, our staff secretary had one in his safe, and we were able to get it to Westmoreland's aide when he landed.

I don't think the lieutenant even had time to wash the cordite and mud out of his hair before he was standing at attention, watching Superman himself pin a medal on his shirt.

While no one begrudged the lieutenant's getting a prize, we

in the Marine headquarters questioned the wisdom of passing out such high standing medals before all the facts were known.

Visiting wounded soldiers and Marines in hospitals and awarding them Purple Hearts was one thing. Awarding a Silver Star six or seven hours after the skirmish seemed to be pushing it a bit.

With this in mind, let me tell you a war story. This is a verbatim copy of the official citation.

CITATION:

For conspicuous gallantry and intrepidity at the risk of his own life above and beyond the call of duty while serving as a helicopter gunship pilot attached to Marine Observation Squadron Six in action against enemy forces near Quang Nai, Republic of Vietnam, on 19 August, 1967. During an escort mission, Major (then Captain) Pless monitored an emergency call that four American soldiers stranded on a nearby beach were being overwhelmed by a large Viet Cong force. Major Pless flew to the scene and found thirty to fifty enemy soldiers in the open. Some of the enemy were bayonetting and beating the downed Americans. Major Pless displayed exceptional airmanship as he launched a devastating attack against the enemy force, killing or wounding many of the enemy and driving the remainder back into a tree line. His rocket and machine gun attacks were made at such low levels that the aircraft flew through the debris created by explosions from its rockets. Seeing one of the soldiers gesture for assistance, he maneuvered his helicopter into a position between the wounded men and the enemy, providing a shield which permitted his crew to retrieve the wounded. During the rescue the enemy directed intense fire at the helicopter and rushed the helicopter again and again, closing to within a few feet before being beaten back. When the wounded men were aboard, Major Pless maneuvered the helicopter out to sea. Before it became safely airborne, the overloaded aircraft settled four times into the water. Displaying superb airmanship, he finally got the helicopter aloft. Major Pless' extraordinary heroism coupled with his outstanding flying skill prevented the annihilation of the tiny force. His courageous actions reflect great credit upon himself, and uphold the greatest traditions of the Marine Corps and the United States Naval Service.

Now let me tell you Steve Pless's version of what happened that day.

At the beginning of this chapter, I stated that very few people admitted that they wanted to win big medals. Steve Pless was one of those very few.

Not only was he open and honest about wanting to win a Medal of Honor, he worked at it as well.

He carried with him at all times a tape recorder, which was rigged to plug into the UH-1E Huey radio system, and he had a clamp attached to his flight helmet to which he could attach a movie camera. Camcorders had not been invented yet, or he would have had one of those too.

I saw his home movies. In the citation, it mentions that the aircraft few through debris created by explosions from its rockets. That debris was human, and it was not a pretty sight.

He knew that recommendations for big medals had to be verified by witnesses, and he meant to provide as much verification as he could.

The operative words in the citation were *downed* and *stranded*. A cold reading of the citation suggests that some soldiers had stumbled into a large Viet Cong force, and this simply was not the case.

What had actually happened was this.

An army helicopter was flying along the beach, out of harm's way, transporting some army enlisted personnel. The engine of the UH-34 began to act up, and the pilot, a major, elected to land on a desolate strip of beach to see what the problem was.

Upon landing, the pilot ordered the soldiers to form a defensive position around the helicopter while the crew chief checked the engine. The beach looked pretty deserted, and he didn't expect any trouble, but just in case some bad guys did take a shot at them, he wanted the soldiers out there with their rifles.

There were some bad guys. A lot of them. They objected to an American helicopter landing right in front of them, and they attacked.

The helicopter engine was running, and so the pilot did what he thought was the logical thing. He pulled the collective into his armpit and took off!

The enemy weren't bayoneting and beating "downed" Americans. They were bayoneting and beating "stranded" Americans.

This pissed Steve Pless off.

When Pless originally heard the call for help, he and the flight of transport helicopters he was escorting were returning to Marble Mountain from a canceled medevac mission. They had launched to haul some wounded out of a firefight, and for reasons unknown to Steve, the mission was canceled.

But this meant that he had not expended any ammunition and that he still had enough fuel to answer a distress call.

He detached from the formation and headed east, toward a strip of seacoast sand dunes and ironwood trees we called Barrier Island.

At this point I should further explain why he carried a camera and a tape recorder. A month or so before, he had faced the real possibility of a court-martial because of an incident in which it was claimed that he tried to shoot down a U.S. Air Force plane. This gets a little complicated, so follow me.

In this episode, Steve was flying gunship escort for an emergency extract of a Marine reconnaissance team that had run into a large and unfriendly group of Viet Cong in the hills west of Da Nang.

After a lot of shooting and bombing, the eight-man recon team scrambled aboard the transport helicopter, and the planes flew back to base, and that should have been the end of it.

But when the Marines disembarked from the transport, they discovered to their dismay that they didn't have all eight Marines. One was missing.

While people stood around scratching their heads and wondering what to do, Pless wasted no time. He cranked up his Huey and flew on the red line back to the area where they had picked the team up.

On arrival, he was stunned to see an air force FAC plane circling the area and a pair of F-100s orbiting overhead. This meant only one thing. The FAC was about to run an air strike.

Steve's immediate problem was one of communications. The air force planes were operating on one of their tactical radio frequencies, and Pless did not know what it was. I had a similar problem in 1970 involving the rescue of one of our crews in Laos.

He switched to the guard channel, the universal emergency channel which is guarded by everyone. He called, but he got no response. In desperation, he flew directly into the target area and began orbiting as he searched for the missing Marine.

The air force pilot couldn't help but see him, and finally came up on the guard channel to warn Pless that he had better get out of the way because he was about to run an air strike.

Here's where it got complicated.

Pless had to put a stop to the strike, but he couldn't tell the air force pilot why because the enemy had our radios, too, and he had to assume that the Viet Cong were listening in on the guard channel and would know that there was a wounded Marine down there.

The air force pilot, of course, had no way of knowing that. All he knew was that he saw enemy activity in the area, which there certainly was, and that some crazy Marine was getting in the way and screwing up the operation.

The radio conversation between the two got pretty ugly and came to a head when Pless yelled out on the guard channel for everyone in the world to hear, "If you make one move toward that area, I'll blow your ass out of the sky!"

Perhaps in defiance, perhaps just out of curiosity, the forward-air-control plane turned into the target area. Pless, afraid that he was rolling in for a rocket-marking run, raised the nose of his Huey as high as he dared and fired a smoke rocket in the general direction of the FAC.

The air force pilot must have thought Pless was insane, but he did abort the air strike. In a few minutes, the gunship crew spotted the Marine, who was indeed wounded, landed, and hauled him aboard.

They flew the Marine back to Charlie Med, which was the navy's version of MASH, and the Marine was saved. And from that day on, Pless never flew without his tape recorder.

He didn't get court-martialed either.

After that episode, Steve Pless's reputation was pretty well established. Everybody talked about him, and a growing number of people had doubts about wanting to fly with him. He never kept it a secret that he intended to win a Medal of Honor, and a big chunk of the squadron decided that they didn't want to be there when he did.

Steve was the product of what today we call a dysfunctional family. He was raised in a military school, Fork Union in Virginia, and he enlisted in the Marine Corps immediately after graduation. The Marine Corps was his life, and in his young mind, heroism was the ultimate status symbol. He was smart enough to get into flight training without any college, and did his first tour in Vietnam as a transport pilot, flying H-34s. In order to get back to Vietnam as quickly as he could, he volunteered to go as a forward air controller with the Korean Marines.

He spent six months with the ROK Marines, then joined VMO-6 and started flying Hueys, which were the ultimate warrior helicopters in 1967.

Steve Pless was an aggressive pilot.

Heading toward Barrier Island and the daring rescue, he got all of his electronics recording equipment working as he called the army pilot and found out what had happened. He dropped down to treetop level, and was able to make his first attacking run without being noticed because he had started from a downwind position and the Viet Cong couldn't hear him coming.

After he drove the enemy back into the trees, he tried to get the army pilot to land with him in order to pick the soldiers up in a minimum amount of ground time. But the army pilot would not. According to Pless, the army pilot said he couldn't land because it was a "hot zone."

Pless's reply was not complimentary. He landed, as the citation read, and his crew scrambled about, dragging bodies to the Huey. He kept the enemy away by raising the gunship a few inches into the air and moving the nose left and right with the rudder pedals as he squeezed the trigger. This traversing machine-gun fire repelled most of the enemy.

The one soldier who was alive got aboard first, just as Pless spotted an enemy soldier approaching the helicopter from the right. Pless pointed at the enemy and shouted for the soldier to get on the right door gun and shoot him.

The soldier only had one arm that was working, so he wrapped a leg around the M-60 to steady it and squeezed off a burst that did the job.

Pless saw another enemy soldier creeping up on the left with a satchel charge of explosives, too close for the plane's guns. He was able to get the attention of his copilot, who was helping to drag a body to the plane, and pointed to the approaching sapper.

This was the only part of the story Steve told with a smile. According to Pless, the lieutenant knew only one way to shoot a .38 pistol, the way he had been taught by Sergeant Major Hufty on the pistol range in Pensacola.

The lieutenant unholstered the .38, cocked it as though he were back in Florida, took careful aim, holding the weapon with both hands, and squeezed off his rounds as though he was still on the fifteen-yard line doing rapid-fire practice.

The enemy sapper expired, and the satchel charge blew up without doing any damage to the helicopter.

The takeoff was the hairiest part of the entire episode.

The citation refers to the helicopter as being overloaded. This is an understatement. Anyone who has ever flown a fully loaded Huey gunship knows that in hot weather it is always overloaded at takeoff and has to be dragged off the ground.

The plane was not designed to be a gunship. The ''change seven'' kit, which added the forward-firing guns and rockets, took the gross weight of the plane up into the dangerous area, and the extra ammunition and spare gun barrels alone created a hazardous situation. Add extra people, and Pless's gross load was supercritical.

Pless turned into the wind and started skipping along the sand. The Huey had no wheels, just skids. Frighteningly, he ran out of beach before he had enough forward speed to fly, and so he kept on skipping, right out into the water.

The crew started throwing everything overboard that wasn't bolted to the plane. Ammo cans, canteens, armored vests—everything went. Someone—Pless said he was glad he couldn't remember who—suggested that they jettison the dead bodies. That, of course, was rejected.

They finally got airborne and flew to the naval support activity hospital just across the road from Marble Mountain. The bodies were unloaded, and the wounded soldier was rushed to the emergency treatment center, and then Pless lifted the lightened plane over the road and into the squadron area.

When he inspected the plane, he expected to find it riddled with bullet holes. Surprisingly, there was only one hole in the entire plane, in the gear box right beside the tail rotor. One inch to the left or right would have caused the helicopter to crash.

But Steve Pless had accomplished what he set out to do, and the rest, as they say, is history. Except for the political intrigue.

It took almost a year for the Medal of Honor to be approved. One of the reasons for this was that the army major who caused the problem in the first place had been awarded the Silver Star for his participation in the action before all the facts had been discovered.

Had the citation included all of the details, the army would have been greatly embarrassed, and so what you read must have been the result of exhaustive staffing and sanitization.

The only words that missed staff scrutiny were *downed* and *stranded*, and I like to think that they were left in the citation intentionally, perhaps as a cryptic apology to everyone who knew what really happened that day.

MARKSMANSHIP

The most important thing a Marine owes the American taxpayer is to be able to hit what he's shooting at.

So said my drill instructor during the summer of 1952 when I was a naval aviation cadet in Pensacola.

Of course, this was the same man who explained to us that a particular marching movement was "Did in three counts," and then demonstrated—"one, two, three, four!"

My very first encounter with this man of steel dealt with marksmanship.

"D'ja ayver far 'n Aim Mon rahful?" he barked as I stood mystified in front of his desk.

It took three tries before I understood that he was interested in my background in riflery, particularly any experience I might have had with the M-1.

I learned two things that day: that if I ever decided to become a Marine I had better learn to appreciate marksmanship, and that if I was ever going to get along with Marines I had better learn to understand southern accents.

I also learned not to laugh when a drill instructor made a mathematical error on the drill field.

When I first started flying with VMO-2, three months before I actually joined the squadron, I was disappointed in the marksmanship of some of the pilots. I watched a lot of air strikes from a distance in those early days, learning from the combat-seasoned veterans as they controlled bombing and rocket attacks on enemy positions, and the one statement that galled me the most went something like this:

"From my smoke, drop twenty meters south."

Now, if you were dropping a stick of thousand-pound bombs, twenty meters would be a respectable CEP (circular error probàbility), and if you were dropping from thirty thousand feet and even came within twenty meters of the target it would have been blind luck. But when a pilot was pumping out a white phosphorous rocket from a slant range of around fifteen hundred feet, twenty meters seemed to me to be downright unprofessional.

I was convinced that the only people in Vietnam who seemed to be able to hit what they were shooting at every time were the hospital corpsmen. They administered two or three hundred shots a day, and they got to be real good at it. Practice, practice, practice.

In 1970, the Marine Corps' close-air-support war was not all that dangerous. The enemy had moved their big guns away from Da Nang, and I personally felt that a man ought to be able to take his time and hit what he was aiming at. When I assumed command of VMO-2 in January, and did away with the onerous thousand-foot-minimum-altitude restriction on OV-10s, one of the first things I did was to encourage marksmanship.

I put out the word unofficially that I didn't think it was necessary to bring ammunition back after a flight. This didn't include white phosphorous rockets, which were expensive and critical to our mission, but high-explosive rockets and bullets and twenty-millimeter shells were plentiful and belonged out in Indian country somewhere—preferably sticking into or out of enemy soldiers, but certainly not back on the flight line.

Within a month I began to hear some encouraging sounds.

"Where do you want the bombs, Hostage?"

"On my smoke would be nice, pardner."

By the time the weather got hot, so had VMO-2s marksmanship, and by June, the bomber pilots expected us to put the marks on the targets.

We practiced constantly, and shoot-off competitions became common, providing just about as much fun as military pilots could ever expect to get out of life. Whenever two of our pilots found themselves airborne with nothing to do except bore holes in the sky, they would find an abandoned plantation building or the hulk of a dead airplane or vehicle of some sort, get clearance from whatever regiment controlled the area, and start another round in the Great Southeast Asia War Games.

There was a dead amphibious tractor down on Go Noi Island that was popular, and crashed helicopters and fixed-wing airplanes abounded. But my favorite target was one of the windows of an abandoned plantation house, ten or twelve miles southwest of Da Nang. If a rocket sailed cleanly through the window, the smoke from the explosion was orange because of all of the crushed tile inside, tile which had at one time been the roof.

Most of the captains in the squadron had always been great marksmen, and it was with them that I competed. I avoided taking on the majors, partially because I thought that any competition among senior officers was in bad form, and mainly because the executive officer, K. D. Waters, would wax my fanny every time.

I didn't take on the lieutenants either. Losing to a young lieutenant, six months out of training command, was something I didn't really need.

On my best day, I put four out of five rockets through the five-foot-square window of the plantation house. Regrettably, Captain Denny Herbert shot five out of five that day, and I had to buy him drinks all night.

One of my more embarrassing marksmanship experiences took place with a lieutenant watching, and I use the story to this day in counseling young hotshots on the dangers of writing checks with their mouths.

First Lt. Peter Colt and I were out in Indian country on a deep reconnaissance patrol one morning, searching the hills and valleys and rivers along the Laotian border. We used two planes for these missions, taking turns at the high-cover position while the other plane swooped and snooped down among the trees and rivers.

Peter was skimming along an olive-green river, searching for signs of human activity in that remote jungle, when he passed by a raft that was rather poorly concealed in the riverside foliage.

It was a small raft, three logs lashed together and about ten or twelve feet long. He pulled up sharply and exclaimed over the radio, "Skipper! Did you see that raft?"

I saw it. I flipped the switch to my left rocket pod and rolled in.

"You mean this raft?" I pickled off an HE rocket and hit the raft squarely in the lashings at one end, which caused it to fan apart.

"Wow! Good shot, Colonel!"

I was rather pleased with myself, too, and satisfied that my reputation as a marksman had just been enhanced, and then I made that most fatal of errors:

"Wanna see me do it again?"

Oh, male ego! Why do you make us do these things?

Well, sir, let me tell you . . . I couldn't hit the other end of that raft for all the tea in China. I took three or four shots at it, and Peter did too, and we finally gave up and continued on our patrol, pretending that we didn't have time or fuel to waste on trifles.

Something similar had occurred a few years earlier when I was flying F-8 Crusaders out of the Marine Corps air station at Kaneohe Bay in Hawaii, and I should have known better because of it. I was a captain in VMF-232 and had only recently joined the squadron after a ground tour as a forward air controller with the 1st Air and Naval Gunfire Liaison Company (ANGLICO), where I got to jump out of airplanes a lot, but had flown only four hours a month in the station Beechcraft at NAS Barbers Point.

We were in the middle of a three-day air-defense exercise when I took off at about two in the morning on a supersonic intercept mission. I scrambled into the night in afterburner, and stayed that way throughout the intercept—which after that twenty minutes of flight, I was looking at a low-fuel warning light. The F-8 only held 8,600 pounds of fuel.

Now, in peacetime, night flying is one of those things a pilot does, not because he wants to, but because he has to. There's nothing dangerous about it, it just cuts into your liberty time something fierce. And when you do give up an evening at home, you want to log as much time as you can so that you don't have to do it again too soon.

To return to base and land after twenty minutes, then, seemed to me to be counterproductive, and so I called for a steer to an in-flight refueling tanker that was orbiting just north of Maui.

I hadn't refueled in almost two years, and I had never done it at night before, but I pulled in behind that C-130, plugged in on the first try, and sucked up a load of JP-4 as though I had been doing it for a living.

The word got around the squadron quickly. "Hey, this guy, Moriarty. He's pretty good. Hadn't been on a refueling hop in two years, etc." My ego was refueled, too.

The next afternoon I was airborne, practicing missile intercepts, when I got a call instructing me to run over to the refueling area and take a few practice stabs.

The weather was perfect, not a cloud in a sky that was so blue a man might think about joining the air force, and if it hadn't been for the curvature of the earth, I could have seen all the way to Alaska. My wingman and I joined up on the exact same tanker, and I took the exact same drogue I had refueled from so early that morning.

I extended my probe, and moved in with all the confidence of an experienced marksman—and proceeded to reenact a scene from *The Three Musketeers*. Lunge, parry, thrust. I fenced with that thing like D'Artagnan fighting off Cardinal Richelieu's entire palace guard. The eighteen-inch drogue basket finally surrendered, and my battered probe slurped up a tank full of fuel, but I suffered acute embarrassment in full view of the entire population of Maui. Fortunately, my marksmanship with guns and rockets in Vietnam was better.

While the ability to put a rocket precisely on target was ego-satisfying, a more difficult and professional form of marksmanship was the ability to put someone else's rocket on the target.

This is what the air-control business was all about. It didn't take any great talent to fire a white phosphorus rocket into some clump of trees, tell the A-4 pilot to hit it, and orbit somewhere safe while he worked his tail off doing the best he knew how.

A good controller got into it with the bomber, sometimes right beside him, sometimes on top of him. Dropping bombs within fifteen or twenty-five meters from friendly troops was no place for casual kibitzing.

You have to understand that when I, or any other VMO-2 pilot, controlled bombing and rocket air strikes, the instant the weapon left the bomber it belonged to me. The term "cleared hot" didn't mean go ahead and drop it and let's see where it hits. It meant that the bombs were going to hit what I intended for them to hit.

Let me describe to you some of the methods I used for close-in bombing and napalm drops. I guarantee that you will never find my procedures listed in any official manual. Remember also that some of the things we did applied only to the Marine Corps' war in the Quang Nam Province in 1970, where we had total mastery of the skies, and large antiaircraft weapons were no longer available to the enemy.

In order to ensure accuracy, I wanted to be as close to the bomber as I could get at the moment of release. A few feet off his wingtip was a good place to be.

Once the bomber pilot saw where I wanted his bombs, we were able to establish his pattern, which was pretty much like a landing pattern. As he started his approach turn, I would mark the precise target again, generally with white phosphorus rockets at the six and twelve o'clock positions. This not only pointed out the confines of the target, but also fine-tuned any correction to his run-in heading.

After firing the rockets, I had to bend the OV-10 around in a hard G turn so that I could be in a position to see exactly what the bomber pilot was looking at when he got to the drop point. This was just as hard on the hemorrhoids as a pullout from a steep dive, but there wasn't enough time to do it any other way.

When the bomber rolled his wings level in his run, he called just that. "Wings level" meant that he was lined up and ready to drop. At this point, I had to be able to assess how accurate he was going to be, and the only place for that was right on his wingtip.

This took some doing. He was doing about 450 knots, and because of that tight turn, I was probably down to around 120— tops. And so I had to position myself to be at his drop point when he got there.

If he looked good, I'd key the mike and give him permission to drop. "Cleared hot" was all I had to say. He would "pickle off" his bombs, while I pulled up and away to avoid the "darts" from his bomb blast.

If for some reason he was not lined up properly—and in jets that only occurred with new, inexperienced wingmen—I'd key the mike and start yelling at him. The words: "Negative! Negative! Abort! Abort!" generally got a pilot's attention and prevented him from punching the little red button on the top of his stick.

On the rare occasion when we came upon a situation where a wingman wasn't up to the airmanship required, we simply told him to orbit while the leader did the job.

In a napalm attack, the jet ran in much lower over the target, and I found that a point directly over the bomber was the best place to be. I would brief the pilot that I wanted him to release the napalm when I yelled "Now!" or "Mark!" When he was "wings level" in his run, I would call "Stand by" two or three times, and then when I yelled "Now!" he was to pickle off the fire bombs.

To get in position, I would go through the same procedure as in a bombing run, except that I would aim for a position directly above him. Also I would be almost inverted, sometimes absolutely upside down, which irritated the hell out of the aerial observer in the back seat.

The bomber would whiz by under me, and just as he reached a point where I could see plainly how momentum would carry the napalm, I'd yell, and he'd pickle. To people watching the maneuver from the ground or from a helicopter, it looked pretty scary because I would only be about a hundred feet above him, but it was not that bad. All I had to do was release most of the pressure on the controls, and the stable OV-10 would whip back to an upright attitude.

If there were bad guys on the ground shooting at the bomber from the side, I did something else that was disquieting to aerial observers.

I didn't worry too much about the enemy directly under the drop. Common sense would have them trying to bury themselves in a hole somewhere. But even if they did have a death wish and tried to shoot at the plane, the chances of them hitting something moving that fast were infinitesimal.

Bad guys off to the side, however, could get an angle on the plane as it pulled away from the target, so they had to be encouraged to keep their heads down. I had to shoot at them as the bomber flew past.

To accomplish this, I would clear the bomber from a position a bit further away from his wingtip, my position over the friendlies, and keep the nose of my plane pointed at the enemy.

As the bomber flew through my gunsight, I squeezed the trigger. I kept the ''pipper'' on the trailing edge of the bomber's tail without pulling hard Gs—which meant that there was no way for the bullets to hit the bomber. In this way I was able to strafe the enemy position during that critical moment when they might be able to draw a bead on the plane.

I really liked that tactic, but the younger pilots were afraid to try it.

Probably the worst marksmanship I ever saw involved an air force Arc Light bombing run.

B-52s from Guam and Thailand flew massive bombing raids almost every night, carving huge swaths out of the jungles of South Vietnam, and someone got the bright idea one day to use such a raid to prep a helicopter landing zone.

We had planned to insert a rifle company into a zone pretty far out in the hinterland early one morning, and instead of using our A-4s and F-4s to prep it and neutralize the zone from booby traps and buried explosives, tons and tons of bombs from B-52s were going to do the job just minutes before the dawn landing.

It made sense to me. Arc Light raids had never presaged an infantry assault before, and we had been assured that B-52s always hit their targets.

I got out there at first light to control the operation, and the devastation was truly incredible. The load from one B-52 created an area of destruction about the size and shape of a long, wide runway. Nothing but brown, muddy craters and tangled tree stumps remained, where a few minutes before lush, green jungle had thrived.

The entire moonscape where the bombs had hit was impressive. But what really grabbed my attention was the fact that not one of the bombs had hit the landing zone. One bomb had been close enough to throw some dirt on it, but that was the extent of the zone prep. I called in some F-4s that had been assigned as high cover for the landing, and we did the job with Rockeye bomblets—and of course, we lost whatever advantage of surprise had been hoped for.

Wing G-3 later yelled at me for using such expensive bombs on something as simple as a zone prep. I thought that was interesting, but I cannot recall arguing with them on the obvious inconsistency of complaining about me using expensive bombs when the taxpayers had just paid to send a B-52—and the B-52 missed! I probably had a list of things I was trying to wheedle out of them at the time, and I didn't want to piss them off, so I didn't argue.

I never maligned the air force on that one either. Had the bombs been released about a half a second earlier, a lot of bombs would have detonated where they were supposed to. But a helicopter landing zone was hardly a fair target for an Arc Light mission.

By the spring of 1970, the two A-6 Intruder squadrons in MAG-11 had lost their contracts to fly against the "Wall of Steel" around Hanoi, and like all aggressive corporations in trouble, they were busily trying to diversify themselves. Bombing bulldozers on the Ho Chi Minh trail at night was rapidly losing its charm, and they wanted a piece of the local action.

With their incredible bombload capacity, they hit upon a plan that emulated the B-52 Arc Light raids. They started doing the same thing themselves, and called their small scale operations "Flash Light" raids. We do not know whether or not they ever hit anything.

Our A-6s could carry fifteen one-thousand-pound bombs, and

while they might have been some of the ugliest airplanes ever invented, they surely could deliver. While it was not an everyday occurrence, we sometimes used them to carve helicopter landing zones out of the jungle. This was an incredible stunt for the day. Thousand-pound bombs with daisy-cutter fuses could do the job in five or ten minutes.

Through a process called offset bombing, where the plane used an object miles away for its reference point, the A-6 had the electronic ability to make identical bombing runs on a single target, one right after the other. The pilot and his bombardier/navigator simply plugged the information into the computer, and the plane made repeated runs until they turned off the machine. This meant that a plane could make five or ten bombing runs on the same square yard of real estate. For 1970, this was worth watching.

A daisy-cutter fuse was nothing more than a four- or five-foot extension screwed onto the nose of a bomb. It caused the bomb to explode before it touched the ground, which meant that it would do serious damage to a lot of trees.

By putting the two capabilities together, an A-6 could carve a landing zone because, close as they were, no two bombs landed in exactly the same square inch.

It got a little boring to watch, an airplane making the exact same bombing run ten times in a row, but explosion by explosion, a clearing would begin to emerge as the smoke cleared. Expensive, but effective.

As a taxpayer, I might have objected to the use of thousand-pound bombs to carve a helicopter landing zone out in the middle of nowhere. But that marvelous offset bombing capability of the A-6 had already solved one of my more vexing problems—how to hit the enemy in the jungle when we couldn't see them from the air.

I had a personal, and some say unnatural, love for a weapon called "Lazy Dog."

For reasons never made quite clear, Lazy Dog was deemed inhumane as a weapon and removed from the inventory after only limited use in the very beginning of the Vietnam War. It was silent, and it was deadly, and it played hob with enemy morale. But we had to fight our war without it.

Lazy Dog was a canister bomb that ripped apart at a designated altitude and rained .45-caliber slugs. There were thousands of slugs, with tiny little fins to keep them from tumbling, and when they hit the ground they were traveling at terminal velocity, which was the same rate of speed a .45-caliber bullet would attain six feet in front of the gun barrel.

There was no explosion when the canister ripped open, and when it was dropped over the enemy in the jungle, the results were frightening.

I only heard of one survivor, a Viet Cong porter who was with a group of about a dozen enemy soldiers moving through the jungle at night. He was eventually captured, and told interrogators that all he heard was a whooshing sound, then all of the leaves fluttered down from the trees, and everyone around him was lying on the ground, dead. No noise, just death.

I devoted a lot of time and effort in designing a method for delivering Lazy Dog in the jungle.

I first got interested in the weapon a few years before we went into Vietnam. I had been part of an air/ground exercise in Thailand, during which the air force and the Marine Corps spent a few weeks yelling at each other about whose system of close air support was better. We were impugning each other's manhood, while the Thais and the Australians looked on, laughing their asses off. We won the fight, and we managed to sell the Marine Corps system of close air support for use by SEATO, the Southeast Asia Treaty Organization. But it wasn't much of a victory, because SEATO dissolved as soon as a war got started.

At a reception to mark the end of the exercise, an Australian Air Force officer presented me with a challenge that was to keep me busy for months.

"You only figured out the easy stuff, Michael, my boy. How about coming up with a way to mark a target in the jungle? What do you do when you're on the ground under a sixty-foot tree canopy, and you want to mark a target that's a thousand meters away, and under the same canopy?"

I went back to Hawaii, where we had some great jungle out in the Kahuku training area, and I went to work. What I came up with became known as "Moriarty and his goddamn balloons."

I had to figure out a way to put a visual reference point above the jungle canopy—something similar to the brightly colored panels forward air controllers used on the ground. Smoke didn't work. The trees diffused it too much. But balloons might.

The theory involved running balloons up through the canopy to form a run-in line for the jet attack aircraft. There would be four balloons, the one nearest the target a red one. That's where I would stand with my radio.

The jet would fly over the balloons in the proper direction, and all I had to do was run a time-rate-distance problem with a stop watch. "Time. Standby. Mark!" Piece of cake. The bomber would put a napalm bomb into the treetops, and the rest of the flight would swoop down and eliminate the enemy.

That's when I formed an association with Lazy Dog—which, of course, was the perfect weapon for the elimination of human beings under a jungle canopy. I promoted the project as a vehicle for Lazy Dog delivery.

The theory of my balloon markings and the practical application thereunto were not without frustrations.

I got my balloons from the artillery people in the 1st Marine Brigade at Kaneohe Bay, which was why they were red and white. Balloons were what the cannon cockers used to figure out the wind and whatever else affected artillery rounds.

We did not have access to helium tanks, or any other easily transported gas tanks, and so we were stuck with using this antiquated artillery equipment. They made nitrogen gas for their balloons by sticking some chemicals in a garbage can full of water, and so we had to do the same thing. Think about the practicality of that, especially in hilly jungle!

We had to solve the problem of what kind of string to use on our balloons. Communications wire was something we had plenty of, and so we tried a single strand of that to anchor the balloon. Wrong! By the time the balloon got near the tree tops, sixty feet of communications wire weighed as much as the balloon, and the damn thing started dropping back to the ground. I went out to a sporting goods store and bought some fishing line.

How many balloons would be necessary? At first I thought three would do the job, but then we discovered that the density of the canopy cover prohibited our getting three balloons up in a straight line. We needed four to ensure a visible line of direction.

How about nighttime? The meteorologists at Kaneohe Bay put up night balloons all the time, and they used a water-chemical generator that lighted a bulb which was tied to the string just under the balloon. We found that by extending those wires from the generator to the light bulb, we could put the light inside the balloon itself. They looked really neat at night, but once again it didn't seem practical in hilly jungle.

After a month or so of working on all of this, we were ready to put on a demonstration.

Capt. Jim Loop, who had just left ANGLICO, was in VMA-214, the Blacksheep Squadron, at Kaneohe Bay, and he was selected to run the airborne portion of the exercise. He knew exactly what I was trying to do in that he had been in Thailand with me, and he was anxious to see it work.

We drove out to Kahuku early one morning and hauled that damn garbage can full of water up and down the hills in our weapons carrier until we got to the heaviest jungle canopy. That part of Oahu may all be condos today, but in the early sixties, the Kahuku area had some great jungle, with fantastic orchids.

We inflated the balloons with nitrogen gas and ran them up through the canopy. Jim Loop reported that four of them were exactly the right number to form a dotted line toward the target.

I had sent a team to the target area we had selected, and they were to listen to the time-rate-distance problem on the radio and ascertain that the A-4 was indeed over the target when I called the mark.

We were all set, and Jim Loop rolled into his low-level run that would carry him along the axis formed by the three white and one red balloon, and point him to the enemy.

The sleek A-4 Skyhawk streaked along the treetops, headed right for my balloons, all lined up perfectly—and the jet intakes swallowed four balloons, three white ones and one red one.

I never forgave Jim Loop for that.

A few days later, at the bar in the Camp Smith officers club, I bemoaned my balloon problems in the presence of some people from the CINCPAC staff. In the early sixties, the lowly little Air and Naval Gunfire Liaison Company was located in the same building as the commander in chief, Pacific, the old Aiea Naval Hospital, where our pistol range had once been the morgue.

After they expressed amusement at my sad story, a navy captain pulled me aside and told me quietly that the problem my balloons were designed to solve was about to go away. That was the first time I heard about the offset bombing capability of the A-6.

All a ground commander had to do was turn on an electronic signaling device, which was about the size of a suitcase in 1970, and the A-6 could do the rest.

Sure was a lot easier than carting a garbage can full of water just to watch some clown swallow the balloons. Sadly, however, the world never got to see the wondrous glow of my balloons at night.

Because I was the squadron commander in VMO-2, I was often called upon to conduct aerial tours for generals when they didn't have all day to see the countryside from a Huey.

You all do understand that the UH-1E Huey helicopter was the slowest flying machine in the world. It could perform a lot of missions, but it didn't perform any of them at an impressive rate of speed. One day back in the States, I was flying a Huey westward from Tucson to Yuma, Arizona, and a Greyhound bus passed me! Absolutely true. I was bucking a headwind, and the Interstate speed limit was still seventy miles per hour, and that sucker passed me!

Anyway, the generals had their lists of things they wanted to see, and I had my list of things I wanted them to see, and sometimes the generals got to see a lot more than they had bargained for.

One day I was flying the new assistant division commander around when he insisted on my making a low pass over the reconnaissance outpost on Hill 258. Those were the guys who dropped their pants for us. I was never able to explain that satisfactorily, and General Simmons was not amused.

Anyway, most of my points of interest were displays of bombing professionalism, and I mention them here because in 1970 dive-bombing was still an art form.

In addition to obvious points of pride like the A-6 bomb-created helicopter landing zones, I was particularly fond of an area of total devastation in the jungle no larger than a municipal swimming pool and filled with water the same color. It didn't look like much until I explained that the bombing that created the square pit had been done by two F-4 Phantoms, each making two runs—that in four separate bombing runs nothing missed the target. The pilot was someone whose name I have forgotten but whose personal call sign was Mauler.

A reconnaissance team had stumbled upon an enemy staging area, a small compound of huts well concealed under the trees, and they asked me to take it out. I ordered up a pair of F-4s, and when the jets were overhead, the Marines on the ground set fire to the huts and ran like hell.

The foliage was so dense that the smoke was barely visible. I marked the spot with a white phosphorous rocket as soon as the recon team was well clear of the area, and the Phantoms performed one of the slickest jobs of surgery I ever saw.

From there, I flew the generals over to Antenna Valley at the western end of the Que Son Mountains and showed them the scars of an F-4 strike that saved the lives of many Marines and involved professionalism and heroism so great that VMO-2 wrote the Phantom pilot up for what we hoped would result in a Navy Cross.

The weather had been horrible when that strike went in. The cloud layer had been below the tops of the hills surrounding the valley, and at first glance, Maj. John Morris of VMO-2 was certain no visual bombing was possible. But the lead F-4 pilot found a way down through a hole in the clouds and decided he could do the job if his pullout from the run was straight up. Not east or west, but straight up!

He did it twice. He twisted down through the holes in the overcast, dropped his Snake Eye bombs while heading straight at the side of a mountain, and pulled up vertically through the weather using afterburner to clear the tops of the hills, which were invisible in the clouds.

He and John Morris broke that enemy attack all by themselves, and it was a banner day for Marine Corps aviation.

The greatest single feat of marksmanship I ever witnessed was performed by a VMO-2 pilot, Maj. Carl Olsen, who relieved me as commanding officer when I rotated home. He hit a target the size of a man's head with a rocket.

A rifle company from the 1st Marines had flushed a covey of NVA troops, and one of the enemy soldiers had dived into a river to escape. The current carried him downstream, and he was out of small-arms range when Major Olsen arrived on the scene.

The company commander asked him to eliminate the fleeing enemy, and Carl told him that he would be happy to oblige, but that he was out of ammunition and had only one rocket left.

Carl saw the head of the man, now well downstream, took aim with his one rocket and fired, and the rest is history.

Hell of a shot. Of course there was no way to show that to the generals, but you can be certain I worked it into the conversation.

I really enjoyed conducting tours for infantry commanders and showing off what 1st Marine Air Wing could do. Today, ground commanders can pretty well expect "smart" weapons to remove surgically any enemy in front of them. But in 1970, eyeball dive bombing and rocket shooting were finely honed crafts.

Let me tell you about the day I almost blew the top of a mountain away with some thousand-pound bombs. I didn't mean to. It just worked out that way.

Picture it: a north-south ridgeline with a sizable, flat bulge near the middle.

The 51st ARVN had put a battalion into the eastern side of that flat spot, where they set up a base camp and ran patrols throughout the ridgeline. Unfortunately for them, the enemy did not want them there, and the government troops were getting bloody noses every time they stuck them out.

The enemy had to be removed from the area, and the method we chose for accomplishing the task entailed what we on the working level called a "Blivot Drop," but which has been recorded in the history books as Operation THRASH LIGHT.

I will describe the Blivot Drop firebombing raid in the next chapter, but before we could do that, we had to get the ARVN troops out of the way.

We were going to pull the battalion out with Marine helicopters, and I had a sizable roster of fixed-wing bombers on my knee board, both to use as protective cover and to blow away some prebriefed targets after the troops were safely out.

One of the bomber flights scheduled was a pair of A-6s making their first local appearance in the Da Nang area as eyeball bombers since their missions to Hanoi had been cancelled. Not too many of the A-6 pilots had experience in this arena, and so the CO and XO of VMA-242, Lt. Col. Stan Lewis and Maj. Carl Dubac, were flying the planes.

Because of the A-6's unique on-station capability, the ability to hang around for hours and hours without running out of gas, we had decided in the briefing that I would save them for last. They were armed with fifteen thousand-pound bombs apiece, and I planned to put that tonnage of hard bombs on what we thought to be a bunker complex. To my embarrassment, I would forget the size of those bombs in about twenty minutes.

My show was scheduled to begin at 0600. As fate would have it, the Viet Cong had scheduled their appearance two or three minutes earlier. Either that or their clocks were fast.

Just as all of the various aircraft were checking in on the radio, the enemy attacked. This is what the newspaper said:

AIR ATTACK REPELS REDS

DA NANG—A massive bombing attack by 1st MAW attack aircraft recently repelled a heavy attack on Special Forces and ARVN troops 35 miles south of Da Nang.

"Our mission was to provide cover while Thuong Duc Special Forces and an ARVN battalion were being extracted," said Lt. Col. J.M. Moriarty (Pensacola, Florida), VMO-2 commanding officer and pilot of the OV-10 controlling the action.

Just prior to the extraction a large enemy force launched a heavy attack with small arms and automatic weapons.

"Their timing was disastrous," Lt. Col. Moriarty stated. "We had an overwhelming superiority of air power available at the time."

The instructions of a radio operator assigned to the unit were so precise Lt. Col. Moriarty was able to direct air strikes within 15 meters of friendly positions.

"Despite the heavy volume of ground fire our aircraft on station were able to pinpoint their ordnance with devastating accuracy and the enemy withdrew," Lt. Col. Moriarty continued.

As a result of the close coordination between ground units and the aircraft, the helicopter extraction was completed without any further incidents.

There was a lot of accurate bombing, no doubt about that, but what caused Charlie to cut and run was a lapse of memory on my part—the size of those damn bombs.

The radio operator mentioned in the article was an Australian advisor to the 51st ARVN, and one of the bravest men I ever worked with. In stopping the initial assault, he marked the enemy with smoke, and I blasted away with twenty millimeter until I got some A-4s headed downhill with 250-pound Snake Eyes.

He called me to complain that my twenty-millimeter shell cases were falling on top of him and that they hurt. That's when I discovered that he was marking the enemy positions with hand-held smoke grenades! A man can only throw one of those things so far.

Then he called and asked me to stop the A-4s from pulling out so low. "Lost one the other day because of that," he explained as calmly as he might have spoken standing belly-up to the bar in the officers club, "and I'd hate to have another on me conscience!"

We bombed and strafed. The A-4s and F-4s bombed, and I strafed. In dodging the enemy's return fire, I pulled a stunt that morning that I had been taught seventeen years earlier while I was a cadet in flight training.

On a rainy day in 1953, when we could not fly, a navy flight instructor taught us some of the tricks of the trade used in attacking enemy ships in the Pacific during World War II.

"The Jap gunners had been taught to lead the nose of our planes as we pulled away from the ship," he explained, "and so, what we did was stomp hard on a rudder pedal and fly away in one hellacious skid, damn near flying sideways. The gunners led the nose, which wasn't pointed anywhere near the direction we were actually flying, and we dodged a lot of bullets that way."

I hadn't spent one minute thinking about that since I first heard it so many years before, but the human brain seems to have a way of storing survival tips.

When I shot at the enemy, he shot back at me—which was fair, but not a whole hell of a lot of fun. As I pulled off target, I jammed the left rudder as hard as I could.

Sure enough, the tracers whizzed by well to the left of me, just the way my flight instructor had said they would. Wow! Was I ever impressed with myself.

Like the Ancient Mariner, I told my tale to everyone who would listen for about a month after that, and because I was the squadron commander, the lieutenants and captains were polite enough to listen. God, how I must have bored them! But it kept me from having to explain how I damn near blew everybody away.

We beat off two attacks, everything calmed down, and I called in the helicopters to commence the airlift.

And sure enough, Charlie mounted a third assault. And all I had left was that flight of A-6s.

I put the helicopters on hold, called down the A-6s, and set up an attack on the position from which the enemy had come. I planted a white phosphorous rocket on a trail slightly downhill on the west side of the ridgeline, and pulled around to monitor the bomb run.

The lead A-6 was lined up perfectly, and I cleared him to drop—and found myself flying wing on a stick of five one-thousand-pound bombs!

My brain was thinking five-hundred pounders, and even at that I was pressing the safety limits. When I saw the size of those bombs, only about twenty meters away from my left wingtip, I demonstrated hand-eye coordination of Olympic proportions.

I switched the radio to FM frantically and keyed the mike button as I pulled away with all the strength in my right arm. "Put your f——king heads down!" I screamed.

Well, sir, when those bombs hit it was one of the most impressive experiences of my life. My little airplane was rocked by bomb blast with a jolt like a sledge hammer. The entire valley shook. The OV-10 went inverted for an instant, but I was so busy pulling Gs that it didn't make a whole lot of difference. I pulled around to see the entire area cloaked in smoke. Debris flew everywhere.

The aerial observer and I looked on in silence as the dense, acrid smoke lifted. What would we see? Were any friendly troops injured? How much of the ridgeline was left?

Five distinct craters, brown and ugly and still steaming from the horrendous blast, appeared where before the enemy had mounted their attacks. I was hesitant about calling the second A-6 that orbited above.

The Australian advisor spoke first. "Uhh, you aren't going to do that again, are you, mate?"

"I hadn't planned on it."

"Good," he said with a sigh. "I think we can begin the airlift now."

As the newspaper said, we completed the airlift without any further incident.

THE GREAT BLIVOT DROP

Nineteen seventy was the year of the Blivot Drop, one of the true innovations of the war in Vietnam. Locally created and locally produced, it was a major drama about which very little has been recorded in the history books.

This amazing method of carrying fire and destruction to the enemy was born in January of that year, nurtured and tested during the spring, executed in June, and abandoned before the year was out.

It was abandoned for several reasons, not the least of which was the fact that 1st Marine Air Wing ran out of garbage cans.

Let me tell you about the Blivot Drop from beginning to end. It's a fascinating story of innovation, ingenuity, and heroic efforts, involving the combined assets of 1st Marine Air Wing with outside logistics help from III Marine Amphibious Force.

BACKGROUND

In the early days of the Marine Corps' war, back in 1965, we were faced with a worrisome problem regarding our newly developing airfield at Chu Lai, some sixty miles south of Da Nang. Overlooking that coastal base, which was being constructed right on the sands of the South China Sea, was an east-west mountain ridge from which it was feared Marines would receive continuous harassing fire similar to that which the French had received at Dien Bien Phu in 1954. In fact, the new fortress at Chu Lai was sometimes referred to derisively as "Dien Bien Phu East."

The air force had a simple solution to our problem. They would defoliate the mountain and eliminate all cover and concealment. If the enemy couldn't hide, he couldn't set up his rockets. And because no one could think of a better way to do it than by firebombing the mountain, they were given the go-ahead.

Now, this was in 1965. No one had thought of Agent Orange yet. They would turn to that later as a result of what I am about to tell you, proving that one total fiasco can indeed be followed by an absolute disaster.

The air force's solution entailed firebombing the mountain until it was completely denuded, and so they did. For hours and hours, plane after plane flew over the mountain and unloaded incendiary fire bombs and anything else that would start a fire. Soon the entire ridgeline would be ablaze.

The smoke was visible for miles, and the heat from the burning mountain intense. So intense, in fact, that it created its own thunderstorm. Which put out the fires.

This humbling lesson led to a search for a better way to get rid of cover and concealment, one which would not be self-destructive—and the rest, as they say, is history. I will admit, however, that had I been involved in the problem at that time, I too would have been in favor of a chemical that could be sprayed over enemy territory and which would cause the plant life to strangle itself. What could be the harm in something as simple as that?

SITUATION

How best to employ the impressive lifting capacity of the giant CH-53 helicopter.

When the CH-53 Sea Stallion arrived in Vietnam, it was considered so precious, so expensive, that the Marine Corps would not permit its use as a tactical flying machine. It was looked upon as a helicopter version of an ordinary transport plane that could land in places the C-130 could not, and it was employed accordingly.

This caused great anguish and gnashing of teeth on the part of the pilots who flew them. They lived among the tactical helicopter pilots in Marine Aircraft Group 16, men who flew boldly into the jaws of death daily, and an ego problem of great proportions gave rise to a demand on their part for a piece of the action.

An example of their embarrassment: CH-53 pilots earned a leg on a twenty-mission Air Medal each time they landed in a safe and secure landing zone, and there was one particular mission that resupplied regiments and fire support artillery bases all over the 1st Marine Division's tactical area, and which required exactly twenty landings. One day's flying equaled one Air Medal, and it was an extremely popular mission among senior officers who popped up from all over the wing to fly in the copilot's seat once a month.

In the MAG-16 officers club at night, one had only to listen in order to locate the tables occupied by CH-53 pilots. While most of the bar buzzed with dramatic narrations of that day's war stories, the pilots who flew the "Heavy Haulers" invented new and aggressive uses for their airplanes, and the later the hour, the more inventive the concepts. Turning the helicopter into a giant gunship was very popular during the 1969-70 monsoon season.

Late one rainy night in January, just after I joined VMO-2, but before we moved to the Da Nang Air Base a few miles away, four of us sat around in Lt. Col. Andy Andrus's hut, cursing the monsoon weather and discussing those same CH-53 concepts over a bottle of fine cognac—which meant that as the evening grew on, we became more and more brilliant. And it was there that the Blivot Drop concept was hatched.

All of us were squadron commanders, although Andy Andrus had just left his squadron and was now the group operations officer. As our blood-alcohol counts increased, the seriousness of the war decreased.

Andy was a pioneer in the CH-53 program and had led the first squadron of them into Vietnam. A few days earlier he had been talking to some Korean Marine officers who had told him of a demonstration they had seen in which an army CH-47 helicopter had dropped some fifty-five gallon drums of napalm on a target, after which a gunship ignited the mess with a white phosphorous rocket. Andy was smitten with the idea and convinced that the CH-53 was the logical vehicle to do the job.

The rest of us were an easy audience. At that stage of the bottle, we could have become enthusiastic about almost anything.

He proposed that a load of fifty-five-gallon drums of napalm be carried to a target area in a cargo net slung under a CH-53 and dumped from some altitude which would ensure that they broke apart upon hitting the ground, splatting the jelly-petroleum mix all around. The mess would be ignited by a white phosphorous rocket fired from either an OV-10 or an AH-1G Cobra gunship.

We discussed this at length, and by the time the bottle was empty, we were convinced that we had revolutionized warfare.

The label Blivot Drop was applied that night, and it stuck. A blivot, as everyone knows, is defined as two pounds of fecal matter stuffed into a one-pound bag.

After a couple of days of cold sobriety it still seemed to be a good idea, and we knew we were on to something.

The wing Commander at the time, Maj. Gen. Gay Thrash, loved innovation as well as the next guy, and he gave the go-ahead to MAG-16 to work out the details and find out whether or not the concept was practical.

We selected an open area of terrain between the airfield and the famous old Marble Mountain itself, and went to work.

My role was minor. We had just moved VMO-2 from Marble Mountain to Da Nang, and all I did was show up on time and fire a willie peter rocket into the goo once it had splattered. Getting the barrels to fall properly required a great deal of trial and error, however, and the CH-53 people busted their tails working it all out.

I'll never forget the sight of one CH-53 pilot trying to rid himself of a barrel that had gotten hung up in the cargo net after a practice drop. It just wouldn't come loose from the net that sagged under the plane, and we all flew out over the ocean to watch him jerk the helicopter up and down as though he was trying to shake dog crap from the bottom of his shoe. I didn't know a helicopter could do that and still keep the rotor screwed on. On his third or fourth try, the drum of napalm finally fell free and splashed into the South China Sea, and I machine-gunned it into submission as the helicopters flew back into the airfield without having to jettison a valuable cargo net.

Twenty drums of napalm per cargo net dropped from a thousand feet seemed to be the best solution. The drums would burst properly when dropped from eight hundred feet, but one thousand feet was chosen as a drop altitude to appease those who wanted the expensive helicopters to remain out of small-arms firing range.

Tactically, the flights would entail a three-plane V formation, and the only problem remaining was one of accuracy, a simple one-potato, two-potato calculation as it turned out.

As is the case with most military operations, the tactics were simple, but the logistics were not.

The barrels had to be assembled and filled with napalm and staged on cargo nets, and this had to be done where the dangerous mixture was far enough away from men and equipment, yet still in a secure area. A short, crosswind runway at the south end of the Marble Mountain Air Facility was selected as the staging area so that if the Viet Cong did manage to blow it up, the worst that would happen would see a lot of sand turned into glass.

MISSION

Find an appropriate target.

During the first week in June, a massive air strike was developed to destroy what was believed to be the headquarters for all enemy activity in the local area, an organization which the Viet Cong called "Front Four."

The heavily forested target area was about forty miles southwest of Da Nang, on the southern face of steeply rising terrain that was capped by a high plateau.

Beginning early in the morning, A-4 Skyhawks and A-6 Intruders and F-4 Phantoms would make repeated air strikes, and for the first time the CH-53 would make its appearance as a tactical plane and firebomb the hillside.

VMO-2 had nothing to do with the location of the target, and we were not as familiar with the area as we might have been. I personally considered the high ground north of the targeted area to be a more likely site, mainly because a couple of days earlier I had spotted what I was certain was a basketball court under some trees there. Of course, we were never able to find it again, and I had to keep my mouth shut lest someone question my sanity.

Because the hillside was steep, it was decided that the firebombing would take place about halfway down in hopes of starting a fire which would sweep upward and burn out the spot that had been "pinpointed" electronically.

It was a grand morning of bombing and rocketing and firebombing, and everyone had a marvelous time—and to the best of my knowledge we never hit a thing.

Toward the end of the raid, when the excitement of the chase had waned and the command-and-control helicopter had gone home, I still had a flight of F-4s overhead which had been scheduled for targets of opportunity.

Nobody seemed to care much, and so I took the opportunity to hit an alternate target, which I just happened to find in the high plateau to the north in the vicinity of the NVA basketball court. I probably didn't hit anything there either.

The results of the firebombing were not good. It was pretty much like tossing an egg against your refrigerator door; all the mess was downhill from where it made impact. Also, the mountainside was so wet at that early hour of the morning that we couldn't get a really good fire started.

As far as I was concerned, the only value of the raid lay in the fact that we had been able to work out the tactics and logistics for the Blivot Drop. Everything else was a waste of time.

We ran four waves of the three plane flights that morning, which dumped 240 barrels of napalm on the steep slopes, and we worked out the timing and control and aiming procedures. We now knew how to do it, but never again would we schedule a Blivot Drop so early in the morning, or on such steep terrain.

But a mountain ridgeline? Now, there was a perfect target!

Ever since we found our first indications of an enemy buildup in the mountains above Thuong Duc, intelligence gathering had made a stronger and stronger case for a raid there. The place was crawling with bad guys, and they weren't even keeping it a secret.

Early one morning, on a 76-Alpha flight, I was approaching the Thuong Duc area at first light in hopes of catching Charlie with his pants down, when we received a frantic call from the Special Forces outpost there. They were under a heavy mortar attack and wanted me to put a stop to it.

I put on full power and called the Direct Air Support Center for some bombers as I raced to the scene. I knew where the Special Forces camp was, but I had no idea where the mortars were coming from, and so I asked what I thought to be a perfectly logical question. Had he, I asked, been able to perform any crater analysis, a procedure whereby the angle of the mortar fuse could be used to determine the direction from which it was fired?

When a mortar round hits the ground and explodes, the fuse generally remains intact, and by inserting sticks into the remains of the fuses, a guy who knows what he's doing can get a good estimate of the direction of fire. Did he, then, perform crater analysis?

"Man!" he yelled, "if I stick my head out of this hole, I'll *be* crater analysis!"

That was amusing, but not a whole hell of a lot of help. The aerial observer and I picked out some locations that were in the vicinity of the approximate range of a sixty-millimeter mortar, but all we did was bomb and strafe a lot of trees.

There was no serious damage, and none of the villagers had been hurt, but the attack pretty well proved that something had to be done out there.

Thuong Duc was the responsibility of the Vietnamese Army, and so the first response was to insert a battalion from the 51st ARVN Regiment into the middle of the mountain ridgeline to find the enemy.

They did, and they got their clocks cleaned.

The next step was a joint ARVN/1st Marine Air Wing action.

The plan was fairly simple. We would heli-lift a fresh ARVN battalion into positions at the southern tip of the ridgeline, then fly the empty helicopters to the central position and evacuate the now decimated unit. This is what we were doing when I thought I had almost blown them and the mountaintop away.

The next morning we would use the Blivot Drop to burn the ridgeline away in a systematic progression of firebomb drops which would be followed by the ARVN troops as soon as the ground cooled.

I'll never forget the formal briefing for the operation at wing headquarters. It was scheduled for 1400, just a few hours after we had swapped the ARVN battalions, "without any incident," and K. D. Waters and I arrived early, mainly because it was a hot day and the briefing room was air-conditioned.

The wing headquarters building was the same structure that had housed III Marine Amphibious Force headquarters when we first arrived in 1965, and the briefing room was the exact spot where I had toiled away day and night as the director of the command center.

Major Waters and I took seats in folding chairs in the back, which put us above and behind the soft, padded chairs in the front row which were reserved for colonels and maybe the assistant wing commander. For the first time I noticed that the floor tiles were identical to the ones in our office at VMO-2.

As we waited, two young Marines entered the conference room, carrying a large aerial photograph mosaic. The clerks propped it up on an A-frame in the front of the room, beside an oversized map of the Da Nang area and directly in front of the general's richly padded swivel chair with two stars embroidered in the upholstery.

A highly polished and freshly scrubbed captain from wing G-2 (intelligence) marched into the room and stepped up on the front tier with the colonels' chairs. He snapped into a parade rest and appraised the positioning of the mosaic.

"A little to the right, Marines. That's well." He seemed satisfied, left the room, and K. D. and I wondered where the captain might have gone to school. The inevitable oxymoron regarding military intelligence was discussed.

We waited some more, and K. D., who always had excess energy, decided to inspect the map and mosaic. He plodded down the steps and went over to the briefing aid, and within seconds found the outlet he had been seeking.

"Jesus H. Christ! Will you take a look at this? This is the wrong ridgeline!"

I joined him at the photograph and studied it with some amusement. Both of us had practically memorized the terrain, and there was no question that the mosaic covered another ridgeline entirely, one which lay just west of the target area.

Major Waters was livid, and his comments on the photo squadron were not complimentary. I tried to make light of it, but K. D. wasn't buying.

"Doesn't really make a big rat's ass, K. D. We know where we're going to drop the stuff, and that's really all that matters. Let's ignore it and let the briefing officers make their brownie points with the general. We can ask for post-action photography, and then the whole world will know."

He might have persuaded me to blow the whistle then and there, but the door flew open at that moment and the room filled quickly with briefing officers and senior staff officers and the commanders of the units involved with the Blivot Drop. At precisely 1400, the general himself walked in, everyone snapped to attention, and I discovered that I was the only person in the room wearing a flight suit. Everyone else was starched and polished. The wing commander, Maj. Gen. Gay Thrash, nodded and smiled, and I tried to hide behind the guy in front of me. The general sat down in the chair with the stars.

"Good afternoon, General." A tall, hawk-faced briefing officer whipped his hand with his pointer and cleared his throat. "Tomorrow morning, 1st Marine Air Wing, in conjunction with the 51st ARVN Regiment, will remove the enemy threat to the Thuong Duc Valley in a coordinated air/ground effort . . ."

It went on like that for about thirty minutes, with all of the briefers pointing to the map of the wrong ridgeline. I thought at first that K. D. was taking notes, but it turned out that he was working on a watch bill, or something similar. He couldn't stand being bored.

But we both came up with a start when the senior briefer announced that the operation was to be code-named Operation THRASH LIGHT.

First there were the air force Arc Light bombing missions. Then came the A-6 Flash Light missions, which were miniature replications of the B-52 raids—and just as useless. And now "Thrash Light!"

Major General Thrash winced. The things people would do to suck up to their bosses.

For the record, that was the only time any of us ever heard that code name until the history books were published years later. To those of us who invented it and executed it, it would always be a Blivot Drop.

EXECUTION (PLUS COMMAND AND CONTROL)

The Blivot Drop was scheduled to begin at 0700, a compromise between air and ground factions that was settled finally by the meteorologist. Ground commanders clamored for the operation to begin at dawn—not for any particular advantage, but rather out of a sense of tradition. Aviation planners, on the other hand, wanted to wait until later in the morning, when the foliage would be dry and easier to ignite.

The aerology officer, a warrant officer, settled the matter, explaining the high probability of thundershowers in the middle of the afternoon. The operation was to last for eight hours, and it was wiser to chance some morning dew than to try to start a fire in the rain. Many of us remembered the air force fiasco in 1965, and we supported the compromise.

I took off at 0610 in order to check the weather before the helicopters launched on the exacting time tables.

Dawn was just beginning to illuminate the mountains to the west as we climbed for altitude, and soon the coastal lowlands would bustle with activity.

Cook fires shimmered around camps in the field as infantrymen filled their stomachs before setting out on the long day's patrols. In a distant valley, I could see a lone flare drifting down into the bowl of darkness, and the rivers to the west began to take form as the rising sun chased the stars away.

I called the wing operations center. "Joyride? Hostage Six

airborne at one zero. Mission Eighty-two. My Echo Tango Romeo, Whiskey Charlie.''

I estimated my time of return to be when completed.

Over the years almost everything in the war had been reduced to a code, much of it a waste of time. Using the letter *R* for radio, for instance, ground Marines now referred to their radios as Romeos. *T* for tank became Tiger, became Pussycat, and sometimes I wondered if wars weren't designed for twelve-year-olds. Highways were ''red lines,'' dirt roads were ''brown lines,'' and rivers were ''blue lines''—just the way they appeared in the funny papers, the colored maps.

''Roger, Hostage Six. Joyride copies Mission Eighty-two. Thank you for calling Joyride.''

The aerial observer was busy in the rear cockpit, switching from frequency to frequency on the FM radio in order to get artillery clearance through the regimental areas. The 5th Marines were trying to run as many artillery fire missions as possible before their guns were silenced for the eight hours of heavy helicopter traffic through their turf, and I had to make a wide detour.

The weather in the target area was good when I arrived—some early morning mist in the river below, but nothing more. I called to my backup pilot, Lt. Ken Ellison, who took off twenty minutes behind me and who would relay messages to the CH-53 pilots who waited nervously in their cockpits.

''Hostage Dragon? Hostage Six. The mission is a *go*.''

I eased the power levers back and orbited the ridgeline lazily, studying the terrain for a few minutes before the jets and helicopters arrived. The ARVN battalion at the south end of the ridge looked like a Boy Scout encampment and showed no signs of preparation. They were eating whatever it was Vietnamese ate for breakfast in the field, and they appeared to be in no hurry.

I decided to run the first flight of A-4s right smack in front of the ARVN wire instead of holding them in reserve. The planes were armed with napalm, and the close-in fires would give the CH-53s a better picture of the target.

I instructed the aerial observer to warn the ARVN, but I did not turn up the volume on my FM radio receiver. I let the AO listen to the singsong shouting of the Vietnamese as they all got together on the same frequency.

I adjusted the sync of the engines as I banked over the ARVN camp. I would have to direct the A-4s in on a course almost perpendicular to the narrow ridgeline to keep the loaded aircraft from running in over the friendlies' heads. I maneuvered to a run-in heading that would cover as much of the target as possible and still run parallel to the ARVN lines. I flew the course and wrote down the compass heading: 048 degrees.

Ken Ellison, a tall, handsome Princeton graduate whose first name was Ketron, called from ten thousand feet and announced that he was anchored overhead. In addition to being my backup, he would also marshal the many flights of jets and pass them down when they were needed.

His call was followed by that of the first flight of A-4s, and the attack jets joined Ellison's OV-10 at ten thousand feet.

Tension began to mount. I would start the action as soon as the first flight of CH-53s crossed the IP and checked in on the radio. It would take them six minutes to fly from their initial point to the target, and I briefed the A-4 pilots on the runs I wanted from them.

I waited. A lone Huey whirred in from the east. I had been warned that the wing commander might come out to watch.

"Hostage Six? This is Peppermint, inbound from the east. I have Moment Six aboard." Andy Andrus loved that call sign, Peppermint. Moment was the call sign for the wing, and of course Six designated the commander.

"Roger, Peppermint. Come on in. The water's fine."

I wondered if we didn't have our priorities a little screwed up. A CH-46, even if it carried only one or two troops, required a gunship escort, but an unarmed Huey carrying a general didn't.

I was starting to feel pregame jitters and stomach butterflies as I searched the river valley for the giant helicopters and their deadly loads of napalm. Soon I caught sight of the first flight of three just entering the area from the flat Arizona Territory. The napalm looked so innocent hanging from the bellies of the planes, like ordinary resupply cargo.

"Dimmer One Dash One approaching the initial."

I recognized the voice of Lt. Col. Charlie Block, the CH-53 squadron commander. The helicopters neared the jagged and mostly submerged remnants of a bridge which we had chosen as the initial reference point.

It was 0654. Perfect timing. It would be three in the afternoon, eight waves later, before Colonel Block called in as Dimmer Eight Dash One.

"Roger, Dimmer. Continue." Then I called the A-4 flight leader.

"Okay, Tomcat. Come on down and let's go to work. I'll put out marks at six and twelve o'clock."

The lead A-4 armed his switches and maneuvered to a roll-in position—0655.

The aerial observer called the ARVN advisor and warned him to keep the soldiers' heads down.

"Hostage Six in for the mark."

I rolled into a dive on the 048 degree course, took aim, and planted a white phosphorous rocket twenty meters from the barbed wire at the northwest corner of the camp. The second cloud billowed equally close to the northeast corner.

"Tomcat has your marks. Rolling in now."

"Roger, Tomcat. Careful now. Don't drift to the right."

I watched the A-4 carefully and maneuvered my plane so as to be directly overhead when the jet raced in low for the drop.

"Wings level."

"Continue, Tomcat."

I strained against G forces. I did not clear the A-4 "Hot." A few degrees variance could be disastrous—0656. The CH-53s were getting closer.

Abruptly, I horsed the OV-10 into inverted flight, and held the plane upside down with top left rudder and forward stick. Only fifty feet separated our planes as the jet thundered underneath.

"You're hot! Standby. Mark!"

The napalm tumbled to the ground, and the A-4 streaked out into the broad valley to the east. I released the unnatural control pressures, and the OV-10 snapped around in a steep right turn.

"Dash Two rolling in." Sunlight reflected off the second A-4's wings as it turned in.

"Okay, Dash Two. Along the left side of your leader's hits. To your left. Steady. That's it. You're hot. Stand by. Mark!" 0659.

"Right on, Dash Two. Okay, Dragon, send them home."

I was already turning to the south as I spoke, and I didn't have time to think about the A-4s any more. The CH-53s churned inbound, flying a thousand feet above the ridgeline. They would be over the drop point in less than a minute. No time for me to climb to much altitude. Damn! I should have thought of that.

"Okay, Dimmer, turn in to the ridge in front of the friendlies and drop on the other side of the fire. I'll mark the spot. Don't overfly the friendlies, now."

"Dimmer, roger!"

The voice spat tacks. How could I even think he would overfly the friendlies?

"Scarface? You ready?" I called to the Cobra gunship pilot who would ignite the napalm and, perversely, I enjoyed the iciness in Charlie Block's voice. Whether he had planned to overfly friendlies or not, he sure as hell wouldn't now.

"Scarface Eleven is ready, willing, and able, pardner!"

God! That was all we needed then—a mouthy Cobra pilot.

I was unable to climb to an altitude high enough for a good rocket shot. I horsed the OV-10 into a shallow run from about six hundred feet above the ridge and calculated a gunsight lead for a really bad angle and airspeed. *Whoomph!*

Perfect! The white phosphorous cloud billowed almost in the exact center of the ridgeline and ten meters north of the fires. Hell of a shot, Moriarty!

Lieutenant Colonel Block flew up the western edge of the ARVN camp, flanked on either side by wingmen, and the cargo nets swayed with the heavy loads of napalm as he turned in. The white smoke from my rocket slid under his nose.

"Now!"

The front straps of the cargo nets fell away as the crew chiefs of all three helicopters tripped the release switches. Down rained the napalm, sixty drums of it.

"Bombs away!"

Block sounded as though he were having fun.

The napalm splattered as the drums smashed into the ground and flattened on impact. The jelly oozed into every hole and crevice.

The Cobra pilot fired a searing rocket into the center of the slimy napalm, and it erupted instantly into a raging holocaust. He felt the intense heat through the gunship canopy as though he had opened a furnace door, and he wasted no time turning back toward the initial point where he would pick up the third wave of helicopter bombers.

"Man, that stuff's hot!"

I lined up for my next marking run, and this time I was able to get enough altitude for a respectable shot.

"Dimmer One Dash Two turning in."

"Roger, Dimmer. Continue."

From here on it was easy. I fired another rocket, and the second wave of CH-53s dropped their loads. Another Cobra, Scarface Five this time, torched it off.

The third and fourth flights repeated the process then took up a course for Marble Mountain, leaving over a hundred meters of ridgeline burning, completely devastated. I flew low over the charred and still-burning ground looking for evidence of the enemy and hoping I wouldn't see any. I didn't mind greasing a guy in a fair fight, but this left me a little empty.

I called Lieutenant Ellison.

"Okay, Dragon. Send down your first load of hard bombs."

Thirty-five miles away, at the Marble Mountain helicopter base, the seldom used crosswind runway was a frenzy of activity. The little runway was the staging area for the blivots, and was dotted with stacks of fifty-five gallon drums of napalm, piled on nets like cans in a grocery store display.

Lieutenant Colonel Block led his flight of three into the refueling area. The planes took on fuel, then air-taxied to the staging area, where each pilot followed the signals of a taxi director and maneuvered to a hover over one of the stacks.

Ground crew Marines, protected from the swirling sand by goggles and ear protectors, swarmed under the huge, screaming helicopters and hooked up the nets. The pilots, on Block's command, pulled up on their collective control levers, and the planes ascended slowly as the nets pulled taut like tow sacks.

Satisfied that the loads were secure, they flew off on the return trip to Thuong Duc as the second wave of planes behind them dropped off their old nets and air taxied to the fuel pits. It was 0735. Block would be back over the target for the 0800 drop.

At ten thousand feet over the target, Lieutenant Ellison played the role of Approach Control at a busy airport.

"Lovebug 523, you're cleared into the bombing pattern. Descend to eight thousand immediately. Lovebug 525, descend to ten thousand. Lovebug 527, descend to twelve thousand."

Odd numbers meant the flights were scheduled. Any flight of jets that was scrambled from the hot pad to meet some emergency was assigned an even event number.

I took control of the first flight.

"Lovebug 523? Hostage Six. I have your target. Ready to copy?"

"Roger, Hostage. Ready to copy."

"Your target is a ravine on the west side of this ridge. Run-in heading, zero seven two. Pull out right. Two runs. Four bombs each run. Target elevation eight hundred and rising at twelve o'clock. Minimum altitude Papa Delta. (That meant pilot's discretion.) Friendly troops one hundred and seventy-five meters south.''

I briefed the mission by the book, then I put out the mark, and the F-4 pilot put four bombs squarely on target.

"Good show, Lovebug. Dash Two. From your leader's hits, come twelve o'clock, twenty meters.''

After a while you learned to accommodate young jet pilots whose concepts of distances over the ground were invariably wrong. I wanted to move the bombs forty meters, so I asked for twenty.

I ran two flights of F-4s on that ravine, which we had selected as the most obvious escape route for any bad guys who might panic at the fire bombing. The area lay splintered and smoking, and I flew down, low over the target. Nothing. The churned earth was bright green where the bombs had exploded in heavy foliage. The shredded leaves had fallen back to the ground as though nature was impatient to put life back into the soil.

"Hostage Six? Dimmer Two Dash One approaching the initial.''

Time for me to get back to work.

By three o'clock in the afternoon, the Thuong Duc ridgeline was a blackened mess. The only part of the ridge that wasn't black was a big brown spot where a bomb had missed and crunched up the soot.

K. D. Waters and I had traded off, each taking his turns at controlling the operation, and I was there for the finale.

It wasn't a whole hell of a lot of fun. I watched the ARVN troops pick their way through the charred soot and ashes and around the flattened napalm drums, somehow orange from the fires. What a mess—and all because VMO-2 had gotten suspicious over a cook fire.

It would be a couple of days before the body count came in, and everyone knew the Vietnamese commander would inflate the number tenfold.

The history book says the results were questionable. I was controlling the operation, and unless someone lied to me, I'm here to tell you that the body count was zero.

It was one hell of an operation though, and we might have done it again, except that the only fifty-five gallon drums left in Quang Nam Province were a few garbage cans no one was willing to part with. We dropped about two thousand barrels that day.

Hell of a show!

FORCE RECONNAISSANCE AND PARACHUTE JUMPING

Let me tell you a couple of short stories about Force Reconnaissance operations during 1970. I only got to work with them twice, but the two operations, one involving a helicopter insertion and the other a night parachute drop, will point out that while the super grunts had been reduced to a platoon-size operation by the time I got to VMO-2, they were still "Swift, Silent, and Deadly"—as opposed to division recon, which some of our pilots referred to "Swift, Silent, and Surrounded" because of the large number of emergency extracts that required so much of our attention.

In fact, for their last months in Vietnam, Force Recon was actually attached to division reconnaissance, a point some of the more dedicated super grunts would rather forget. But that's an administrative technicality.

In January of 1970, it was still called a company and stationed at our rapidly shrinking base at Hue/Phu Bai, just outside the old imperial city north of Da Nang. They were still performing their stealthy snoop-and-poop missions along the out-of-bounds area on the Laotian border.

On 25 January, just four days after I joined VMO-2, I was part of a helicopter insert package that would put a recon team into the A Shau Valley, Tiger Valley, which had been a major battleground for a couple of years, but was now deserted and part of unclaimed Indian country—which meant that the North Vietnamese pretty well controlled all of it.

Four Cobra gunships and two OV-10s had flown up from Marble Mountain to join four CH-46 Sea Stallions from Dick Bancroft's HMM-365, one of the squadrons still based at Phu Bai, which had once belonged to Marine Aircraft Group 36 before that helicopter group was pulled out and relocated at Futemma on Okinawa.

We briefed the mission in Maj. Alex Lee's Force Recon operations hut, and the tactics were fairly complicated—intentionally so because the whole purpose of the insertion was to confuse the enemy. There were to be six separate landings in the hilltops surrounding the valley.

We would split up into two flights, each with two transports, two gunships, and one OV-10 overhead for whatever support might be needed. Each flight would make three separate landings on scattered hilltops, and Charlie would have to figure out which one, if any, had actually landed Marines.

At that time of the war, the NVA bad guys were making a lot of noise to the effect that they had entire battalions dedicated to the death and destruction of the famous Marine Force Reconnaissance teams. They had printed leaflets stating the fact and had even put it out on the radio. The A Shau Valley was theirs, and they intended to keep it that way.

How serious they were was anyone's guess, but we classified it as pregame hype and didn't give it too much thought—although I suspect that the young Marines who were about to venture out into their claimed domain had good reason to be nervous as hell.

I know for a fact that the team leader was edgy enough to have lost his sense of humor.

When the briefing was over and we were leaving the building to head for our airplanes, I ran into the young lieutenant—literally ran into him.

Those of you who have participated in special operations of this nature know very well the pregame jitters the lower intestinal tract goes through. If you've never done it, just remember how active your bowels were just before a big athletic event, or maybe your first starring role in a play.

On my way to the door, the team leader came out of the bathroom after his third or fourth emergency trip, and was so busy tying his costume back together he wasn't looking where he was going.

I say "costume" because the clothing Recon Marines wore in the field could hardly be classified as uniforms. Everything metallic was either tied down, blackened, or rubberized. The floppy hat had no shape at all, and the greasepaint on their necks, faces, and hands made them look more like some monster that came from the deep than anything human.

The young man let the bathroom door slam shut as he fumbled with his equipment, and charged right into me. He was a big boy who could just as easily have been suited up in a Pittsburg Steeler uniform, and the laws of physics dictated that if either of us was going to bounce, it was going to be me.

I recovered before I hit the opposite wall, and presuming that a huge lieutenant might be apologetic for running down a small lieutenant colonel, I chose to make light of it, considering the circumstances and all.

"Wow!" I exclaimed, marveling at his appearance. "Your mother sure dresses you funny!"

I thought that was pretty funny, but he did not. The whites of his eyes grew until his jolly-green-giant face took on equine proportions, and I knew then that any NVA troops who got in his way were in for a rough go of it for the next week or so. Unless he got his green hands around my throat, which for an instant was a distinct possibility.

Well, anyway, the OV-10s took off first, and we proceeded out to the valley, initially as weather planes. It was monsoon season, and the weather was iffy on the coast, but the valley turned out to be fairly clear with a lot of sunlight, and we called back that the mission was a go.

I was not in charge of anything on this flight. I was flying as a backup to Capt. Denny Herbert in order that I might learn how it was done, and the entire operation was an air show in itself, as carefully choreographed as anything the Blue Angels ever staged.

The scene was an elongated valley, about four miles from north to south and maybe a mile across, with an abandoned air strip at the north end—the same one where that air force major won a Medal of Honor landing his AD Skyraider to pick up a downed pilot a couple of years earlier.

The two helicopter flights went into their shell-game routine, flitting about the mountaintops, landing first here, then there, until even I couldn't remember which flight the reconnaissance team was on.

Captain Herbert and I put on an air show of our own, snarling around the valley and looking menacing. I say snarling, not because we were flying so fast, but simply because that's the sort of noise the OV-10 made.

There were no radio transmissions until the operation was completed and the planes departed the valley. I really liked that. A well-planned and well-briefed tactical flight should obviate the need for radio chatter, and for thirty minutes, ten airplanes darted around in what appeared to be a random, uncoordinated, training mission.

When it involved working with other flights and ground units most of VMO-2's work required a great deal of radio chatter, and this was refreshing professionalism. I wanted to tell that to the helicopter pilots, but we flew the OV-10s directly back to Marble Mountain when we were finished, and I didn't get the chance.

The team was in, and the NVA had no idea where. A few days later they were extracted without incident. The same choreography was used to confuse the enemy so that they would not know where the Marines had been.

Whatever they accomplished was none of my business at the time, and so I cannot report on it. But the shell-game insertion technique was an important development in the art of fighting against guerrilla forces, and I mention it in case we have to do it again someday.

The parachute operations came a few months later, after what was left of Force Recon had been reduced to a platoon-size unit and moved down to the Da Nang area.

There were a series of small villages about thirty miles northwest of Da Nang with the improbable name of Ruong Ruong. When the villagers of Vietnam used up the ground around their huts and animal pens, and the area was no longer habitable, they simply moved a hundred yards or so away and built new huts. And so it was not unusual for four or five village areas to exist under the same name. Intelligence information indicated that the area known as Ruong Ruong was well trafficked by the bad guys, and division thought that it would be a good idea to put a reconnaissance team into the hills north of the villages and find out what was going on.

The area was outside the division TAOR, tactical area of responsibility, and so Force Recon was given the task. The unit commander, a major whose name I have forgotten, thought a night parachute jump into the hills would be an exciting way to do it.

That's where I came in. Not only was the OV-10 a perfect airplane for the airborne delivery of Marines, but my experience in jumping out of airplanes made me sympathetic to the plan. It sounded like a lot of fun to me, too. I didn't have to jump into hostile territory at night. All I had to do was drop them in the right place.

We had to work out the tactics because none of us had ever done this before, and we selected as a practice landing zone the strip of beach north of Da Nang, which Marines had stormed so gallantly in March of 1965.

For those familiar with the area, it was the beach just before you got to the Standard Oil tanks on the way to the Col de Nage, a pass east of Highway 1 and the railroad tracks.

Red Beach received a lot of publicity that day five years earlier, although the only Vietnamese the Marines had faced as they charged off the landing craft were military and civilian dignitaries and a few pretty girls with flowers. More formidable were the television and newspaper reporters, each of whom had to have an exclusive for the six o'clock news.

The flotilla that carried the special landing force had bobbed around at sea for weeks, waiting for Washington to give the order to land, and the reporters got some unexpected responses from the bored and seasick Marines. They all zeroed in on the young man who seemed to be the first across the beach. How did it feel, they asked, to be the first Marine to land in Vietnam?

His answer was wonderful, if not printable. "I'm just glad to get off that f——king ship!"

It was a nice beach, a soft landing zone without a wall of barbed wire close by. I thought the absence of barbed wire was the reason Force Recon chose it. I was wrong. They chose it because they wanted to go swimming, and I got yelled at for dropping them in the water instead of on the beach. You don't break anything landing in the water, although a water landing doesn't do the parachute any good.

The OV-10 could carry four parachutists in the back, in the small cargo compartment that formed the back end of the fuselage. It was rigged for airborne operations when the plane was manufactured, and had a static line running along one side of the deck instead of overhead the way C-130s were rigged. There were red and green signal lights and a doorbell which could be activated from the cockpit. The clamshell door was removed, and the four parachutists crowded into the compartment, which was about the size of your living room couch, facing backward as though they were sitting on a toboggan. Just to be cute, because it wasn't necessary, the Marine closest to the door let his feet dangle outside in the slipstream, which made for some nice pictures that also caused me to get yelled at.

Two OV-10s could carry the eight-man team, and Capt. Larry Ruymann flew as my wingman.

We made two practice jumps and coordinated ringing the doorbells and pulled up simultaneously in order to get the entire team into their chutes in a tight group. The local newspaper gave the parachute demonstrations a lot of coverage, which I did not think was healthy. One of the pictures clearly showed feet dangling out of the back, which was what caused me to be called on the carpet.

In order to prepare the village of Ruong Ruong for overhead air traffic in the middle of the night, I had our night standby package of two OV-10s take off around 0400 and fly over the area in section each morning before dawn so that the villagers and the Viet Cong would get used to the sound. It had worked over Hiroshima in 1945 when those unfortunate people had become accustomed to the single weather plane overheard, and so we duplicated the ruse.

After the second practice jump, we were ready, and all we needed was clearance from the new 1st Marine Division commanding general. General Wheeler, who originally approved the concept, had broken his leg in a helicopter crash about that time, and his relief, Major General Widdeke, had to be sold on the idea anew.

When the new division commander was ready to see us, the colonel in charge of division G-2 (intelligence) escorted the recon commander and me into his office for the briefing. The major used his maps and flip charts with great skill, and the general, one of the toughest looking Marines I had ever seen in my life, was impressed. He had only one question. "What time of night do you plan to do this?"

The major and I answered simultaneously. He said, "Midnight," and I said, "Thirty minutes before first light."

"Come again?" The general looked up in surprise.

We repeated our conflicting answers, the major with noticeable agitation in his voice.

"Explain!" demanded the general.

The major explained that he wanted to execute the drop at midnight in order to give the team time to secrete themselves in the hills before dawn.

I explained that I wanted to do it as close to dawn as possible so that the emergency extract could take place under daylight conditions.

Everyone in the room glared at me as though I had just farted.

"Well," I said, certain that my manhood was in question here, "if all I had to do was drop the team, midnight would be just fine with me. But if they run into a shit sandwich and have to come out, I'm the guy who's going to have to do it. We average about five emergency extractions a month, and we're real good at it. But believe me, General, it's a whole hell of a lot easier when you can see what you're doing."

I'd forgotten that in the earthbound Marine Corps, lieutenant colonels didn't talk that way to generals, but in spite of the faux pas, he got the message.

The mission was scrubbed, and that major never spoke to me again—and I don't blame him one bit. It would have been a lot of fun. But it was 1970, and unnecessary risks were no longer acceptable.

Just to keep things in perspective, let me tell you one more recon story that wasn't all fun and games.

Late one afternoon, I got a call asking me to go to the assistance of a recon team in the area we called Charlie Ridge, about fifteen miles southwest of Da Nang. They were on their way out of the hills following a three-day patrol, but because they had some prisoners, one of whom had to be carried, they wanted me to help them find a pickup spot closer than the one they were scheduled to use. It was growing late, and the prisoners, especially the wounded ones, were slowing them down. I had to find someplace close by so that they could be picked up before it got dark.

The only suitable area I could find necessitated their climbing a tall hill, and even that piece of ground was going to require some zone clearance before a helicopter could land. They agreed, and I called the Direct Air Support Center for assistance. They scrambled some Hueys from HML-167, call sign Comprise, that carried a new invention called the TRAP weapon, which was in limited supply and under evaluation.

I never did know exactly what TRAP stood for, but it was a small bomb that could be dropped by hand from a helicopter and would cut down small trees. It had a small parachute to make certain the bomb hit straight down, and a daisy-cutter fuse about a foot long to ensure that the explosion took place a couple of inches above the ground.

The bomb itself consisted of a lot of banded steel, pretty much like the spring in your rotary lawn mower. When it went off, the explosion forced the steel coil out to a distance of fifteen or twenty feet and cut down small trees.

The Comprise Hueys came out and did the job with four of the experimental bombs, and now it was simply a matter of getting a team of tired Marines to the zone.

I could hear the exhaustion in the voice of the radio operator, and I felt a bit helpless. The zone was absolutely the closest site I could find, but time was growing short.

Suddenly I was startled by a request from the radio operator. "Request permission to kill these prisoners."

My jaw dropped down around my torso harness somewhere. I had never heard anything like that in my life, and don't think I ever will again.

I thought a while before I answered. "If you need some help," I finally said, "I can get a rifle company out here in about thirty minutes!"

I didn't know if I could or not, but it was the best answer I could come up with at the moment.

The radio operator answered that they didn't think that was necessary, and we continued to orbit the trek, sometimes seeing them, sometimes losing them for a few minutes.

They were working their way up the hill when I lost sight of them for about five minutes. I called.

"The pickup helicopters are inbound, but I've lost sight of you. What's your position?"

"We're standing here at the edge of the hill . . . beside these freshly dug graves."

End of story. The helicopters landed and picked up the team plus one prisoner, a female. I'll be honest and tell you I never pursued that one. I don't even recall the team's call sign, and I don't want to.

MY DAYS AS
A FEARLESS PARA-MARINE

I have made several references to my experience with airborne operations, and I think it appropriate at this juncture to explain it all.

All company grade Marine aviators were required to pull a tour of duty with the infantry during the 1960s. Most were assigned to the Marine divisions as forward air controllers for a year, but some of us were lucky enough to draw assignments with an unusual organization called 1st ANGLICO—1st Air and Naval Gunfire Liaison Company—based at that time at Camp Smith, in Hawaii.

Born out of necessity during World War II, ANGLICO was designed to provide forward air controllers and naval gunfire spotters to the army when they were committed to an amphibious assault, during which they would depend on the navy and Maine Corps for their air and gunfire support.

ANGLICO teams were constantly being deployed to army and allied units for training exercises, and in 1961, one of them was assigned to the famous 503d Airborne Battle Group, based on Okinawa in preparation for a possible assault in Laos, which would have to be supported by Seventh Fleet.

According to Capt. George Boehmerman, the team leader, the battle group commander was delighted to have them aboard for the operation, but wondered how the Marines were going to accompany the Airborne forces. "We're going to jump in," he said. "How do you all plan to get there?"

George, and his assistant, Wendy Grubbs, suggested that it sounded like a lot of fun, and if the 503d would be good enough to teach them how, the ANGLICO unit would jump in with them. Pretty gutsy.

They were put through a crash course in about three days,

and while the assault never took place, airborne operations suddenly became part of ANGLICO's mission.

I checked into the company on the same day that a message arrived from Headquarters, Marine Corps modifying the mission to include this activity. Because I was the newest arrival and had a whole year ahead of me, I was offered the job of forming an Airborne unit.

Who could turn down such a wonderful opportunity? Well, it turned out that a lot of people did, about an hour before I walked through the door. Most subscribed to the theory that it was senseless to jump out of perfectly good airplanes. The senior aviator in the company likened the activity to practicing bleeding.

But three of us volunteered. With me in the project were John Archbold, who was killed in a helicopter crash in Vietnam in 1969, and Terry Armentrout, whom we saw on television a lot a few years later when he became one of the major aircraft accident investigators for the National Transportation Safety Board.

Virtually all of the enlisted Marines in the company volunteered, and we got to handpick a team of some of the finest young men I ever had the pleasure of working with. With us also were a Marine lieutenant, Rob MacIntyre, who was an artillery officer, and a navy lieutenant, Chuck Howell, who was a naval gunfire expert.

The only other airborne organization in the Marine Corps at the time were the Force Reconnaissance companies, and I worked closely with their representative, a Major McAllister, in formulating our tables of organization and equipment.

Finding the jump school took a bit of doing. Major McAllister thought that Force Recon could do the job right there in Hawaii, and I thought that in-house training was a good idea, too. But we were finally persuaded by the army to use one of their schools, because, after all, it was with them that we would be operating.

I wasn't too thrilled about going through that ordeal. Fort Benning, Georgia in the summertime wasn't my idea of fun. But even that was ruled out in favor of our training with the 503d on Okinawa, simply because it was cheaper. If we went back to the continental United States, the Marine Corps would have to foot the bill for plane tickets and temporary additional duty money. Okinawa was almost a freebie.

So, instead of Fort Benning in the summertime, we got to enjoy Okinawa in August. Lordy, but wasn't that unpleasant!

The airborne instructors couldn't believe their good fortune. For three weeks they got to train Marines! They got to insult us, harass us, bully and embarrass us, and get even for every injustice, real or imagined, that had ever been perpetrated by Marine Corps public relations offices.

To this day, every time I see a man in a white T-shirt and blue baseball cap, a cold shudder runs down my back.

After our 0500 calisthenics and morning run, often accompanied by a considerable amount of puking, we would change into fresh, starched utility uniforms and fall in for our morning inspection, which preceded the morning's training session.

I was the leader, and stood out in front of the two units, the air platoon and the naval gunfire platoon. The senior instructor, a West Point lieutenant, approached me, saluted smartly, and held out his hand. I took off my captain's bars, which he put in his pocket, and for the rest of the day, we belonged to him.

At the end of the day, totally wilted, we formed up again in the same formation, and he returned my bars and dignity. He saluted smartly, and I was once again in charge until 0500 the next morning.

Two weeks of that sucked, but I sure got good at doing push-ups.

A series of push-ups was the standard penalty for minor infractions, and I got more than my fair share simply because I was the leader. If a lance corporal was caught leaning against a post and was ordered to make love to that post for his flagrant violation of discipline, I had to intervene and object that such punishment was not germane to the business at hand. And of course, I was offered the opportunity to take punishment in the lance corporal's stead. And of course, I had no choice in the matter, except that I was allowed to do push-ups in lieu of whatever penalty had originally been decreed.

I came away from jump school with a seventeen-and-a-half-inch neck and a forty-six-inch chest—which I thought looked a little silly on a guy who was only five feet nine and a half inches tall. After I left ANGLICO and joined Marine Fighter Squadron 232 at Kaneohe Bay, I returned to a normal size—which was just as well, because in August of 1964, I had occasion to eject from a burning F-8 Crusader and shrink three-quarters of an inch. I have been short and dumpy ever since.

My first jump was fascinating. It was from a giant C-124,

which I do not recommend to anyone. Because I was the leader, naturally, I had to go first. I shall never forget standing in the door, waiting for the light to turn green, and screaming into the slipstream, "I'm a fighter pilot! What the hell am I doing here?"

I bounced on that first jump. I do not know how high, but I definitely bounced. I thumped down in a sweet-potato field in the Yamatan drop zone, bounced, and then twisted my ankle in a drainage ditch, running after my parachute to collapse it. John Archbold broke his leg ricocheting off the old runway there, and Terry Armentrout tore up his knee so badly that he had to get the rest of his qualifying jumps over the water.

I never really understood that. I have seen pilots eject from airplanes over terrain that was totally unknown, crash down into rocks seven or eight thousand feet high, where the air was thin and the chute traveled much faster, and walk away with nothing more than skinned knees. We trained and trained, and learned all of the tricks of the trade, then landed in a designated parachute drop zone under school conditions, and pretty well wiped out all three air controllers. I was the only one of the three pilots who got to finish walking upright, and as soon as we finished jumping, my sore ankle swelled up as though it had been just waiting for me to stop using it.

The folks in the 503d were a decent bunch, and they wanted us to have as many jump-qualified forward air controllers as possible, so they arranged for Terry Armentrout to get four water jumps to complete his qualifications. They did it in an hour!

They flew him out over the ocean in a helicopter, dropped him into the water, then flew down and scooped him up with downed-pilot rescue gear. As the helicopter climbed for altitude, Terry buckled into a fresh parachute, and they repeated the exercise.

Up and down, four jumps, four scoops, and a wet but happy Marine pilot earned his jump wings. Unfortunately, John Archbold was locked up in the hospital, and while we could smuggle booze into his room, we couldn't smuggle him out to get some water jumps. Besides, the cast was up over his hip, and even if we had managed to do it, we suspected the nurses and doctors would have noticed.

After we returned to Hawaii, our jumps were all made over Mr. Dole's fallow pineapple fields, a softer drop zone than anyone could imagine, unless one was unfortunate enough to land on the spears of a pineapple bush that had grown back.

I'll never forget the morning of our first "home" game when I jumped wind dummy. That's the guy who goes first, makes no corrections with his chute, and determines which way the wind is going to take the chutes.

It was our first jump after training, and the wind that morning was blowing from the south toward the Kamehameha Highway. I scootched myself out of the helicopter and floated down, not making any corrections, and it occurred to me that if I didn't pull on some of the risers in one direction of another I was going to land in one of two places: either in the middle of the Kam Highway, or on top of a Tasty Freeze stand. It was 0700, and the traffic on the highway out to Schofield Barracks was pretty heavy, and so I elected to break a rule and try to steer that damn parachute back into the pineapple field.

I did, barely, and thumped rather ingloriously into the red soil, directly in front of a group of Marine dignitaries who had come out to witness the first organized Marine parachute jump on the island of Oahu.

It was the perfect spot for a good line, but my brain wasn't up to clever remarks at the moment. I stood up and released my chute, gathered it together, and approached the colonels. "I suppose," I panted as I dusted the red clay from my utilities, "you're wondering why I called this meeting . . ."

I didn't get a laugh.

But we were Airborne Marines, and it was fun being a pioneer. No one had ever seen jump wings and naval aviator's wings on the same shirt before, and I was just about the cockiest kid in town—until one day a navy captain flushed me at the Camp Smith gas station with a simple question, "Why the jump wings? Are you famous for not bringing them back?"

I wasn't the only hotshot para-marine to be embarrassed. One of the young Marines in the unit—I can't remember his name— went home to somewhere in the Middle West on leave just after we completed jump school, and caused himself no end of grief when he wrote a check with his mouth about what a highly skilled parachutist he was.

He got to drinking with a parachute demonstration team that was going to put on a show at a fair just outside of town, and he so convinced them of his skills that they invited him to jump with them the next day. They loaned him a parachute, and it wasn't until the plane climbed to altitude that he learned that the jump was to be made from several thousand feet, with the jumpers free-falling to around fifteen hundred feet before pulling the rip cords.

Now, he had never done anything but army parachute jumping, with his chute being opened on a static line as he left the plane. He had never in his life done a free-fall jump, and a few seconds after exiting the plane he panicked and pulled the rip cord, and landed about ten minutes after the rest of the group, literally in another county.

He cut his leave short after that and returned to Hawaii where he still had some friends who appreciated him.

Because of the airborne experience, I got to go through Special Forces training at Fort Bragg in 1964, while the school was still at Smoke Bomb Hill. That was fun too, and my only regret is that I didn't stay around long enough to get picked up in the Skyhook rig.

Skyhook was a nifty contraption that was designed to pick up downed pilots before long-range helicopters with in-flight refueling capabilities were invented. The rescue plane dropped a kit to the downed airman, who inflated a blimp-shaped balloon and strapped himself into a harness attached to the balloon by several hundred feet of strong bungee rope. The plane flew into the bungee, and a rig that extended from the nose snatched it, cut away the balloon, and hauled the man in with a winch.

I got to fly copilot in the Skyhook Caribou during an Armed Forces Day parade flyover, and I had enough suck with 5th Special Forces so that I was on the list to get my body jerked off the ground the next time they put on several demonstrations in a single day. But I was homesick for Hawaii and went back to the islands as soon as I finished my schooling.

I was there at Fort Bragg for the revolution, which very few people knew about.

John Kennedy, the patron saint of Special Forces, had only been dead a few months, and the Department of the Army was determined to get the renegade forces in the green berets back into the fold. Under "Saint John's" aegis, Special Forces had become more and more special, and by the spring of 1964 the officers were trying to get themselves full blown branch status.

One morning all of the Special Forces officers showed up wearing on their left collars not their regular insignias, but crossed arrows, representing Special Forces. The army always did believe in dressing up their uniforms a little bit more than was really necessary, but I thought the arrows looked pretty neat. Pretentious, but neat.

That lasted about two or three hours, long enough for some-body to snitch to Washington and for the Department of the Army to send a signal ordering them to take them off.

That was about the same time that the troops in Special Forces decided to change their uniforms.

One morning they all showed up wearing jungle fatigues, which we would all wear a year later when we got to Vietnam but which none of us had ever seen before. These were the all green ones, not the ridiculous camouflaged "tree suits" soldiers and Marines have been forced to wear for the past twenty years.

They wore the suits the way they were meant to be worn, with the jacket hanging loose and with black metal rank insignias and their name and service tags embroidered in black, the way they're worn today, and you'd have thought they had planned to overthrow the government the way Department of the Army reacted.

"That is an army uniform!" Washington screamed, "and you will wear it as such! You will wear a pistol belt around the jacket and wear proper rank and unit markings!"

So, the next day the special warriors wore the pistol belts and displayed stripes and colorful unit markings and patches all over the jacket, and in general went back to looking like Wurlitzer jukeboxes, and that pretty well took all of the fun out of it. We Marines commiserated with them the most because we were used to looking like mud hens when we went to the field.

It certainly was a shame that Washington had to pay a snitch to call them on the telephone each time Special Forces tried to pull a fast one.

But Special Forces did a lot of neat things then, as they do today, and I always considered my time with them as valuable training. I just didn't know how valuable it would be at the time.

A CHRISTMAS STORY
AND OTHER TARGETS
OF OPPORTUNITY

Let me tell you my Bob Hope Christmas story. I didn't see Bob Hope, you understand. I didn't even hear him. This story just happened to take place while he was clowning around at the Freedom Hill amphitheater on Christmas Day of 1969.

Except for the general who has to attend, senior officers do not go to Bob Hope shows. The next time we go to war and Bob Hope shows up to do a show, someone is going to give you tickets, and you must not use them. You must give them to the enlisted Marines. Don't forget that. It's one of the traditional rules of etiquette people forget during peacetime.

I was not yet a member of VMO-2 on Christmas Day, and maybe that was the reason I had a 1600 (4:00 P.M.) takeoff. If you're going to screw somebody out of the Christmas cocktail party, make sure you do it to somebody who doesn't have any control over your fitness report.

As far as the war was concerned, there wasn't much going on that afternoon. The Christmas cease-fire ran from 1800 (6:00 P.M.) Christmas Eve to 1800 Christmas Day, and we weren't allowed to shoot anybody for another two hours.

After takeoff, I checked in with all of the controlling agencies and flew out into the middle of the Arizona Territory, trolling for somebody who might be able to make use of me. I couldn't fly north. Bob Hope was putting on a show, and we weren't allowed to fly near there lest our noise disturb the show.

Cobras were allowed to fly near there. The security was tight around such an internationally famous American, and the Cobras had to snoop around and miss the Christmas party, too.

Of course, Bob Hope was probably the one person who didn't need any security. The other team wouldn't dare harm a hair of his head, because it might have provided the spark to unite the American people behind their government.

Anyway, I was motoring around the countryside, and the only thing of interest was Charlie Dunbaugh's HMM-364 Christmas helicopter.

HMM-364 pilots called themselves the Purple Foxes, and their CH-46 helicopters all had roundels on the tails that featured a grinning purple fox which I think they copied from Disney's J. Worthington Foulfellow. Around the circumference of the roundel were the words: "Give a shit."

That was a little crude, and in a few months the wing was going to order them to change the wording, but at the time everyone enjoyed it—if only because in 1969 one did not see that word too often.

The Christmas helicopter was just that. It was loaded with nothing but ice-cold beer, and everywhere it landed at Marine encampments in the field, enough beer for everyone was passed out over the tail ramp by Charlie Dunbaugh himself in a great Santa Claus costume. One of the highlights of the war as far as I was concerned.

Around five o'clock I got a call from another OV-10 pilot asking me to come over and help him out. He had some "Gooners" holed up in a cave, and he wanted me to come over and relieve him on station because he was running low on fuel and it was time for him to go home.

The cave was on a river bank just south of Hill 55 in an area we called the Vegetable Garden. I didn't see any cave until it was pointed out to me. The mouth couldn't have been more than eighteen inches across, and it was behind a bush. But the other pilot swore to me that three Gooners had run in there, and it was up to me to take care of them when 1800 rolled around.

And so we set up an orbit around the little cave, and I felt very much like a house cat that spent hours waiting beside some place of concealment that might—or might not—have been the refuge of the mouse or lizard it was chasing at the time.

At about five thirty we called the First Marine Regiment, headquartered on Hill 55, and ordered up an artillery fire mission for six o'clock. They worked out all of the arithmetic; the time of flight of the rounds would be thirty-seven seconds, and so they would pull the lanyards at five fifty-nine and twenty-three seconds.

We waited and waited, and really felt stupid sitting over a cave on Christmas Day waiting for six o'clock to come so that we could blow the piss out of three bad guys who might or might not be there, just like the lizard the cat never caught.

At moments like that we appreciated the OV-10's single side band radio. Most of the time the radio was a waste of money and added to the weight of the plane. But when a pilot was really bored, he could always tune in Radio Australia, and that afternoon we listened to some lady read a Christmas story.

At last, five fifty-nine and twenty-three seconds came. The cannon cockers pulled the lanyards, and at precisely 1800 the rounds hit with considerable accuracy.

End of story, except that the pilot I relieved hadn't seen the enemy run into the cave. They were spotted by the pilot HE relieved on station . . . Which means that one third of VMO-2's assets that afternoon were dedicated entirely to three bad guys, real or imagined, who popped into a cave around noon time.

Did we kill them? I have no idea. The artillery mission belonged to the First Marines. So much for Peace on Earth, Good Will Toward Men.

Let me tell you about the time I attacked a whorehouse. I can't be certain that it really was a brothel, you understand, but all the evidence pointed to it.

I got a call one morning from a section of Marine tanks that were rumbling around the flatland southwest of Da Nang and scaring the hell out of people, pigs, and chickens—everything but the water buffalo that looked upon M-60s as competitors. There wasn't much use for tanks, except as mobile artillery, and so I think the local commander was winging it and making up his tactics as he went along.

The tanks were restricted as to where they could roam. This area was where old French plantations had once produced bananas and such, and where canals had been dug for water transportation. The canals ran straight as arrows and made ninety-degree turns, and probably served as property lines for the plantations in addition to providing a means of transportation to move produce to the Da Nang market.

The canals were not very wide, but certainly wide enough to keep the tanks contained in their assigned areas. As a result, the call to me that morning was one of frustration. I cannot recall the tank commander's call sign—I'll call him "Tiger"—but he sounded very much like a little boy whose ball had gone over the fence and into my yard.

"Tiger. This is Hostage Six. What can I do for you?"

"Hostage Six. Tiger. You see where the canal comes in from the west and does a ninety-degree turn to the north? There's a hootch right at the bend, this side of the road. Tin roof. Banana trees growing all around it."

"Pretty hard to miss, Tiger. What do you need?"

"We saw some gooners go in there. We can't get to it from here, so what I want to do is blow it away with ninety millimeter. And I want you to kill anybody who runs out. You copy?"

"Loud and clear. You have clearance for this?"

"Affirmative."

This was a new one on me, although the principle appeared sound. Still, it was pretty close to civilization, and I had the aerial observer check with division to make sure the tank commander didn't speak with forked tongue. Sometimes the people on the ground got carried away, and we older folks had to save them from their own enthusiasm.

Division gave us a green light, which meant that there weren't any friendlies in the area, and we laid our trap. When I was in a position to roll in, the tanks would each fire one round of ninety millimeter at the hut. Assuming that an enemy soldier running away from such an assault would head west, away from the U. S. Marine positions in the area, I positioned myself for a westerly run along the little dirt road that paralleled the canal and armed my twenty-millimeter cannon, having emptied my four 7.62 machine guns earlier, hosing down some shrubbery for a rifle company a few miles to the south.

I pulled up into a barrel roll, which would end up in an attacking run to the west, and told the tanker to fire. They did, and of course created havoc all through the peaceful and bucolic neighborhood.

Chickens ran squawking in every direction, and a dog took off down the road to the west. Suddenly a human form burst from the smoke and chaos and began a footrace with disaster up the narrow dirt road to the north.

He was running ninety degrees to my flight path, not at all in accordance with my plan, and I stomped on the right rudder to turn the plane to the north in hopes of getting at least some angle for the shot. I put the pipper on the running figure as the plane returned to balanced flight, and my thumb mashed the firing button on top of the stick just as I got a good look at the fleeing enemy soldier.

Maybe it was the color of his skin. Maybe it was the M-16 he was carrying in his left hand. Maybe it was the sight of a man trying to run and pull his pants up at the same time.

I horsed back on the stick just as the twenty-millimeter cannon chugged off its first round. The thumb-sized shell went well over the American's head as a result of what I considered to be the greatest hand-eye coordination of my entire life, and some army guy was saved from what might have been the most expensive piece of ass of his life.

The lady of the house was also unhurt in the surprise attack, and when I turned back to assess the damage, she was standing in front of the heavily damaged structure, buttoning up her blouse. She didn't look real happy.

I suspect that had either she or the soldier been standing up, the ninety-millimeter shell would have been fatal, and so her professional position had saved their lives—but I doubt if she got paid.

End of story. I don't really know that the "John" was an army soldier. I told the tank commander that so that he wouldn't feel bad about almost greasing a fellow Marine, but the guy didn't have on enough clothing for a positive identification.

Another across-the-river incident wasn't so humorous. I was flying the 76-Alpha dawn patrol one morning and was directed to an infantry platoon from the 5th Marines immediately after takeoff. I raced down to their position on the Thu Bon River as fast as my little OV-10 would carry me, expecting to find Marines under attack. I called the DASC en route and alerted them to the possibility of having to scramble some bombers from Chu Lai, and arrived over the area ready for a fight.

There wasn't any fight going on at all, but there were a lot of pissed off Marines in the process of breaking camp on a river bank directly across from a sizable village.

"Two Alpha One, this is Hostage Six. What can I do for you?"

(I have no idea of the name of the unit or its call sign. Obviously there is no Alpha Company in a 2d Battalion.)

"Hostage Six, Alpha One. I want you to take out that ville." The voice of the platoon commander was cold and steady.

"The whole village?"

This was as stunning a request as the one from the recon team that asked me for permission to kill its prisoners.

"Affirmative, Hostage Six. A sniper from that village killed one of my Marines last night. I want you to level it."

By this time I was over the village in question, looking down at the hustle and bustle of a farming community early in the morning. Women were already hanging out the wash, and little kids were chasing dogs and chickens, and men were trudging out into their fields. It was a good-sized village, as I said, and the rifle company had camped directly across the river in clear view of most of it.

I presumed that the platoon commander's request was a grandstand play in front of his Marines and that he was counting on me to modify the scope of his intent.

"Well, let me see what I can do for you. How about pointing out the hut from which the shots were fired. We'll go to work on that while you're getting your troops saddled up and on the road."

He pointed out the part of the village that was most likely the source of the rifle fire, and I got clearance from the controlling agencies to perform minor surgery on the compound.

The aerial observer handled the ground portion of the strike and got Marines from other units into the area to act as blocking forces along all of the paths leading away from the village, while I got a section of F-4 Phantoms with full loads of 250-pound Snake Eye bombs launched from the hot pad at Chu Lai.

The blocking forces moved into their positions at about the same time that the F-4s arrived overhead, and I went to work.

First order of business: get the women and children out of town. This was easy to do. The only problem was that they never moved quickly enough.

When villagers in the Marine Corps' area of responsibility saw an OV-10 snooping around their backyard, with a flight of Phantoms or Skyhawks orbiting overhead, they knew immediately what was about to happen. A white phosphorous rocket planted in the village square, or some other spot close by but away from people, confirmed that, yes, it was their village I was about to damage.

In a very short period of time, people were on the thin roads that lead to the west, herding their children and pigs and chickens along. It was an exodus that they had experienced many times. I grew impatient, and I remember flying low along one of the thin dirt roads, and motioning to them with my hand to hurry up. Wasted effort, but harmless enough.

We saw two youngish looking men limping along, stiff-leggedly, and we told the Marines blocking that particular path to check them out for the old rifle-down-the-pants trick.

After about fifteen minutes, the village was clear, and the F-4 pilots were growing impatient, so I put a white phosphorous rocket on the hut that had been singled out as the source of evil. The jets made two runs apiece and left a big hole where an hour earlier people had slept.

Two figures dressed in black took off running to the south toward the hills and ran into a blocking force—and were dispatched. That proved that there really were bad guys in the village, and the air strike was legitimate.

It wasn't what the platoon commander had asked for, but it was all he was going to get out of me.

I tell this little story to illustrate the emotional differences among people waging war. If VMO-2 had been the controlling squadron over the village of My Lai for instance, maybe army Lieutenant Calley wouldn't have been able to vent his frustrations on innocent women and children. He would have called for the destruction of every man, woman and child in the village, but someone with a cooler head, someone who had not just lost some soldiers to snipers from the village, would have taken charge.

FUN AND GAMES

In order to appreciate this chapter, you must bear in mind that we males never grow up, we only grow older. If you keep that thought, most of what I'm about to tell you will make sense.

I want to tell you about the games people played in Vietnam. Not little games, like poker and acey-deucey—or piddling little athletic contests like softball and boxing—not even small wars that pitted squadron against squadron and kept lieutenants busy for days, although some of those were a lot of fun. I'm talking about major conflicts between huge air groups, with separate campaigns, that brought all of the available tools of warfare into play and provided fun for the participants for weeks on end.

We Americans learn our games early in life, and virtually all of the competitive games played in Vietnam were variations on that great pastime of boarding schools and summer camps all over the world: capture the flag.

When writers referred to the British Empire's successes as having been forged on the playing fields of Eton, they thought they were referring to the gentlemanly rules of conduct of cricket and football, but they were wrong. The playing fields, on sunny afternoons before tea time, were where young British gentlemen learned to put on an act. The game that prepared the Brits to rule most of the world was their version of capture the flag, a game which took place at night and taught the down-and-dirty game of stealth, deception, sneakiness, and foul play. They just didn't admit this until they formed their first commando units in 1941.

The rule for capture the flag is simple. Find out where the enemy keeps the flag, and steal it.

There are always some local ground rules. No one is supposed to get hurt, but the littlest and wimpiest kid always picks up a few bruises. You're not supposed to hide your flag, but some kid always dumps dirt and leaves on it, which is generally the reason he gets the bruises in the first place, because it's the littlest and wimpiest kid who's put in charge of flag security, while the brawnier and fleeter boys are out doing dirty deeds in the dark.

There are probably a few additional rules when the game is being played at coed schools, and which deal with other forms of contact sport that can be played in the dark. But those are simply sidebars to the true story of capture the flag, jungle-rules edition.

Now, it has been said that idle hands are the Devil's workshop. The person who first said that two or three thousand years ago probably was not thinking about a group of Marines away from their families for long periods of time, but he might just as well have been. He was probably grumbling about the idle young men hanging around the forum, leering at his daughter and trying to look up her toga. But he could easily have been predicting the plight of a bunch of Marine pilots in 1970 who had too much free time on their hands.

Infantry officers didn't have this problem, you understand. The poor grunts were too busy fighting off the flies and mosquitoes, trying to cook a meal over a heat tab, and hoping to find something to drink that was colder than the water in their canteens. No, the problem of what to do with free time was one common to pilots who had comfortable, air-conditioned living spaces and an air-conditioned officers club, who had a mess hall serving three hot meals a day, and who had cleaning and laundry women who came in six days a week to make their beds and wash their clothes and shine their boots.

These pitiful pilots didn't have to worry about basic survival, except for the occasional moment of stark terror when they were required to perform aggressive aerial acts against people who had guns and bullets and sharp objects. They had everything provided for them, and when they were not strapped into a cockpit or performing their collateral ground duties around the squadron, their time was their own—except that they couldn't go anywhere.

The Devil had a lot of shop time in Vietnam and was altogether willing to provide on-the-job training.

On a big night out, a group of pilots might borrow the commanding officer's jeep and drive over to another unit's officers club to visit friends, but the difference between air group's officers clubs was negligible. The Seabees who built them only had two floor plans to work from, and there was precious little difference between one air group's officers club and another group's staff NCO or enlisted club. The building materials were identical from club to club, gray stone quarried locally and a tin roof which could be replaced quickly after a rocket attack. Any choice of places to visit were pretty much like choices among McDonald's hamburger stands.

A few journeyed over to the naval support activity hospital to chase nurses, but that was not a common occurrence. In fact, the whole purpose of VMO-2's illegal, three-day R & R trips to Udorn, Thailand, was to keep the pilots from chasing nurses in Da Nang, thus allowing them to give the war their undivided attention.

So, let me tell you about some of the games pilots played in combat. Competitive games. Corporate games, if you are willing to compare an air group to a sizeable corporation.

One-upmanship does not disappear when squadrons and air groups move into the combat arena, but the means of competition grow enormously. Any time you take a group of males away from the responsibility of life and plunk them down in a summer-camp environment, they're going to think up ways of entertaining themselves. And when you make available to them such marvelous toys as those which exist in combat zones—free of charge, so that the families back home will never even get a bill—then Satan is well pleased.

On the squadron level, the game is so simple as to be one dimensional. It's fun, but there is no depth, no peripheral side play.

I'll give you an example, and tell you about a simple game of capture the flag between the C-130 squadron, VMGR-253, and our sister squadron, VMO-6, both of which were based in Okinawa. I became personally involved in it, but only in the most innocent way.

The "flag" in this case was a three-foot wooden statue of a raccoon, Tanuki, the Japanese symbol for happy-go-lucky, which the transport squadron had honored as its mascot since the days when they flew old R4Q-1 Flying Boxcars out of Iwakuni, Japan.

The Tanuki was wired to light up, and there was a doorbell imbedded in the base, which the squadron commander could ring when it was time for someone to buy a drink. The duty officer was charged with delivering it to and retrieving it from happy hour each Friday evening—after which security was not so great. I would estimate that over the years Tanuki had been stolen fifteen or twenty times—twice while I was in the squadron in 1958.

One night in July of 1970, the lieutenants of VMO-6 stole the critter, and the next night the lieutenants of the transport squadron retaliated by stealing the VMO-6 squadron commander's jeep, putting it on a C-130, and flying it to Vietnam.

The night action on the part of the C-130 pilots, I understand, was a classic exercise in stealth, technology and timing, with the jeep being hot-wired and driven to the flight line just as a C-130 was turning the turbofan engines for a scheduled trip to Da Nang, driving across the tail ramp just as it was time to taxi. I had to take the transport pilots' word for it, however, because it all took place in the middle of the night, and no one was awake to be deceived.

I thought that was pretty cute, and it was at that point when I was invited into the game. Our own squadron jeep became part of the ransom note.

The two C-130 pilots who flew the jeep into Da Nang stopped by our squadron later that morning, one of them carrying a Polaroid camera, and insisted that I lend them my jeep for a half hour in order that they might prepare a ransom note with photographic proof of their triumph. They convinced me that there was some modicum of honor among thieves, and returned the jeep to me exactly when they said they would, with a duplicate Polaroid picture, which I still have.

The picture showed the back ends of the two commanding officers' jeeps, VMO-2 and VMO-6, and featured the tire covers as proof of the deed. Between the jeeps stood two attractive Vietnamese girls wearing flowing *ao dai*s and holding up crudely lettered signs with arrows that designated the jeeps as COMBAT and NON-COMBAT.

Presented with photographic evidence the next evening, VMO-6's skipper capitulated, the jeep and the Tanuki were returned, and a splendid party was held to celebrate the occasion—which was the whole point of the kidnapping in the first place.

This sort thing happened all the time, and was of little consequence. It was fun, perhaps even exciting for the lieutenants, but it was so predictable that VMO-2 tried to stay above it all.

Of course that superior attitude did not deter us from stealing our share when targets of opportunity presented themselves.

On the local scene in Da Nang, the ''flag'' was generally a squadron logo, and because sneaking around in the middle of the night could get a man shot, the capturing had to be accomplished in public, often during a USO floor show.

Each time a floor show was booked into the MAG-11 officers club, generally after playing the enlisted and staff NCO clubs first, the tables were lined up in rows, one squadron to a row, and covered with huge, green linoleum cloths. The revered logo of the unit was placed in front of the squadron commander's place of honor at the head of the table.

The logo was generally built around a model of the squadron's airplane or patch. The Marine air base squadron, charged with keeping the camp running and the facilities working, didn't have any airplanes, and so their statue featured a model of a defueler truck, which they called the Pee-Pee pumper, and which was used to pump effluents out of the second-rate sewage system the group was forced to use. But generally the logo was a one-of-a-kind treasure which the squadron worshipped to one degree or another.

We didn't know about any of this when we arrived. MAG-16, the helicopter group that spawned us, hadn't gone in for signs and logos, and when we arrived for our first party night with the MAG-11, we came empty handed, and were roundly jeered for our lack of social graces.

We were quick to adapt to new situations, however. The lieutenants made up a play in the huddle, and stole the Tomcat logo of VMA-311 out from under the nose of their commanding officer before the evening was half over.

Until that night, the existing procedure for stealing logos had been pretty straightforward. Lieutenants sidled up to the target, pretending to be part of the crowd gathered at the bar behind the tables, grabbed the objet d'art, and ran for the door. Not terribly sophisticated.

We had aerial observers in our squadron—infantry officers— ex-football players and heavyweight wrestlers. It seemed so logical to use our beef as blocking backs and door guards. Even though we came to that first party totally unaware of the traditions, we hit on a play that set the standards of sophistication for months to come and saw the ''steal'' enhanced by a forward pass, two laterals, and a hand-off—plus massive downfield blocking at the backdoor by two of our observers who were so big they just barely fit into our airplanes' cockpits when they flew.

The VMA-311 skipper cried foul with great vehemence, of course, and expressed utter distress that VMO-2 would do such a dishonorable thing. And of course, I grinned at him and lied through my teeth.

In truth, he wasn't as upset over the actual theft as he was over the fact that we didn't have anything for them to steal in return. We ransomed it back for a case of champagne, and he grumbled the whole time, even as he helped drink it. I became acutely aware of my squadron's boorish ways and etiquette deficiencies. I had to dream up a logo and procure it before another party night came around.

Deciding on an appropriate statue took all of ten seconds. Procuring it took three days. When the next lieutenant left for his visit to the fleshpots of Thailand, he carried with him fifty dollars and instructions to buy as many carved wooden elephants as my money would afford.

You've seen the elephants. They stand about ten inches high, and you can pick them up in any import shop for about twenty bucks. In Thailand in 1970, fifty dollars brought about a dozen of them, and I kept the box hidden in the hangar until the next time the club featured a floor show.

An hour before show time on the evening of a floor show, I drove the box to the club and parked the herd of elephants under the protective linoleum of the table assigned to VMO-2, and for the first time, deigned to sit at the head of the table, as prescribed by tradition.

When the air group had assembled, we got the crowd's attention by banging on a glass or something, and I showed off the handsome elephant and made a dedicatory speech, designed to tempt every lieutenant in the club. I have no idea what I said, but I could see the lieutenants squirming at the other tables, and I milked the speech for all it was worth. I sat down, and we settled back to watch the fun.

Soon the lieutenants of the rival squadrons were whispering to the captains and majors and lieutenant colonels. Within an hour, the first elephant was stolen from its place of honor, directly under my nose.

And we did not move a muscle to prevent it.

Our "elephant security officer" reached under the table, grabbed a replacement, and placed it in front of me while I pretended not to notice. Again the air group's squadron commanders cried "foul."

That was too easy. Jet pilots and engineers all had brains that worked from a zero abstraction level, and every college graduate in the wing except the PE majors could put one over on them.

But I had learned from an expert, after all. Col. Heywood Smith of the helicopter group, MAG-16, had been my mentor, and duping aeronautical engineers was something helicopter pilots did best. Consider, if you will, an episode involving the total humiliation of the jet pilots of MAG-13 based at Chu Lai.

For most of 1970, the helicopter air group was led by Heywood Smith whom we used to see on television a lot when he was Lyndon Johnson's aide. Heywood was bright, innovative, and very competitive, and when it came to humiliating other air groups he had no peers.

Once upon a time, he and some of his helicopter pilot henchmen paid a courtesy call on the F-4 Phantom pilots of MAG-13. Ostensibly, the visit was a social one in which representatives of the helicopter community were to join with the fighter pilots at Chu Lai during their Friday afternoon happy hour. But there wouldn't be any story to tell if Heywood had stuck to the script.

If you wanted to catch somebody's country by surprise and bomb its fleet out of existence, you did it on a Sunday morning. But if you wanted to destroy a Marine air group, you invaded during happy hour, when everyone who wasn't flying was in the bar drinking and singing and yelling and telling each other heroic lies.

The helicopter group's invasion party, well briefed and thoroughly trained for espionage, loaded into a huge CH-53 one Friday afternoon and flew down to Chu Lai where they were greeted warmly by the MAG-13 group commander and his staff, and transported to the officers club for an evening of camaraderie. Or rather, most of them were. Some of the helicopter pilots had more pressing chores to attend to, and remained with the helicopter under the guise of being designated drivers, backup pilots for the actual crew. They remained with the helicopter until everyone was out of sight.

Later, this raiding party borrowed a vehicle on their own, under pretenses of making a run to the mess hall. When a decent interval of time had passed, they, too, headed for the officers club, stopping along the way only to replace a sign.

Borrowing liberally from the bravado of the navy's replacement air group at NAS Miramar in southern California,

MAG-13 had erected a self-serving sign at the entrance to their living area welcoming all to "Fighter Town." In an incredibly short period of time, indicating that the raiding party had practiced a lot, the sign was replaced by one identical in color and format. The only difference was that the new sign, in traditional Marine Corps scarlet and gold, welcomed a visitor to "Pussy Town," the adjective referring to wimpishness, of course, and not to anything carnal—which was totally lacking at Chu Lai anyway.

The new sign, ten feet by fifteen feet, with lettering fully a foot high, was not discovered until two days later, so splendid was the art work. Heywood Smith not only had balls, he also had a great paint shop.

But that clever coup was an afterthought, definitely not the highlight of the visit. Nor was the diversionary tactic of "inciting to riot" in the officers club of great importance when Heywood stood at the bar and slandered the entire air group, using a hand-held bullhorn to ensure that even the noisy lieutenants in the back were properly insulted.

All of the aircraft at Chu Lai were being used as bombers, the F-4s as well as the A-4 Skyhawks, and it galled Heywood that the F-4 pilots would still call themselves fighter pilots.

He announced grandly (he had worked for Lyndon, remember, and knew how it was done) that he wanted to buy a drink for every fighter pilot in the club. The cheering response to this, predictably, was boisterous, and when it subsided he slapped a one dollar bill on the bar, and added, "And I expect my change!"

Well, that got everyone's attention, as it was supposed to. The screaming and yelling and claims and counterclaims kept everyone busy long enough for the highly skilled terrorists to accomplish their intended mission.

Outside in the parking lot, the raiding party quietly stole the group commander's jeep while the helicopter pilots warmed up the CH-53 just as night descended.

When the sun came up the next morning, long after the helicopter pilots had departed for home, the MAG-13 group commander finally found his jeep—on top of a hangar.

He had to get the army to retrieve it for him—and they dropped it.

That was fun, but the story I wanted to tell involved a running feud between MAG-16 at Marble Mountain and MAG-11 at the big Da Nang base, where we had only recently moved our OV-10 squadron.

MAG-11 was a composite group with F-4s and EA-6s belonging to the photo and electronics countermeasures squadron, and two squadrons of A-6 Intruders in addition to our OV-10s and some two-seated TA-4s. I don't recall that there was any animosity between the jet group and the helicopter group. I think the feuding arose simply because Heywood Smith was bored, and these were the only two air groups in the immediate area.

ROUND ONE

On a Sunday, the MAG-11 group staff and the squadron commanders were invited to journey to Marble Mountain on the sands of China Beach to spend a relaxing day at Heywood Smith's beach house.

God bless the Seabees. It really was a nice house, and the construction battalion commander liked it so much he built one for himself, just like it, and right next door—except that his had a basement bomb shelter made out of a conex box.

There were about a dozen of us on the invitation list, and to save us the trouble of driving over in our jeeps, a CH-53 picked us all up at the wing helicopter pad, only a few hundred yards from our living area compound.

The weather was hot but delightful, with the steady tropical ocean breeze off the South China Sea wafting across the lanai and through the rooms of the spacious beach house. We sipped our fruity rum drinks in comfortable beach chairs and were lulled into ecstasy by the roaring and hissing of the surf. I almost forgot that I was looking at the surf through the ugliest barbed-wire fence ever seen this side of Buchenwald.

It was a nice day. The barbeque was hot, and the drinks were cold, and the swimming and surfing refreshing. As the sun began to set and it was time for us to go home, we loaded into jeeps for the short ride back to the flight line, where we found that the CH-53 scheduled to carry us back to Da Nang was not available, but a pair of CH-46s were.

Dutifully, we clambered aboard one of them and took off, with the second helicopter flying escort, normal procedure for CH-46s. The Cobra gunship escort seemed unnecessary, but it gave us a feeling of security.

Five minutes later, about the time we should have been landing at Da Nang, we were shaken out of our alcohol-induced reverie by the wail of warning sirens, and the helicopter began to plummet rapidly toward the darkened countryside. The crew chief yelled for us to prepare for a crash, and the plane banged down roughly in the middle of some farmer's sweet-potato patch.

The copilot came back from the cockpit and told us what a close one that had been, adding that there was a backup helicopter. If we would walk three hundred yards across the field to where it had landed on a road, we'd be back home in a matter of minutes.

And, of course, as soon as everyone was halfway to the second helicopter, the pilots of both planes pulled up on the collectives and took off, stranding the group commander, his staff and squadron commanders out in the middle of nowhere, in the dark, and without weapons.

Actually, we were only about a mile outside the gates to the air base, in a very secure area abutting the heavily traveled road that connected us to 1st Marine Division headquarters. Colonel Smith had arranged to have a MAG-16 six-by-six truck arrive at the scene as soon as the helicopters took off, and everyone was home safely within an hour. But our group commander, Colonel Pommerenck, was spring-loaded to the pissed-off position just the same, and the feud began at that very moment.

Now, I tell this story to aspiring naval aviators in order to describe the differences between the helicopter community and the jet community. Because of the selection priorities in the Naval Air Training Command, most of the student pilots who qualified for the more glamorous jet "pipeline" were engineers of some sort. One of the selection factors involved ground-school grades, and the students who were more proficient in math and physics had the edge. The English and history majors generally ended up flying helicopters. All of this meant that the helicopter community had a distinct advantage in the area of creative thinking, and the tightly disciplined engineers weren't too good at the subtle nuances of clever feuding. Colonel Pommerenck was a splendid air group commander, who would soon be a general, and he was a marvelous human being as well. But he was, after all, an engineer, and didn't stand a chance.

ROUND TWO

In order to retaliate properly for the marooning of his group staff in a sweet-potato field, the MAG-11 commander decided that night on a plan designed to embarrass the helicopter group commander in front of his own people. It wasn't a very good plan, and some of us tried to get him to accept the fact that we had been properly snookered and forget it, but he was having none of it.

On Tuesday, Black Tuesday, the day of the 1st Marine Air Wing commander's weekly conference, when Heywood Smith would drive over from Marble Mountain and park in the wing headquarters compound just as he did every Tuesday, the MAG-11 motor transport people would exact the group's revenge.

Their preparatory efforts were exhaustive, and they worked into the night determining the exact amount of fuel it would take to get a jeep to the middle of Freedom Bridge that connected Da Nang to the coastal community and Marble Mountain, where the motor would sputter and die and Colonel Smith would need a tow. And, of course, the tow would come from a MAG-11 vehicle.

The plan really sucked. When Tuesday arrived and Colonel Smith left his jeep and went inside for the conference, MAG-11's people rushed the vehicle to the motor pool and drained all but the required amount of fuel from the tank. They then painted the jeep in a dozen different and bizarre colors and returned it to the wing compound, dispatching simultaneously a MAG-11 tow truck to Freedom Bridge to lie in wait.

Well, those of you who majored in English and history know right away what happened. Heywood emerged from wing headquarters, took one look at his jeep, and went back inside and picked up a telephone. He called over to one of the CH-53 squadrons, which dutifully sent a plane to the wing helipad. Within minutes, he and his jeep were safely back at Marble Mountain without anyone of note having seen it. Great toys, those CH-53s.

But victorious or not, one good turn deserved another, and Heywood called his raiders into conference. This campaign was supposed to be MAG-11's retaliation, and instead MAG-16 had emerged triumphant. But upstarts had to be punished, if only to keep them in their places.

It was the paint that bothered Heywood. Painting a military vehicle in psychedelic colors simply wasn't done. If MAG-11 was interested in paint, he was going to show them paint. You could see why Lyndon Johnson liked him so much and promoted him to the rank of colonel five years ahead of his contemporaries.

ROUND THREE

After a decent interval, maybe a week or two, and at a time when most of the MAG-11 group staff was busy somewhere else, the helicopter group struck. It was a scene right out of Colonel Hogan's Stalag 13 on television.

A six-by-six truck with no discernable tactical marks on it pulled into the MAG-11 compound, showed proper paperwork to the sentries, and proceeded to the group commander's house. (The Seabees had built a house for Colonel Pommerenck, too, but in truth, it wasn't nearly as nice as the beach house.)

Out tumbled a group of ten or twelve lieutenants from the helicopter group, pilots dressed in grungy coveralls, each carrying a paint bucket and brush, and a couple of them carried ladders. Within twenty minutes, they had painted the group commander's house . . . in much the same color scheme as had been used on Heywood Smith's jeep.

Colonel Pommerenck was pretty put out about it all, especially the big bull's-eye they painted on the roof.

The lieutenants, God bless 'em, were the willing tools who made the combat tour so much fun. These were youngsters, only two years removed from the college campuses, who had not yet been molded into the conservative, corporate mind-set of the profession, and who still remembered how to make a game out of the dreariest of situations. But occasionally a general would fool you. Let me tell you about the arrival of the air wing's new chief of staff in July of 1970.

In the Marine Corps, the chief of staff is the colonel who makes an organization work. He is senior to all of the other colonels, generally hand-picked by the wing commander, and wields enormous power as he implements and coordinates all of the important stuff that goes on in an organization as large as an air wing. Even in combat, he occasionally got stuck with a lot of the petty bullshit, and I recall a week-long hassle over the proper length of sideburns, where even squadron commanders were caught up in a confrontation over the relative geography of a Marine's eyes and ears. But generally the chief of staff busied himself with weightier stuff.

I don't know how other services handled the arrival of a big wheel, but 1st Marine Air Wing greeted all incoming generals and chiefs of staff at planeside with a brass band and welcoming committee made up of his friends and anybody who had a burning need to start sucking up early.

Jake Sloan, the new chief of staff, and the same guy I woke up at the beginning of the war to get things started, was Maj. Gen. Al Armstrong's choice as the man to come back to Vietnam and end it. A fairly senior colonel now, Jake was the one man with the charm and administrative talent to carry out the unpleasant duties necessary to sending people and units home while magically keeping the remaining units happy and combat capable. I believe every staff officer in the wing showed up with a personal agenda.

Jake Sloan was one of the most popular officers in all of Marine Corps aviation at the time, and the crowd of well-wishers and lobbyists that met the plane that afternoon was the largest I ever saw outside of a Bob Hope show.

When I arrived at the Da Nang Air Base passenger terminal for the festivities, I was invited to join General Armstrong's personal entourage in the air-conditioned VIP lounge. I was impressed. I had been in that building at least a dozen times— it was the only place in Da Nang where you could get a decent pizza—and I never knew there was an air-conditioned VIP lounge.

We stood around and made small talk, and I felt self-conscious again as I compared my baggy and rumply oversized flight suit to the freshly starched jungle utility uniforms of the general and his staff officers. I took comfort in the fact that I was probably the only guy in the room who wasn't there to make points, but at moments like that, one still feels that the world is a tuxedo, and he is a pair of brown shoes.

We sucked on orange soda pop as we waited for the American Airlines DC-8 to pull up to the massive wooden air force terminal building. The only person in the crowd whom I did not know was an attractive blonde woman, thirtyish, with an Australian accent. Some staff officer's girlfriend, I suspected. She was dressed in a loose fitting muumuu like the ones my wife used to wear around the house when we lived in Hawaii, and her presence was a mystery to me.

The general's aide, a young captain with one of those godawful high-and-tight haircuts that eluded completely the skirmish over sideburn length, came into the room and announced that the airliner was on final approach. People began to stir and move reluctantly toward the door and the scorching heat that was intensified by the acres of black tarmac around the terminal—everyone except the aide and the Australian lady. Amid chuckles and knowing glances from the general and his intimates, the aide produced from nowhere a huge, fat bed pillow and handed it to the Australian lady as he bent over to remove the blousing garters from his trouser cuffs. The rest of us decided not to leave just yet after all, and a nearsighted major got yucky stuff on his sleeve trying to retrieve his orange soda pop can from the trash barrel.

The Australian lady took the pillow and garters into the ladies' room, and emerged only moments later, looking extremely pregnant. More chuckling and a lot of sexist side comments, and we proceeded, semi-ceremoniously, out onto the sunbaked tarmac while the Australian pregnant lady adjusted the pillow and practiced waddling.

The plane arrived, the engines whined down, stairs were rolled up to the doors, and the band began to play. When people went home from Southeast Asia, the band played "California, Here I Come," but when dignitaries arrived, the band was pretty much on its own. I have no idea what they played that afternoon. It was lively. I remember that.

As soon as the stairs were in place, the Australian lady scampered up with agility rarely seen in pregnant ladies. The DC-8's door opened, and a stewardess, squinting in the sunlight, did a double take that could have landed her a fat contract in a Mack Sennett movie. I suspected that a pregnant Australian lady was pretty close to the last thing she expected to see at that exact moment.

But the astonishment on her face was nothing compared to the stunned look on Colonel Sloan's face when he emerged into the sunlight and the pregnant Australian lady threw her arms around his neck, and screamed out for all of Southeast Asia to hear, "Jake, darling! You got back just in *time*!"

I was standing about three feet from General Armstrong at the time. He sighed, hands clasped behind his back the way confused people do when they want to look like things haven't gotten completely out of control. He rolled his eyes skyward, and said to no one in particular, "Well, so much for pomp and dignity in the 1st Marine Air Wing."

I really liked Al Armstrong.

THOUGHTS WHILE PLANE
WATCHING

On nice afternoons, I enjoyed sitting on the top of one of our aircraft revetments, close to the dual north-south runways of the Da Nang Air Base, where I could pass an hour or two in peace, watching airplanes take off and land. It was hot and noisy, gritty with the red clay dust from the southwest where the war was, but fifteen feet above the asphalt there was always a breeze, and I would find myself happily tapping the heels of my flying boots against the corrugated-steel wall as I watched the planes go by.

If a man couldn't hold a fishing pole, watching airplanes was the next best thing, and the Da Nang Air Base was one of the best plane watching places in the world. At any given time one could see giant cargo jets and graceful airliners, air force and Marine Phantom jets and Vietnamese Bird Dog observation planes, all in various stages of the flying business. Antique prop transports, newly refurbished and bristling with guns, vied for the tower's attention with OV-10s, Marine A-6s, and air force Jolly Green Giant CH-53 helicopters. Smaller VIP helicopters carrying their semiprecious loads of generals and colonels demanded immediate access to some busy area, while an A-4 Skyhawk from a distant carrier limped in from the north with half its tail shot away, the pilot praying to make it to the runway arresting gear.

Supply and resupply winged in every minute. Tons of cargo arrived on C-130s and high-tailed C-141s and interesting DC-8s that belonged to Flying Tigers Airlines and didn't have any windows. Fresh troops arrived, and tired troops departed, on the 707s and DC-8s of small, unknown airlines that took their sustenance from government contracts. Some troops departed on C-141 hospital planes, while others, less fortunate, left in boxes on C-130s.

Shiny Pan American and TWA liners flaunted their commercial glamor at the passenger terminal as perky stewardesses in not-yet-wilted uniforms bid good-bye or hello to servicemen returning from or boarding flights for R & R in Australia or Hawaii. And there were always a few horny lieutenants hanging around the terminal doing their damndest to entice one of the girls into doing her part for the war effort.

One of our aerial observers succeeded one night. I suppose that was a great conquest. But he used my hut!

I had the night standby mission and slept in the hangar that night, and when I returned to my Quonset hut quarters to shower and change in the morning, there was a note pinned to my pillow thanking me for the use of the "apartment." It was written in a flowery, feminine hand, and the perfume lingered for days. I had a hard time being angry.

Sitting on a revetment, I had time to think about pressing problems, and I spent some time pondering what I would do with all of the AK-47 automatic rifles we had collected over the months—this after two flights of air force Phantoms screamed into the air with a throaty snarl of pure power. I loved that sound, and I thought about the day I turned down orders to fly the planes, and decided that it had been one of my better decisions. One of the Da Nang based Phantom squadron call signs was Gunfighter, which caused my mind to wander to the AK-47 problem. I solved that one sitting on the wall.

Just about every time we saved some reconnaissance team's ass, we would be rewarded with a gift for our efforts, and it was always an AK-47, except one time when some team gave us an old Chinese rifle that looked as though it might have been used to shoot at Marines during the Boxer Rebellion at the turn of the century. After every shop and office in the hanger had one or two battle trophies hanging on a wall, we still had a dozen or so pieces of offbeat ordnance sitting in corners and closets and collecting dust.

The answer, of course, was to do exactly what the reconnaissance battalion had done with them in the first place—give them to suckers like me.

I figured this out the moment Lt. Col. Ed Reagan took command of the reconnaissance battalion.

Back in 1965, just before we went to war and were still at Camp Hague in Okinawa, then Maj. Ed Reagan, heavyset, bespectacled, and constantly smiling, completed his overseas tour with the Task Force 79 staff and was getting ready to go home.

His roommate, Maj. Bill Seaton, and I spent a lot of time think-ing of a memorable going-away present, one he would never forget as long as he lived. It didn't have to be nice, just memo-rable.

In one of the Camp Hague PX concession tailor shops that made special-order clothing, there had been hanging for months a wonderful overcoat, which some Marine had invented in a moment of alcoholic, perhaps drug-induced, frivolity and never dared come back to pick up.

Whenever we visited that section of the PX, we examined the coat, and showed it to all of our friends, pointing out with gen-uine enthusiasm all of the special features. It was a tweedy over-coat with no fewer than sixteen pockets, several of which had zippers. There were inside pockets and outside pockets, and every time we visited it, we discovered some new wonderment, not the least of which was a zippered vent we never did fully understand. It was belted and had a buttoned flap similar to a trench coat, and in truth was the goddamnedest garment anyone had ever seen outside the red-light district of a large city back in the States.

After considerable discussion, it became obvious that we had to buy that memorable coat for Ed Reagan's going-away present. There was nothing else quite so garish on the entire island.

Bill Seaton was a world-class shopper, and so he dickered with the owner of the concession until he was able to purchase it for about twelve bucks. Our only problem then had to do with timing. We couldn't give it to Ed too soon before he left, because he could easily lose it, or leave it in the men's room at Kadena base operations, or even refuse to take it.

We spent a lot of time figuring out the exact time to make the presentation. We'd decided that the moment of truth would have to be at a time when he absolutely couldn't refuse it under pain of acute embarrassment.

Bill Seaton took the coat to Kadena Air Base early in the day of Major Reagan's departure, and had the flight operations clerk stow it under the counter where flight plans were filed. As de-parture time neared, we went through normal send-off proce-dures, arriving at base operations at the proper time, and accompanying Ed to the steps of the chartered airliner. I stole back to the operations desk as the party of well-wishers chatted amiably, retrieved the coat only after a command performance demonstration of the zippered pockets to the operations duty officer, and caught up with the party just as the passengers were called to board.

Bill Seaton accompanied Reagan up the steps, holding the wonderful overcoat behind his back, and when there was absolutely no time for any rejection, presented the going-away present.

Timing, it turned out, was everything, and when Ed Reagan returned to Vietnam and took command of the infantry organization we dealt with so much, I knew immediately how to get rid of AK-47s.

Every time a colonel or general visited VMO-2, we had an AK-47 stored out of sight but nearby whatever vehicle awaited the dignitary. When the visit was over and I accompanied the VIP to his jeep, the weapon would suddenly appear, and I never did see the man who could refuse a present at the exact moment of departure. I cared not what the man did with the rifle after he left the squadron area; I knew only that we had reduced our illegal armory by one, and disposition was now someone else's problem.

For some reason, I never did find out what Ed Reagan did with that overcoat five years earlier.

But I digress, which is allowed when you sit on a revetment wall and watch airplanes.

One of the values of small, personal histories is the snippet or two of what the writer was thinking about at the time. The following are some of the things we talked about in 1970:

1. We didn't spend too much time pondering the right or wrong of the war. That would have been a waste of time, but we did discuss what was going to happen when we pulled out of the war.

2. Our solution to winning the war was a simple one. We would stage a wonderful victory parade through downtown Da Nang, have the general give a speech proclaiming victory, climb aboard the ships, and sail away. As it turned out, that's pretty much what we did in the end.

3. We were certain that as soon as we were gone, the North Vietnamese would move in, and considerable time was given to speculation as to what the North Vietnamese Air Force would do with the wonderful real estate we had developed for them.

4. We all agreed that it would take ten years for the Marine Corps to recover its public image; the army would take

longer, simply because there had been more soldiers than Marines to piss off the American public.

5. While we deplored the riots and antigovernment unrest on the college campuses, we felt that many of us, too, might have been looking at the Canadian border had we been youngsters subjected to the same brainwashing that had taken place over the years. College kids of 1970 had been young teenagers when they first received their daily dosage of the war with their dinner on the six o'clock news. By 1970, they were convinced that to go to Vietnam meant that they would die. To go into the army meant that they would go to Vietnam and die. To be drafted meant that they would go into the army and go to Vietnam and die. No wonder they tried to dodge the draft.

These were small thoughts, except for that last one, which took a couple of sessions and a lot of vodka and grapefruit juice. On the other hand, the breach between the military and the news media took an inordinately long time to understand. After all, I was in the middle of it for a while there, and it was difficult to understand what was going on at the time.

When he was plane watching, a man had time to think about the world in general, and also about nothing in particular. It was on such an afternoon that I finally figured out why the war we were fighting so diligently was getting such a bum rap from the news media.

My version of what happened to get us into so much trouble with the press was a simple one because, like most veterans, my head was not filled with facts.

In order to understand the actions of the news reporters over the years of the war, one had first to recognize the nature of the beast newsmen were reporting on, and the brain of that beast was not in Da Nang, nor Saigon, but in the White House and the pentagon.

The long and short of it was that the president and the secretary of defense micromanaged the war. They did this for two reasons. One, they could; and two, they didn't trust the military commanders. One had only to meet the Marine Corps' first III MAF commander to understand why that might have been.

Communications were pretty good in 1965. They weren't great, but they were good enough for people in Washington to get involved with just about any level of command they wanted to. In the "1965" chapter, I related some of those communications abilities. My scrape with an army colonel from the emergency action center in Saigon over a six-digit grid coordinate for the location of a dozen or so Marines—a questionable piece of information he demanded immediately because the White House was on the other phone and wanted it for the president's morning briefing—hints at the fact that from the beginning Washington intended to control the tactical war. But the tale in that same chapter about the international uproar over somebody taking a potshot at a gunboat was of greater importance, and better served to make my point.

That minor incident received major focus simply because the nature of the episode required Saigon attention, which in turn alerted Washington immediately.

At about two or three o'clock one morning, an ensign on duty at a small naval base near Monkey Mountain saw what he believed to be an attack on the air facility at Marble Mountain, and he decided to save the base single-handedly with naval gunfire. Following procedures, he phoned MACV headquarters in Saigon for permission to call in the five-inch guns of a destroyer. Saigon was in instant communications with the National Military Command Center in Washington, and before long, I was having lively telephone conversations with duty officers all over the world.

Because of a scheduling quirk in Washington, Honolulu, and Saigon, all of the watch officers that night were Marine aviator contemporaries of mine. We all knew each other and were able to speak on a first-name basis and trust each other to be telling the truth, and the incident was laid to rest within an hour.

But this was a rare episode. Instant communications were wonderful, but if you didn't believe the guy who was calling, then the best phone system in the world was worthless. And the micromanagers in Washington didn't always believe us—maybe with good reason.

We lied. We didn't lie to the press, at least I don't think we did, but we withheld one hell of a lot of information from higher echelons simply to avoid airing our dirty linen in public.

If a pilot, flying with his head "up and locked," dropped a load of bombs without arming them, and we then had to send an ordnance demolition team out into Indian country to blow them up, we'd report the incident, but we would leave out the bit about the pilot being a short circuit between the rudder pedals and the kerosene handle. That was a training problem, and we would rectify the situation ourselves.

We would still be lying at the squadron level in 1970, but for different reasons. In the chapter on aerial observers, I refer to an OV-10 killing two enemy snipers—not a big thing had the war been a normal one. But those two kills were left out of the after-action report simply because the Marine Corps was at that time lobbying for an additional attack squadron, and every time Washington bureaucrats in the Department of Defense read about the OV-10 being used in the attack role, that information was used to prove that we already had the additional attack capability. Lieutenants and captains could kill Viet Cong—that was simply youthful exuberance. But when the squadron commander did it, the act pointed to a policy change, and could be exploited politically. I don't know whether or not the Marine Corps really needed the extra attack squadron, but I wasn't about to jeopardize the request just because I greased two gooners.

In 1965, III Marine Amphibious Force put out a sitrep (situation report) every night and copies were sent to Saigon and Washington and every high-echelon command with an interest in the war—which was just about everybody. As soon as the report went out on the wire, we prepared another one, which was sent only to Fleet Marine Force Pacific headquarters in Hawaii via a back-channel net, and which included another two or three pages telling extra-secret stuff—or maybe just sensitive stuff—about what really happened, and which we didn't want the rest of the world to know about.

I suspect it didn't take long for the White House to catch on to the fact that military commanders were not telling them everything, and because they insisted on running the war themselves, it was only natural that they would begin to seek other sources of information. Washington often bypassed the high-echelon military commands, and a general who suspected that people in high places were talking to his field commanders behind his back might easily have become paranoid.

Paranoia led to lying—not deliberate lying exactly, more like panic lying, cover-your-ass lying. It didn't take long for the press and television reporters to smell a rat.

News gatherers had egos just like everyone else, and they all wanted scoops. That's how reputations were made then, and that's how they're still made today. They weren't getting any scoops at all attending the carefully staged, choreographed, and sanitized daily news briefings. They had to go out sniffing around for their own stories. They found them; and they reported—or didn't report—them to suit their own needs.

At first, they were pretty decent about it. Try this story on for size. As in the movie, *Cool Hand Luke*, what we had one afternoon was a failure to communicate. A semantics problem.

In the summer of '65, a Marine platoon was busy checking out the population of a village and looking for bad guys, when a young Vietnamese man in black pajamas cut and ran. The platoon commander saw the man running, pointed and shouted, "Somebody stop that man!"

Now, to a young Marine rifleman, the word "stop" carried a connotation that went a little bit beyond "grab" or "detain for questioning." The Marine did as he was told. He pressed his cheek into the stock of his M-14, squeezed off a round, and stopped the Vietnamese man dead in his tracks.

What was that? a horrible mistake, or blatant disregard for human life?

The incident occurred in the early days of the war when the press still trusted us. It wasn't hushed up, but it wasn't reported either, to the best of my knowledge. The platoon leader was relieved and sent out of the country in disgrace, and a reporter I talked to later thought it was simply one of the sad stories of war and a really rotten deal for the young lieutenant.

Or this. Soon after we set up shop in the III MAF command center in 1965, we received two or three .45-caliber "grease guns" to hang on the wall in case we were overrun and had to defend ourselves. No one in the command center had ever fired that particular weapon before. I had never even seen one. The chief-of-staff arranged for all of the assigned enlisted Marines to go to a nearby rifle range one morning and test-fire the guns until they learned how to keep them under control. Forty-five-caliber machine guns tend to ride up on you.

One of the kids let go with his first burst, the barrel started up as advertised, and he fired a few rounds clean over the target area, one of which ended up in the leg of a Vietnamese farmer who was taking a bath in the river behind the range.

The farmer staggered, screaming and bleeding, to the road that ran along the river, and was picked up almost immediately by an army doctor and his driver who happened to be driving by at the time. He was treated successfully.

End of story.

Our watch officer was aghast, however, and ran to the chief-of-staff with the news of the tragedy.

"No big thing," Regan Fuller said calmly. "An accident."

"But what if the press gets hold of it?"

"What if they do? They've been around long enough to know the difference between an accident and an atrocity."

In the summer of 1965, there was a certain amount of trust, but a few years later there was none, and one can be certain that if either of those incidents had occurred in 1970, it would have been headline news.

Here are some examples of how the news media earned themselves a bum rap with the Marine Corps. No one was guilty. Everybody was doing the best he knew how, and it just happened.

In 1965, when we first moved into Da Nang and the surrounding environs, the press moved in with us. For the first six months of our war, the things we did were reported in *Time* magazine accurately. Sometimes we didn't like what we read. Maybe we would have changed an adjective or an adverb and maybe we would have preferred the word "acknowledged" over the word "admitted." But those of us who ran the III MAF command center were in agreement that the news wasn't slanted—at least not in *Time*, which was the only Stateside publication we received then.

We had a nasty disagreement with a particularly cheeky woman from a French news agency, who was forever giving us hell about a lot of unimportant stuff, like a small Confederate flag flying over some bunker out on a hillside somewhere, up at Hue/Phu Bai I think. The power figures eventually agreed with her on that one, and the Marines who lived there took the flag down and said that they were sorry and that they hadn't meant to offend anybody—and she wrote another article saying she didn't believe them.

Newspaper and magazine reporting didn't seem to be much of a problem. It was television we didn't understand. We had seen a sign much earlier that we were going to have trouble with television, and we should have taken it as a warning.

Long before any large numbers of Marines moved into the Da Nang area, there was a small unit, consisting of a helicopter squadron with infantry protection, that went by the improbable navy designation "Task Force 79.3.3.6," but which we called "Operation Shu Fly."

Overseas Marine helicopter squadrons during the early 1960s rotated in four-month increments: a training tour in Okinawa, followed by four months afloat as part of the special landing force, and four months in Da Nang. An infantry platoon protected them in Da Nang, and the fact that the platoon sometimes numbered about five hundred Marines was one of the better kept secrets of the day.

They trained Vietnamese pilots to fly the old H-34 helicopters, and they performed all manner of nontactical chores. During the monsoon floods of 1964–65, they saved an enormous amount of lives as they hauled entire villages, people, pigs, and chickens, to safety from the raging high waters.

One day in early spring, a helicopter was shot down by bad guys. This was around the time we sent in the 9th Marine Expeditionary Brigade. Another helicopter hauled the dead and injured back to Da Nang. A German news team was there to meet the helicopter, and when a dead Marine was off-loaded, one of them stuck his movie camera smack dab in the middle of it all, and captured the blood and gore for whatever news agency he worked for.

This pissed the Marines off. They had no argument with cameramen filming the dark side of war, but they sure as hell weren't going to permit anybody, no matter what nationality, to take pictures of their fallen comrade. Death was a personal thing after it happened, not for publication, and a shouting match ensued.

The Marine Corps public relations officer arrived—a major whose name I have forgotten—and as the confrontation peaked, he quite naturally took the side of the Marines; and the whole thing ended up with the outraged Marine major punching the German cameraman's headlights out. Not a smart thing to do.

Back in Okinawa, the general and everyone else agreed to a man that he would have done the same thing were he in the major's shoes. But still, the poor man was relieved of his duties anyway and transferred somewhere terrible—probably to Korea, where everybody else was sent when he was bad.

I have no idea as to what was done with the film, but the precedent was established.

Pretty soon, television news people moved in to Vietnam in droves, and during the early days of the war, plied their trade the way it had always been done. Just like World War II and Korea, they took movies of airplanes taking off, trucks moving forward, infantrymen slogging into harm's way and grinning at the camera, cargo being off-loaded, and destroyers shooting their five-inch guns at night. The only new item on the list of standard shots was film of a whole bunch of helicopters landing at once, while warriors tumbled out to do battle with international evil doers.

This was okay for about a week or two, but the demand for film had increased dramatically. During World War II and Korea, there had been no television news. Newsreel cameramen only had to provide a few minutes of film every two or three days, because that was when the motion picture theaters changed their bills. Airplanes taking off and troops moving forward were enough to keep Americans satisfied that they were being kept informed and that they knew the face of war.

During World War II, the only times we kids ever saw wounded Americans in newsreels were when Joe DiMaggio or Lana Turner were visiting them in pristine white hospitals and signing baseballs or kissing their smiling and freshly shaved faces. Once—only once—we saw a scruffy, grungy, unshaven GI with a bloody patch over his eye. But he was herding a bunch of German prisoners and squinting with his cold, steely, good eye, and maybe he was squinting because of the cigarette dangling out of the corner of his mouth. He was the indestructible GI Joe.

Twenty years later, with the six o'clock news to be fed, television had a huge appetite. Pretty soon editors were demanding different stuff, and more of it. If the reporters in the field couldn't provide exactly what the editors wanted, then that was what editors were for.

Here's a version of one helluva big stink from a Marine's point of view. I wasn't there physically, I was in the command center back in Da Nang, but the company commander was a friend of mine, and this is the working Marine's viewpoint of a well-publicized story we all believed to be absolutely true.

During the latter part of 1965, Bravo Company, 1st Battalion, 4th Marines was out in Indian country, looking for bad guys, and a search of a village turned up a reinforced bunker under one of the grass huts. The Marines burned the wood and grass superstructure away and exposed the bunker for all the world to see.

Naturally, the company commander radioed back to his headquarters, which recognized the importance of such a cache. The newspeople were invited to fly out and take a look and see that there was a real enemy out there, who used innocent looking places to hide his bullets and grenades and stuff.

In order to show a reasonable sequence of events, the television people wanted to show a hut burning up to expose the bunker, and so one of them handed a Marine his Zippo cigarette lighter and asked him to set fire to a hut, an unoccupied hut to the best of our knowledge. The Marine did as he was told, and the cameraman got the film, and presumably that was the end of the story. Marines find enemy arms cache and burn a grass hut away to expose it.

But that wasn't what appeared on the evening news in 1965. What appeared in living rooms all across America was a bloodthirsty Marine burning down some poor, innocent farmer's hut.

That is the version we in the Marine Corps believed at the time, and the particular newsman, whose face appeared with the film, made the Marine Corps' ''sucks'' list long before Jane Fonda came along in her starring role.

And so, the stage was set. Military leaders thought the press was out to get them, and the press thought military leaders were lying to them, and the president knew damn well that everybody was lying to him. The star-crossed affair stumbled downhill from there. Everyone was doing his job the best he knew how, and it just happened.

In 1970, it never occurred to me that we would overreact in the years to come and just about bar the press from covering operations like the Grenada landing. But it was predictable. People my age were in charge of the tactical units on that one, and they had no intention of being stung again.

By the time DESERT STORM kicked off, after twenty-five years of thinking about it, the news was managed masterfully. But I suspect that if that war had lasted another week or two, the rules would have changed. Mistakes like the friendly-fire incidents would have been magnified; military leaders would have become paranoid; news briefings would have become increasingly sanitized. As Washington began stonewalling the press, the White House would have begun to micromanage the war, and some mighty fine people would have been vilified as bumbling, warmongering incompetents. That's the way the human comedy is played out.

In 1968, when I was the ''Great Santini's'' executive officer in the Marine air detachment at NAS Pensacola, one of my jobs was to make casualty calls on the families of Marines and to be the bearer of bad news. The first two calls I made were about Marines killed by friendly fire; one by one of our own bombs, and the other by an artillery short round.

The Marine Corps was brutally honest on death calls, and it

was the most unpleasant assignment I have ever experienced in my life. But that honesty paid off in the long run. Other services sometimes played with the facts and got their fingers burned.

The two friendly-fire deaths I was involved with in 1968 were small potatoes during the Tet Offensive when so many Marines were dying, but they would have received major headlines in 1991.

There were other thoughts to be examined, sitting on a wall and watching a flight of A-1 Skyraider Sandys launch into the afternoon sun on a downed-pilot rescue mission, real or practice.

The sight of the A-1 Skyraiders gave me the solution to a tactical problem I was working on at the time. I was trying to figure out a way to support an upcoming SOG effort which would insert a team from the CIA sponsored Special Operations Group into some high ground in Laos—hills which were just a bit too far away for the landing to be supported by our AH-1G Cobras, which couldn't carry enough fuel to do the job. I remembered some of the Korean War stories of how the Skyraiders had been used to cover downed pilots then, when helicopter gunships were only a dream.

A division of four aircraft set up a circular pattern around the helpless pilot in those days, and made continuous diving passes into the area in what was referred to as a "bee-hive" maneuver that saw one plane with its guns and rockets pointed downhill at all times. I knew that we had the capability of doing the same thing with our OV-10s.

Four "super gun-birds" with a twenty-millimeter cannon, two SUU-11 Gatling guns, rocket pods, and the four sponson-mounted M-60 machine guns gave us a lot of firepower for close-in support, and I sketched out a pattern on my knee board right there on the revetment before I went running to wing G-3 with my proposal.

The wing operations officer remembered the bee-hive operation from the early fifties, and a meeting was arranged with some of those incredible SOG warriors for the next night, in order that I might present my solution to what was really only a logistical problem. The OV-10 had longer legs than the Cobra.

The next day I led three OV-10s out to some target area, I don't remember exactly where, and we practiced the maneuver until we were satisfied that we could protect a team adequately until a massive cavalry charge arrived to rescue them. We used three planes instead of four, because that was all I could afford to pull out of the day's flight schedule.

That evening, we met with an army colonel from the Special Operations Group, and I made my pitch. I started with the Korean War experiences, and explained just how the maneuver worked, and that we had rehearsed it all just that morning, but the steely-eyed warrior didn't warm up to the proposal. I got carried away and told him that the air force's Sandy Skyraiders performed the same operation every day, and if he didn't like the idea of OV-10s, I was sure that he could work out something with the sister service. His back stiffened at that, and I could swear that he snarled.

He was polite, but he liked Marine helicopters. And so the final solution saw a lot of barrels of JP-4 hauled out to a fire support base close to the Laotian border so that the Marine Cobras could refuel.

Another great idea that never got off the ground.

What was actually growing in the revetments themselves seemed important at the time. The steel walls of the revetments were filled with dirt so fertile that weeds and green things grew almost overnight. Some kid in one of the A-6 squadrons had been caught cultivating a crop of marijuana in one of their revetments a few weeks earlier, and so I made it a point to check periodically and ensure that VMO-2 wasn't producing a cash crop.

Additionally, VMO-2's boxing robes were designed on a revetment. For a while there, Marine Aircraft Group 11 had an ambitious boxing program running, and each squadron was invited to field a team. Our sergeant major designed the uniforms, but I knew what the robes were supposed to look like.

Despite my pugilistic past, I had a hard time getting interested in the fight game. Still, I was determined that win or lose, VMO-2 would have the best dressed team in the ring. We had enough money in the coffee mess fund to dress the fighters handsomely, and we had our robes made by one of the very best tailors in Udorn, Thailand. I cannot recall what they cost, but they were OV-10 green with white satin lining, and the sleeves were extra wide as boxing robes sleeves were supposed to be so that the gloves could fit through. Mine had HOSTAGE SIX written across the back in five-inch letters. I designed them right there on the flight line.

Those were neutral thoughts. Sometimes I would become nostalgic. I often thought about how much I wished the squad-

ron were back at Marble Mountain, on the beaches of the South
China Sea and out of range of those damn rockets. Most of us
in the squadron seemed to have more in common with the English and history majors of the helicopter group than we had
with jet pilot engineers who took themselves so doggone seriously. The earthmen infantry officers of 1st Marine Division
weren't any more fun. I plotted angles to return to Marble
Mountain, where I would have an excuse not to run up to division headquarters twice a day.

That was about as homesick as I would allow myself to be. A
man could think of anything but home when he was alone, sitting on a revetment watching Jolly Green Giant helicopters racing after the Skyraiders, nose low, with the collective control
levers in the pilots' armpits. Maybe there was a downed pilot
somewhere out of country. I wasn't going to worry about it
because I knew where all of our OV-10s were.

Thinking about home was as big a waste of time as thinking
about whether or not we should ever have gotten involved in
Vietnam in the first place.

END OF THE LINE

Over the years people have asked, "If you were such a hot shot, why did you retire after just twenty years?"

That's a fair question, and after as much bogus denial as I think I can get away with, I tell them that Peggy Lee made me do it.

People who are old enough to know who Peggy Lee is raise an eyebrow, which requires me to explain how that could be. Young people who never heard her sing think I'm talking about some girlfriend, and sense a scandal, and this also requires an explanation. I now bare my soul in public. And in a few pages, I'll explain about Peggy Lee.

I left Vietnam in 1970, a happy man. Not only was I going home to my wife and family, but I also had orders to take command of the largest tactical squadron in the Marine Corps, Marine Light Helicopter Squadron 267 at Camp Pendleton, just outside Oceanside, California. I was one cocky young light colonel.

I had received a phone call from wing G-1 (personnel) a few days before I was due to depart Vietnam. Third Marine Air Wing at El Toro, California, was on the other phone, and they wanted to know if I would be willing to take command of HML-267 upon my return. My answer was immediate, a resounding "Yes!" I was one happy fellow. I had not lobbied for this command at all, and I relished the idea that it was a reward for my hard-earned performance in combat.

The fact that I was probably the only inbound lieutenant colonel with anything near the proper credentials might have had something to do with it, but hotshots don't have thoughts like that.

There was a downside to the offer. I had to make a change-of-command ceremony on 21 October, which gave me only a few weeks to gather up my family in Pensacola, Florida, pack up the furniture, and move to Southern California. But that inconvenience was a small price to pay. In the Marine Corps, a man seldom got the chance for back-to-back squadron commands.

I managed to get a phone patch through to my wife. "There's good news and bad news," I exulted. "I've been given command of HML-267 at Camp Pendleton, but we have to be there by 21 October."

There was a lengthy pause on the Pensacola end of the connection, then, ". . . Uhh, what's the *good* news?"

I had been in receipt of orders to 3d Marine Air Wing for several months, and expected a desk job at El Toro. I had promised my wife that I would make every effort to get my orders changed so that I could return to Pensacola and take any billet available in the Naval Air Training Command until I had completed twenty years of service and we could retire. The plan was for me to start working on advanced degrees at the University of West Florida there in Pensacola, get a doctorate perhaps, and begin a new career in education. All this crap about going to Southern California did not fill her heart with cheer.

The year we spent at the University of Southern Mississippi, where I finally got a baccalaureate degree before returning to Vietnam in 1969, was as pleasant a time as a family could enjoy, and we decided during my R & R in Hawaii, in June of 1970, that education was the life for us. My wife was understandably spring-loaded to the pissed-off position over this sudden turn of events.

But she was a good sport about it all. She didn't cry or anything. "You let the Marine Corps turn your head!" was about as angry a statement as I heard during those hectic three weeks. And of course that was true. They turned that sucker clear around in the neck socket.

We had two cars to drive cross-country out to California, and this was a lucky thing because it eliminated about 90 per cent of the conversations, most of which would have been one-sided, and would have caused great anguish and gnashing of teeth.

I don't know what bothered me more during that three-day drive—my conscience or my hemorrhoids. I had flown some six hundred hours during that Vietnam tour, sitting on a hard steel ejection seat and pulling heavy G forces a dozen times a day, and my lower posterior extremities were as important to me on that painful journey as my family and career—and sometimes a little bit more.

There was a house waiting for us when we arrived, and we moved into government quarters at Camp Pendleton—which was something else I had promised we would never do. After getting my hemorrhoids snipped at the base hospital, or whatever gross and humiliating thing it was the proctologist did to me back there, I was ready to go to work.

The day before I was to take command, I had to meet with the wing commander, and so I drove out to the Camp Pendleton airfield, where I planned to turn in my orders and say hello at the squadron before I met the staff car which would carry me to wing headquarters at El Toro, some fifty miles north of Oceanside. I arrived at precisely nine o'clock in the morning, such was my fetish for punctuality. As I climbed the outside stairs to the second deck of the hangar, sirens and horns started blaring and blowing and honking. "Huh?" I remember thinking. "They blow the eight o'clock whistle at nine o'clock here in California."

I opened the door and went inside to see people running around and shouting as though a plane had just crashed. And of course, that was exactly what had happened. It was a good hour and a half before things calmed down and I was able to turn in my orders to the squadron adjutant. No one had been hurt, fortunately, but another UH-1E had just bitten the dust. As I tried to be helpful without getting in the way, I wondered if this might be some kind of signal, a burning Huey instead of a burning bush.

It was. That afternoon the group commander, Col. Merv Porter, accompanied me to the wing commander's office where the general gave me a single instruction. "I don't care if your squadron never flies one goddamn hour," he snarled, punctuating his sentence with a stab of his finger. "Just don't break any more f——king airplanes!"

I thought that was pretty clear.

Later that afternoon, after I returned from El Toro and was maneuvering my little white Mustang out of the squadron parking lot to drive home, I stopped to pick up three young Marines who were standing under the give-a-Marine-a-ride sign. One of them had been a plane captain in VMO-2 at Da Nang, and it was an eye-opening experience as I drove into Oceanside and listened to the young veteran tell the others what a great squadron commander I was, and how I wouldn't put up with any of the Camp Pendleton chickenshit, and how I'd probably do away with formations and stuff, and how they could all relax now and start having fun.

Geez! Two burning bushes in one day, and I was grateful for the warning. The kid really believed that a squadron in the States could be run exactly the same way as a squadron in combat. I was going to be expected to deliver on a performance I was neither willing nor able to give. This was going to be trickier than I had thought, and I had less than twenty-four hours to shift my brain gears into a peacetime, training mode.

The change-of-command ceremonies went off without a hitch, and everybody was nice to us. After a couple of days, I discovered that I was in charge of the most unusual squadron in the Marine Corps—except maybe for HMX at Quantico, which flew the presidential helicopters and had to do a lot of weird things.

We were the sole tenants of the airfield there at Camp Pendleton. We belonged to 3d Marine Air Wing at El Toro, fifty miles away, which meant that I had to attend all of the meetings and social events there. But we were also a part of Camp Pendleton, and I had to attend all of the meetings and social events there too. My wife and I went to a lot of receptions.

Additionally, Marine Light Helicopter Squadron 267 was a misnomer. We averaged about forty flying machines on the flight line, half of them OV-10s, and there were generally eighty or more pilots in the squadron—most of whom were just leaving for, or coming back from Vietnam. Most of them were in love, and pilots in love can drive a CO nuts. Can you imagine how many weddings a squadron commander had to attend when there were that many young pilots in the outfit? Baby presents alone ran into big bucks.

Our main business was training Huey and OV-10 pilots before they went overseas. Because of that intense effort and a cavalier attitude toward flying, and maybe the fact that the pilots were all in heat, the squadron's accident rate was the highest in the Marine Corps. My job was clearly cut out for me, as per the general's pointed instruction, and I went to work on aviation safety immediately. HML-267 didn't have another accident for almost twenty years, although I only take credit for two of those years.

When asked over the years about the one thing I accomplished in my short career that gave me the most pride, I answer quickly that the two squadrons I commanded both won chief of naval operations safety awards. I had seen too many people killed over the years, mostly through operational accidents, and the safety award stickers in my log book are still a source of pure personal pleasure.

One of the most enjoyable things about the tour in HML-267 was that I finally learned how to fly a helicopter, and I am here to tell you that it is just about as much fun as a person can have in aviation. Being able to lift myself off the ground the way I used to do in my dreams when I was a kid was a thrill that never faded. Better yet, in my dreams I had to flap my arms. In a helicopter all I had to do was pull up on the collective control lever.

Learning the mysteries of helicopters was probably more fun for me than it was for most people. I was the squadron commander, and the instructors didn't yell at me so much. And when they did, they were always nice about it.

I worked my tail off trying to master the Huey. While I never got as good as the instructor pilots, I could get it from here to there without running into anything. Hueys were so slow that you could see trees and stuff in plenty of time to miss them.

My first night helicopter landing was aboard a moving aircraft carrier. That was interesting. When you're the CO, people forget that you can be just as green at some things as ordinary mortals. I'll never forget the cry of anguish from the instructor pilot in the left seat when I crept up to the USS *Princeton*, twenty miles out to sea, on an inky-black night, and asked him how the goddamn light switch worked.

Anyway, it was a lot of fun. While I did most of my flying as an instructor in the OV-10, the time I spent in Hueys and Cobras was a highlight of my short career—especially when we went to Yuma.

The Marine Corps air station at Yuma, Arizona, was the one place where a U.S. based squadron could operate the same as a squadron in combat, and we made the most of it. Because of our unique training status, we were able to take Huey and OV-10 detachments over to the desert base every six weeks, fly our tails off, and shoot up all the ammunition in the inventory. I used every excuse in the books to justify my going down there as much as possible.

We were able to introduce a system of night bombing which we had perfected in Vietnam, and which was much safer than a single flare or two which caused target fixation and killed pilots. I am convinced that we saved several lives with that development.

We were able to get Force Reconnaissance teams down there, and practice insertions and extractions, using live ammunition. I like to think that we sent pilots into combat one hell of a lot better trained than I had been two years earlier.

I even got to play with the Huey's door guns. God, what sport! I couldn't hit doodly-squat, and the desert jackrabbit population didn't suffer one bit on my account. But that was ten times as much fun as any video game can ever hope to be.

Shooting the forward-firing change-seven-kit guns bolted on to the sides of the plane was a challenge too. The UH-1E was never designed to be a gunship, and the gun sight was a simple, cross-hair device that looked like one of those rings kids use for making bubbles, and which flipped down over the windscreen when it was time to shoot. The pilot made his fine sighting adjustment by putting a mark on the windscreen with a grease pencil, and then hoped for the best, and that was probably the last time Kentucky windage was ever used in air-to-ground combat, because the Cobras came out of the factory with real gunsights similar to 1960 era fighter planes.

People today ask why there was a cage around the forward-firing machine guns, and the reason was to prevent spent bullet shells from flying into all those external moving parts a Huey had—especially the delicate tail rotor. When we took a detachment of six Hueys to Yuma, we always took along a crate of extra tail-rotor blades, because the guns generally fired faster than the baskets could take the shell cases, and one or two pieces of brass always ended up pranging the back end of the plane. The slightest dent in a tail-rotor blade could cause horrendous vibrations and result in the tail rotor separating from the plane. And so, two or three blades were changed each day.

I dinged a tail-rotor blade one day. I was so intent on not pulling any G force when the firing run was completed that I didn't feed in enough left rudder in the dive, which put the tail rotor in a direct line with the left guns, and I purely pranged that sucker.

Other pilots could get away with that error, but you don't think for one minute that the maintenance department was going to let the cold, steely-eyed commander get away with it. No way!

At the end-of-deployment beer party, a dented tail rotor was presented to me, along with the bill for all the beer which they deemed an appropriate fine for a guy trying to masquerade as a helicopter pilot.

I have made the point in this "instruction manual" that commanding a squadron in combat takes a lot out of a person, and this is true. Commanding a squadron in peacetime, however, can be a lot more difficult, even if you do get more sleep.

In a combat situation, if your personality, stamina, and flying abilities are up to it, running a squadron is a piece of cake, and in some ways a lot of fun. But hear me well when I tell you that all the things that make you famous in combat are only a tiny percentage of what you are going to be called upon to do when there are wives and sweethearts and children hanging on to the Marines in your squadron, and you are called upon to become personally involved with all of them, and understand why Corporal Jones couldn't make it in yesterday morning because his baby had a fever, and he had to take the child to sick bay himself because his wife had to go to work—or had just left him, or just wasn't speaking to any of them—and all of that for reasons that were personal, and Corporal Jones didn't want to talk about it.

I couldn't help but get involved the time a captain returned from Vietnam only to find out that his wife had another man living with her. He got roaring drunk and tried to climb into the house through a window, and the man shot him with a .45— which left a really big hole.

Or, how about the time a young Marine left his wife and child, and moved in with another woman who weighed about 150 pounds less than the wife? Both women wanted custody of the child, and I was supposed to referee the fight, and I wondered just how in hell Solomon got away with some of that crap he pulled.

In Da Nang, it was a kinder, gentler war. Over my term of nine months, I held Office Hours for disciplinary reasons only three times. Once was to hear a case against four youngsters who had been caught going through a hole in the fence to get to the passenger terminal where they bought pizza. Another hearing was for a Marine who went through a hole in a different fence on a "leg run," which I learned was local parlance for getting laid. I assigned him to the night crew because he promised me that night work would keep him out of trouble, but it was all I could do to keep from assigning him to the next planeload of kids going to Thailand, where a young Marine or staff NCO could catch the clap from at least three different women during the eight hours the plane was on the ground, and pretty well take care of his sex drive for a while.

That was not an original thought. Two or three days earlier, I had overheard a conversation between a plane captain and a lieutenant as the youngster helped unload the stuff the pilot had brought back from his three-day R & R trip to Udorn in Thailand. The plane captain was needling the pilot about the inequity of life that allowed officers and staff NCOs to spend three days in Thailand while he was permitted only eight hours—and that during the day. He made light of the situation with the following statement:

"I made the best of it. I got a set of bronzeware just like yours, a new suit, the clap, and some sports shirts."

"Whoa!" said the lieutenant. "You talking about gonorrhea?"

"Yes, sir. Wish I knew which girl it was gave it to me. Probably the third one. I was Superman with that one!"

There was a third Office Hours, but I forget what it was for. It couldn't have been very important. The point is that when a group of Marines were away from home, without dental appointments, nagging wives, or screaming kids, most of the major problems of life disappeared, and everyone was able to devote his entire life to the mission at hand. That was how wars were won.

But not in the States. Let me tell you about a few of the things that occupied my time at Camp Pendleton.

I wanted to start an air-ambulance program for the lonely stretch of Interstate 5 that ran along Camp Pendleton between Oceanside and San Clemente. I wanted to train Huey pilots in night medevac techniques, and at the same time suck up to the people of Southern California. Warmongering Marines weren't too popular in 1971, and it all seemed perfectly logical to me.

That was too frivolous for the legal office—Good Samaritan lawsuits and the like—and the program died at birth. Besides, there were more important legal problems for me to deal with.

In sunny Southern California, kids were forever getting into trouble, a lot of it because of marijuana, which was really, really popular about that time, and the use of which the Marine Corps still insisted was a felony crime.

I had my first run-in with a new wing commander, an unusually ambitious man who believed in leadership through intimidation. I asked for permission to treat first-time marijuana use as a misdemeanor, and handle the problem at Office Hours instead of sending the kid to jail for a while and pulling him off the flight line permanently just because the Marine Corps would not tolerate a drug-crazed maniac working on an airplane.

Well, sir, you'd have thought I was asking the Marine Corps to change its fight song or something. I wasn't any more thrilled about drug use than the next guy, but I also had a barracks detail full of highly trained mechanics who would never again in their Marine Corps lives be allowed to touch an airplane, and our aircraft availability really sucked right about then.

After months of begging and justifying, I was finally allowed to treat first-time marijuana use as a minor offense—only I was on my own, and warned that if higher authority made a big stink about it, the wing commander would deny knowing anything about it. And knowing him, I believe he would have. It was an experiment, and it worked, and it came about simply because I listened to a young captain, who didn't like drugs either but wasn't paranoid on the subject the way we old farts were. That episode seemed to take forever, but served as a solid reminder that age and experience were not always the answers to new problems.

Then I got sucked into a big flap over sideburn length. God, what a waste of time that was! I wanted to hammer out some of the tactics we had developed in Vietnam and put them into manual form before we forgot the important details, but I had to spend my time on the length of a Marine's sideburns. I thought I had left that stupid fight behind in Da Nang.

Long hair was all the rage in the early seventies, and Marines wanted sideburns. Blacks wanted Afros, and were able to get away with it during the day by plastering their hair down with some kind of stickum, then combing it out when they went on liberty. But the young white and Hispanic guys wanted sideburns, and the Marine Corps didn't want them to have them.

I didn't want them to, either, but I got caught in the middle of the controversy because 3d Marine Air Wing, for whom we worked and by whom we were inspected, had one regulation on sideburn length, and Marine Corps Base Camp Pendleton, with whom we lived and by whom we were inspected also, had another. There turned out to be a whole goddam inch of sideburn on the line, depending on whose regulation we followed and the shape of the poor Marine's face.

One regulation—I can't remember which was which—stated

that sideburns would be worn no lower than the corners of the eyes, and the other put the limit where the top of the ear joined the head, and I was in the position of having to follow both rules, which of course, was impossible.

"Pretty goddam hard," I yelled at one chief of staff, "on guys with low eyes and high ears!"

"Pretty goddam hard," I yelled at the other chief of staff, "on guys with high eyes and low ears!"

"How about," I offered, "if we stick a pencil in a guy's ear, and make that the boundary line?"

That took about a month to solve. And then I stepped on my pork on the subject of women going to the Naval Academy.

I had to attend the Camp Pendleton base commander's meeting once a week, and it was one of the few regularly scheduled meetings where I was always the junior guy. Occasionally there would be another lieutenant colonel there, but he was generally somebody's assistant sitting in for his boss. My rank, plus the fact that I was a heathen aviator, tended to detract from the value of anything I said until the subject of women attending the Naval Academy came up.

One day that subject became the sole issue of the conference, and everyone was agreeing with the general about what a sorry state of affairs it was that women were now going to be permitted to attend the alma mater of so many of the officers assembled. When there was a lull in the lamentations, I said that I thought it was a good idea. Don't you know, that got everybody's attention.

I could have kept my mouth shut and saved myself a lot of grief—but no! Lieutenant Colonel Smart Ass had to start talking like a pinko, liberal, Jane Fonda-loving pansy.

After a few minutes of minor uproar, during which my manhood and patriotism were called into question, I was allowed to explain myself.

Camp Pendleton had a lot of female commissioned officers and enlisted Marines working in the various support facilities. There were no women in the Fleet Marine Force, but the base units were staffed with a lot of WMs (woman Marines); and I had to do business with almost all of them. I explained to my inquisitors that I was damn sick and tired of the verbal fencing I had to go through with a woman until we both adjusted to a common language and were able to communicate directly. How efficiently things would be run, I insisted, if men and women were raised in the same school and grew up speaking the same language.

I got no cheers, but then they didn't boo me either.

Then came the flap over dog food. I'm not making this up. I wanted to work on a program to eliminate forward air controllers from an infantry battalion's table of organization and support the earthmen from the air, but nobody would listen to me. But even generals can get involved in a good dog-food argument.

In those antiwar years, there were some mean things going on in Southern California, and we had a lot of airfield to guard. Armories were being broken into, and weapons stolen. There were demonstrations at the main gate, encouraging Marines to do dreadful things, and we had a lot of airplanes on the flight line, which would make one hell of a bonfire.

We also had a lot of coyotes on the base, and the sentries didn't like walking around the huge expanse of an airfield without company. Solution: get some dogs.

Our people who were charged with running the airfield found a ready supply of German shepherds at the local SPCA. Every time they got a new shepherd in, they'd call us and one of our security people would drive over to the pound and pick it up. Pretty soon we had a splendid kennel running. It was inspected by the base veterinarian regularly, and we had a bunch of scary signs around that warned people that the airfield was patrolled by dogs. Pretty soon, people who didn't know us were afraid to come near the place.

The problem was that dog food cost money. We were paying for the Purina out of the squadron coffee mess fund, and sometimes that wasn't enough. People like the squadron commander had to reach into their pockets, and I decided it was time to get the supply side of the Marine Corps to pay for it. I put in a requisition for dog food, and forgot about it.

Well now, I've seen some reactions to some pretty strange requisitions in my lifetime, but this one took the cake. I remember for instance a time in 1962, in Thailand on a joint SEATO exercise, when the army's 9th Logistics Corps put in a requisition asking that a previous request for ten thousand condoms, dry, be changed to ten thousand condoms, lubricated, and justified it by explaining: "Study of indigenous population indicates dry, short bore." Everybody chuckled, and the requisition was filled.

I once put in a request I mentioned in an earlier chapter for an

English-speaking Montagnard on flight orders, and that ridiculous request was treated with dignity. But when I asked for something as simple as dog food, it became a subject worthy of the commanding general's attention.

The Marine Corps didn't have any dogs, you see—unless there were some secret places I didn't know about. We tried them in Vietnam in 1965—in fact, for a while there I was the local expert on the project, mainly because I had read both messages on the subject—but we gave up on the idea when the Vietnamese dog handler went AWOL.

All I was asking for was a small allocation of a couple of bucks so that we could run over to the commissary and buy dog food once a month. Sounded pretty simple to me. But, no! There was an investigation, which became a feasibility study, and then, after a month or two of screwing around, we finally got some money.

The general, the ambitious and intimidating guy I mentioned, came down to visit and made me show him the dogs. They yapped and barked and looked really warlike. And then the general asked, "Tell me, are those sentry dogs or attack dogs?"

"Hell, General, they're just dogs. We pick them up at the pound to keep the sentries company. They chase balls and things, and keep the coyotes away, but I don't think they ever attacked anybody."

I don't think he liked that answer, but we got the dog food.

It wasn't just a squadron commander who was frustrated. The Camp Pendleton base commander didn't have things any better.

At that time, President Nixon had his western White House a few miles up Interstate 5, and Camp Pendleton was tasked to provide support.

There was a helipad at San Clemente, and when the president was in residence, we lost half of our airfield tower operators until he was gone. This meant that while the president was nearby, HML-267 was unable to fly at night.

There was a fleet of maybe a dozen brand-new Chrysler automobiles parked across the road from the airfield in the base motor pool, and when the president was in residence, we had to give up our drivers, which meant that a lot of trucks sat idle while Marines drove White House staffers around. I once asked if it would be possible to borrow one of the bright blue Chryslers when there were no Marine Corps vehicles available, and was informed that vehicle and driver usage was a one-way street.

When the president came to San Clemente, all doctors' leaves were canceled at the base hospital, in case someone at the western White House needed attention.

But the one that got everybody's attention was the requirement for a full colonel to be on duty at Marine Corps base headquarters all night long in case the plumbing backed up at the western White House. Absolutely true. One day, some White House staffer called the service number he had been given to call when some maintenance was needed, and he didn't like the idea of talking to a lowly sergeant, so after that a full colonel had to be available twenty-four hours a day.

Most Marines I knew in 1972 were pretty conservative politically, but there were many who were altogether ready to vote Democratic, just to get rid of the western White House.

So it wasn't just I who was frustrated with the way things were. Being a general officer seemed even less attractive in 1972 than when I suffered the humiliation of being a general's aide in 1959.

Now, let me tell you the part about Peggy Lee. She was a great vocalist, and I had enjoyed her singing for years, but I never dreamed that she would be a determining factor in my life until one fateful night in late 1971.

My career prospects were improving, and some people in Washington even knew who I was. Lord knows, I wrote to them enough, telling them how to run their business, and paragraphs from my letters of instruction were beginning to appear in some of their directives.

I had just received a set of orders to join the staff of the air force's air/ground school, at Hurlbert Field in the Eglin complex near Pensacola, where I would be teaching classes and flying as an air controller on their bombing ranges. I was pretty doggone happy about it all. Two squadrons back-to-back, followed by another flying tour was more than any light colonel could ever hope for—and I hadn't lobbied for these orders, either.

Then the annual generals' conference took place in Washington, and my orders were canceled. Generals used that conference to identify officers they liked for the "fast track," and one of them, I never knew who, added my name to the list.

I received a phone call at home at six o'clock in the morning, California time, the very next day. That woke me up in a hurry. "Headquarters, Marine Corps calling for Lieutenant Colonel Moriarty" was a sentence designed to get a man's attention.

My orders to Hurlbert Field were canceled. I was going to

the War College, and then to the aviation training Desk at Head-quarters, Marine Corps, and wasn't that wonderful?

Geez! Try explaining that to your wife!

Shortly thereafter, the commandant of the Marine Corps, Gen. Leonard Chapman, was in Southern California, making his annual visitations to El Toro and Camp Pendleton, and Dallie and I attended both receptions.

At El Toro he grabbed my hand in the receiving line and cooed all sorts of nice things about what a fine job I was doing. My head swelled maybe an inch or two while my wife smoldered behind her good-sport smile.

General Chapman had a good memory, and the next night, at the reception at Camp Pendleton, he continued to say nice things to me. This meant that after he left, Dallie and I found ourselves invited into a circular conversation among the Pendleton powerful—the division commander, the base commander, and his chief of staff, plus their lovely ladies.

For thirty minutes, we listened and smiled and nodded as generals exulted over the fine show they had put on for the commandant. Half the time was given over to detailed descriptions of the flip charts they had used to demonstrate just how wonderful Camp Pendleton and 1st Marine Division were, and ignored completely how frustrating it was having to worry about President Nixon's toilet, and all in all it was probably the single most boring conversation we had ever suffered through.

After a while, we made our manners and left the officers club. As I steered our five-year-old station wagon out of the parking lot, my long-suffering wife made a chilly observation in the form of a question.

"Is that it? Is that what you want to spend another ten or fifteen years for? To talk about flip charts? Is that really it?"

Possibly just to shut her up, I turned on the car radio.

Peggy Lee was singing "Is that all there is?"

The next morning, I went in to the office early and wrote a letter to Headquarters, U.S. Marine Corps, requesting retirement.

DEBRIEF

Please do not misconstrue my early retirement as a slap at the Marine Corps. I loved it, and I believe I served it honorably. But the idea of sitting behind desks for the next ten years was too painful for me personally, and that is my last lesson for young men and women who might be thinking about a career in military service.

If you are young and talented and still looking for something worthwhile to do in life, you really ought to take a close look at Marine Corps aviation. I can promise only a lot of hard work and excitement, but I can suggest with all confidence that you will have more fun, and experience more sheer pleasure of accomplishment as a Marine pilot than you ever imagined.

Then, after five, ten, or fifteen years, when you're all grown up, make your career choice. Remain aboard for the long haul, and the glamor and prestige of being a Marine colonel or general. Or opt for early retirement at twenty years. It will probably be your choice, and Uncle Sam is very generous to people who have served their country.

When you are young, and immortality is a strong possibility, thoughts of eventual retirement never enter your minds. Hell, when I was a nineteen-year-old kid in flight training, I didn't even know pilots got extra money for flying until my last week in preflight, when some lecturer made a snide comment suggesting that some of us were only in training for the extra flight pay. You can imagine how much time I spent thinking about retirement.

But the Marine Corps, as well as the other services, has a wonderful retirement plan. And while your monthly check won't be enough to live on unless you hang around long enough to be a colonel or a general, it will be enough to pay the rent and allow you to do something you will enjoy just as much as flying—like teaching school.

Think of the stories you'll be able to tell your students when you have run out of lecture material and there are still ten minutes left before the bell rings. That's how this book got started—telling war stories in class.